Longevi ng
Your Bra and Weight in the Game

Longevity Lifestyle Matters—Keeping Your Brain, Body, and Weight in the Game

Arlene R. Taylor, PhD
Steve Horton, MPH **Sharlet M. Briggs, PhD**
Foreword by George E. Guthrie, MD

Success Resources International, Napa, CA

Copyright © 2015 by Arlene R. Taylor, Sharlet M. Briggs, Steve Horton. All Rights Reserved.

Address requests for information to:

www.arlenetaylor.org
stehor123@sbcglobal.net
www.sharletbriggs.com

All international rights reserved. No part of this publication may be reproduced, stored in a retrieval system, or transmitted in any form or by any means—electronic, mechanical, photocopy, recording, or any other—except for brief quotations in printed reviews, without the prior permission from the publisher.

P O Box 2554, Napa, CA 94558-9255 USA

ISBN # 1-887307-45-1

Special thanks to Michelle Nash and Margie Penkala.

Cover picture and cartoons by Seth Foley, Seth Foley Studios
www.sfoleystudios.com

Cover design and production by David O. Eastman.

Acknowledgements

This book would never have been written without the studies and painstaking studies by a host of researchers, scientists, and healthcare professionals—plus the impetus from so many who said, "There has to be a more straight-forward way to be healthier and live longer without spending hours every week running on the treadmill, counting calories, and restricting food."

Our sincere thanks to those who gave generously of their time and expertise reviewing the manuscript and offering suggestions. You know who you are.

Special appreciation goes to Dr. George E Guthrie for writing the Foreword and to Michelle Nash for editing assistance.

Dedication

This book is dedicated to individuals who have chosen to keep their brain, body, and weight in the game! They desire to prevent whatever illnesses can be prevented, embrace the secrets of a longevity lifestyle, and purpose to live in a state of mental, physical, emotional, spiritual, and social healthiness—for as long as possible.

Comments

If you don't start, you will never finish. And if you want to improve your health, you'd better start here! The book *Lifestyle Matters—Keeping Your Brain, Body, and Weight in the Game* informs readers foremost on how to enlist their brains to then engage their bodies in all manner of longevity lifestyle issues.

If your desire is to either nudge or shove your brain and body towards a healthier lifestyle, I highly recommend the principles found in this book. Not only will you receive the benefits of better health (i.e., spending less time and money on healthcare, doctors, and hospitals), you will also most certainly live a longer and happier life. When it comes to healthful living, better late than never, and better today than tomorrow!

—Clarence S. F. Ing, MD, MPH
Medical Director, NEWSTART Program
President, NEWSTART Medical Clinic
California, USA

Powerful. Precise. Practical. This book appeals to both the sentiment and intellect of readers as the authors blend down-to-earth stories with the latest in brain and wellness research to map out a journey that embraces a Longevity Lifestyle. They lay down one of the most important criterion for *Club 122 Longevity*: your brain only WILL do what it *believes* it CAN do. The positive possibilities lie in your own informed skillpower and willpower. Set a higher standard—and reach for it.

—Eric Teo Choon Chew, DrPH
Director Youngberg Wellness Center, Singapore

The authors of *Longevity Lifestyle Matters* provide access to findings from current health and brain research that enlighten readers of the best ways to achieve an abundant life. Scientific knowledge is deftly merged with wholistic principles to engage both the brain and the will into a commitment to healthy choices.

We are also reminded of the truth that longevity without health is meaningless, achieving what few books on health have done: offer an informed balance between the health of both mind and body.

Short of that perfect blend, there is no abundant life.

—Prudence Pollard, PhD, MPH, RD
Vice President
Employee Services and Research
Professor of Management
Oakwood University
Huntsville, Alabama 35896

As *Longevity Lifestyle Matters* so clearly portrays, all decisions and lifestyle choices originate in the brain. The chapters offer factual information from current research, visual and narrative inspiration, and practical suggestions—that are very doable—on how your brain and body can best collaborate for mental, physical, spiritual, and emotional health.

The book speaks to all people that what's in the brain and mind both directly and indirectly affects the body. Long term!

—Nievelyn Sison, Health Coordinator, Dubai
Email: nievelyn_antemano@yahoo.com

This book could not be more timely! From the Foreword to the final page, *Longevity Lifestyle Matters* is a book about truths humans must face to extract the most out of each day for as long as possible. That's longevity at its best.

Amidst the noise of false progress (which has led to unprecedented rates of depression and sadness—and which many try to bandage with more "things" —) the authors invite you to hear that authentic voice in your head that helps you brave on against the false guilt and pseudo-evidence about why you can "have it all" with no consequences.

Take this well-researched path to discover that honest child within you that played fair, loved well, and exercised all the time because it was *fun*. Enjoy the trusted roadmap your own brain offers to make the best of the time you have left. With these guiding principles, it's easier than you can imagine to live a longer life and actually find *joy* in the journey.

—Oscar E. Streeter, Jr, MD, FACRO
Clinical Professor of Radiation Oncology,
University of California, Davis, School of Medicine

Because of reviewing *Longevity Lifestyle Matters—Keeping Your Brain, Body, and Weight in the Game,* I have personally renewed health decisions that helped me once lose 60 pounds and keep the weight off. In addition, I picked up knowledge to improve daily longevity choices. Instead of only citing research and methodology, the authors have included many stories, which add a different twist that I believe will be appealing to a broad spectrum of readers. I look forward to re-reading the book and working with the *Companion Notebook.*

I also plan to encourage friends and family members who are struggling with weight and health issues to seek the guidance provided in this book. It will make a wonderful present to my mom, who is 82 years young and not a day too old to learn a few new health tricks!

—Scott Tangerman, D.D.S.
Dentist, Bakersfield, CA

Publisher's Reminder

This book is not a medical, psychological, or biological text. The information and resources herein are for general educational and informational purposes only and do not present an in-depth treatment of specific research findings or topics. They are not intended to take the place of professional counseling, medical or psychological care, recovery therapy, or personalized recommendations from healthcare professionals.

You are advised to consult your physician, therapist, or other healthcare professionals including registered dieticians and certified exercise physiologists and trainers before you make lifestyle changes or implement new exercise strategies.

The publisher, author, contributors, and editors expressly disclaim all responsibility and any liability (direct or indirect) for adverse effects, (actual or perceived), from the use or misuse of concepts presented herein.

The stories are about real people and real questions and real life experiences—disguised to protect confidentiality, of course.

If you find errors / typos in this book, please know that they are there for a purpose. Some brains really enjoy searching for mistakes.

Table of Contents

Change your life today. Don't gamble on the future, act now—without delay.

—Simone de Beauvoir

Foreword

"If you keep doing what you are doing, you will keep getting what you got."

Science has made quite clear the relationship between lifestyle choices and many of the diseases of the so-called "developed" cultures. While many of us are aware of these relationships the actual application of what we know into our behavior and habits often lags behind.

We would prefer a quick and "easy" fix. We expect science to solve our chronic health problems with a procedure or a pill when much of the cause lies within our own lifestyle choices. We turn to impossible and even sometimes-painful quick fixes to lose the weight, fight the pain, and solve our problems.

When these fail to enable us to reach our goal we often blame our dis-ease on the genes we inherited, falling into a hopeless and helpless state bordering on depression because we have no control over our lives. We can see nothing but doctor bills and procedures and inevitably, an uncomfortable death.

This often leads us to seek a little comfort from the very lifestyle practices that caused the problems in the first place. And the illness worsens, confirming our fears.

But in order to really solve our health problems we will need to change what we are doing. Healthy choices are of primary importance in restoring health that has been lost because of poor lifestyle practices.

For some of us the connection between our chronic discomforts and our lifestyle choices has not been elucidated. Not even our health professionals know for sure how to "fix" us with modern technology. They may offer some promise of improvement, or a slowing of the process, or even just a numbing of our pain, but there is no cure.

Regardless of our condition, our bodies and brain work best when they are treated as they were designed to function. For many chronic diseases there may be significant improvement and even cure when the best lifestyle choices are made. Diet, activity, thought patterns, hydration, rest, and emotions all work together in obtaining and maintaining optimum health. To reach this state we need both accurate knowledge and the ability to make the best choices.

This demands the best from our brains and our emotions.

In this fine volume the authors provide an easy way to understand and look at the best of modern science as well as a clear and practical path to a healthy lifestyle.

As you read you will learn interesting facts, but you will also be given practical exercises to improve both your thinking and your behavior. As you make the first few steps recommended in this book you will feel the improvement and it will make the next steps easier to take.

Success fosters success.

The steps are really not hard and the reward is great.

So get ready to *experience* this helpful book. Don't expect to just read it.

Take a chapter or two at a time and put the recommendations into practice. You will be building a healthier way of thinking as well as developing the skills needed to move you safely to the healthiest and happiest life available—and that for the long term.

Remember, "A long journey begins with the first steps."

There are no "magical" quick fixes.

There is no "magic" to restore health.

There is no safe "crash diet."

The best answer to many of our personal and even national health problems lies in a change in our lifestyle.

One definition of insanity is, "doing the same thing over and over and expecting different results."

For your health to actually improve, something needs to change. Your healthcare professional can help to guide you with wise use of technology but you will be the one most responsible for changing your lifestyle.

Stop the insanity and let the authors guide you on this portion of your journey to optimum health.

—George E Guthrie, MD,
MPH, CDE, CNS, FAAFP, FACLM
Assistant Director,
Florida Hospital Family Medicine Residency
President-elect,
American College of Lifestyle Medicine

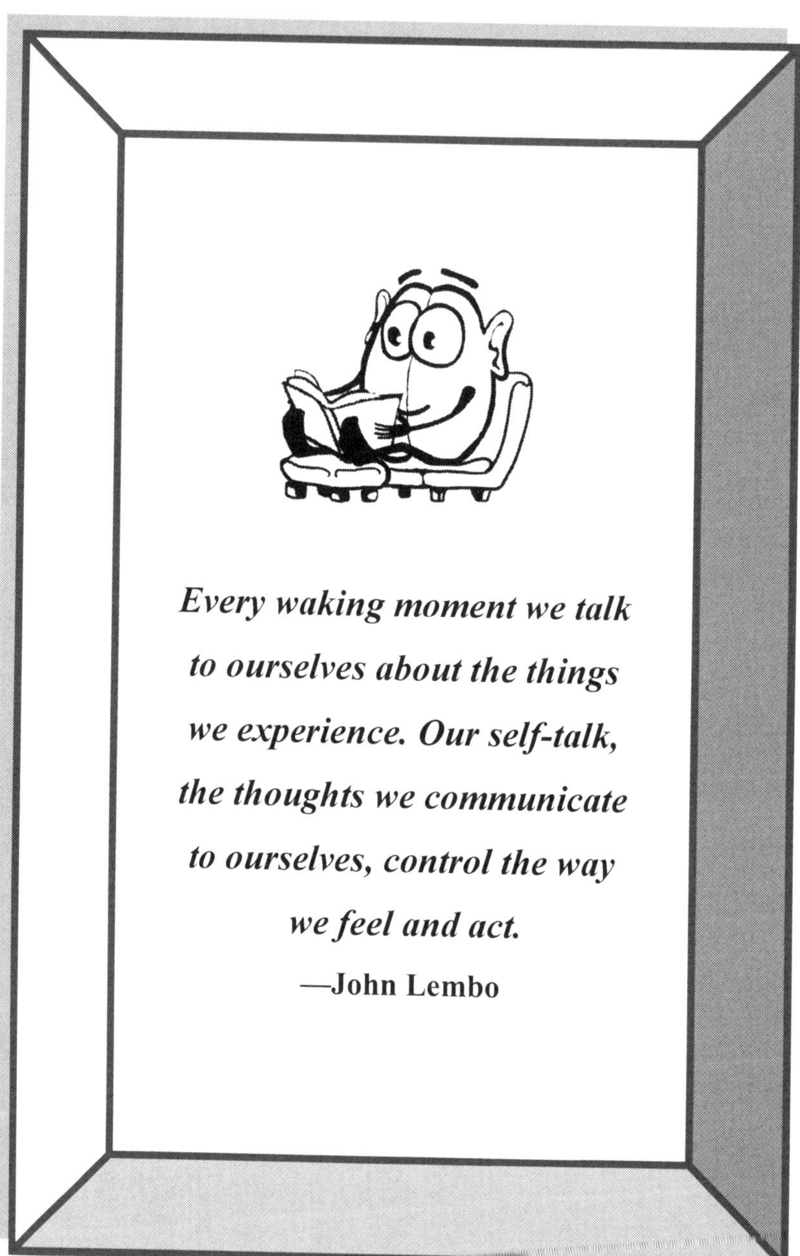
Every waking moment we talk to ourselves about the things we experience. Our self-talk, the thoughts we communicate to ourselves, control the way we feel and act.
—John Lembo

Prologue

The sign in the overflowing waiting area of the Emergency Department read: *Those who are too busy to take care of their health are like mechanics who are too busy to take care of their tools.*

Your "tools" are your brain and body. Without them you would not exist on this planet. But there is such a thing as *existing* and such a thing as *thriving.* And they are light years apart.

Some don't seem interested in taking appropriate care of their brain and body, preferring to do whatever feels good at the moment. Others are interested but unsure what to do that will make a difference. A few have spent time sifting through research papers, attempting to understand the data, weighing the pros and cons, trying to identify how best to avoid disease and injury whenever possible. They hope to maximize their time on this planet by practically applying proven strategies for health and longevity.

Collective wisdom highlights the importance of each person taking personal responsibility for his or her own brain and body. The question is: *How does one go about accomplishing that*? Understanding what really makes positive contributions to health and longevity can be a bit of a puzzle. Some would say more like a deep dark hole. Study conclusions are often controversial and contradictory, which can be confusing, discouraging, and even crazy-making.

For every study that recommends one course of action, there's usually another that labels that fraudulent or at least flawed. For every published data table or graph listing ideal weights, there is some other "authority" to cast aspersions on the numbers.

For every professional who suggests paying careful attention to nutrition, there will be others quite sure that food and drink have a minimal impact on overall health.

For every recommendation to exercise at least sixty minutes each day, another advertises a new piece of equipment or activity that purports similar benefits in under five minutes a day.

For every cooking show that implies you can enjoy whatever you want *and* still retain your health, another contradicts. For every study that shows wine can benefit one's cardiovascular system, another says that it increases the risk for some types of cancers.

For every advertisement for yet another *miracle* pill, liquid diet, injection, prepared pre-purchased meals, exercise equipment, or *magic* something or other to help avoid the need for roomier clothing, there are those who gloss over serious risks to mental and physical health and insist that *big is beautiful.*

For every grandparent who slips sodas, candy, cookies, ice cream, cake, and pizza to the grandchildren, another is horrified and provides less sugary treats. For each child who plays outdoors every day, others are sedentary, sitting like little lumps in front of their big flat-screen television, using computers, smart phones, and iPads, twittering and tweeting on multiple social-media sites.

What is the scoop?

Is there a real deal?

For starters, there is no charm-paved yellow-brick road, no magic wand to fully prevent what may be preventable. Neither is there a one-step strategy that achieves long-lasting health and wellness by popping a pill, downing a drink, sniffing or snorting some supernatural substance, or getting a shot.

This alone stops those who are not interested in health unless it's fast, easy, and aligns with their present lifestyle. They don't want to consider anything that delays gratification or imposes any self-discipline. Add to that the perceptions about lifestyle, and longevity that each human brain harbors—many absorbed prior to age five—that have triggered deeply entrenched beliefs and habits often difficult—but not impossible—to alter. Take food, for example.

In his book *Breaking the Food Seduction,* Dr. Neal Barnard points out that when many infants and toddlers begin to taste solid foods, they often like fruit and rice cereal instantly. And sweets. Oh, my, do they learn to love sweets in a nanosecond, including desserts and sugary drinks. To the point that they will often gravitate to any food high in sugar content.

And meat? Not so much.

Many children, as they begin eating solid foods, are unexcited about meat and shy away from it. Although, as Dr. Barnard points out, before long most will eat meat as a habit, with life-long consequences. Meat appears to possess subtle drug-like qualities much like those of

sugar, cheese, and chocolate. When meat touches your tongue, opiates are released in your brain. Meat, sugar, cheese, and chocolate (to name just a few) reward you, rightly or wrongly, for eating these calorie dense foods, thus pushing you toward making it a habit.

In a 2000 survey of 1,244 adults, one in four Americans were unwilling to give up eating meat for even one week in exchange for a hypothetical reward of $1000.

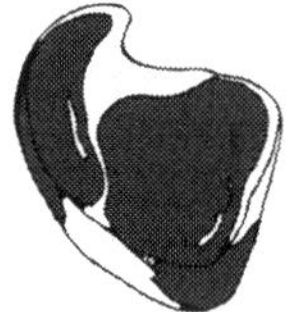

Interestingly, Asian and Hispanic Americans were more likely to accept the hypothetical reward (fewer than 10 percent refused) while 24 percent of Caucasians and 29 percent of Blacks were unwilling to do so.

Think of health as having life in your years for as many years as possible.

The definition of health adopted by the World Health Organization (WHO) in 1948, which incidentally has not changed since then, reads: "Health is a state of complete physical, mental and social well-being and not merely the absence of disease or infirmity."

And what about the *determinants* of health, so-called? Scientists generally recognize five main determinants of health in any given population.

The five determinants are:

- Genetics and epigenetics
- Individual choices and behaviors
- Social environments
- Physical environments
- Health services (access to quality health care and health insurance).

These determinants-of-health factors do have an impact on disease and longevity. However, as Doctors Michael A. Roisen and Mehmet C. Oz point out in their book *YOU: The Owner's Manual,* 70 percent of how long and how well you live is in your hands.

Do you understand the significance of that estimate? That is both good news and bad news.

W. Edwards Deming, PhD, has been quoted as saying: *Learning is not compulsory—neither is survival.* Choose to continue learning, with the goal of moving from surviving to thriving. And if you are already thriving, continue learning how to do so—by design. Not intermittently. Consistently.

> *Now the game. Your game. The one that only you was meant to play. The one that was given to you when you came into this world. You ready? Take your stance. Don't hold nothing back. Give it everything.*
>
> —The Legend of Bagger Vance (movie)

How do you stay *in the game* that only you were "meant to play"?

Some would say: Take care of your body. Eat right. Exercise. Sleep well. Health, after all, is your greatest wealth. Persius, a Roman poet and satirist of Etruscan origin (34 AD to 62 AD) has been quoted as saying:

> *You pray for good health and a body that will be strong in old age. Good—but your rich foods block the gods' answer and tie Jupiter's hands.*

Others emphasize improving your mind: stimulate your brain, get educated, read, memorize, do brain aerobic exercises, be a life-long learner.

Buddha, ancient India's spiritual teacher (c. 563 BC to 483 BC) wisely combined the two:

> *To keep the body in good health is a duty. Otherwise, we shall not be able to keep our mind strong and clear.*

Getting a little closer to home, according to President John F. Kennedy:

> *Physical fitness is not only one of the most important keys to a healthy body. It is the basis of dynamic and creative intellectual activity.*

Take care of your body. That's where you live, as Jim Rohn puts it.

Of no less importance, take care of your brain. That's where you think.

And manage your weight, because either way—too thin or too fat—it will impact both brain and body.

Exactly how to do this, however, is grist for the mill of argument, controversy, and the impetus behind the scores of *weight-loss diets* and the thousands of pages written about them—to say nothing of hundreds of cookbooks that purport success: just "follow the recipe."

Fortunately, emerging research shows clear links between lifestyle and chronic illnesses and provides data on risk factors, along with suggestions for how to stay younger longer while growing older and how to proactively prevent some physical and mental diseases.

Strategies that have been shown to work long-term versus those that don't seem to have much staying power or are relatively ineffective are being identified. Furthermore, research on how some strategies appear to be more efficacious than others is growing by leaps and bounds. More and more individuals want to keep their brain, body, and weight *in the game.* Is this just science fiction or wishful thinking? Likely not!

The Age of The Dinosaurs is long past. It is now the Age of the Brain. Thanks to brain scanning equipment and other state-of-the-art research modalities, every human being with a functioning brain—and that includes you—has an opportunity to look at life and health in a new way. You are capable of changing your brain, which in turn can impact your mind, body, health, aging process, and potentially even your longevity. And, largely due to neuroscience, you can learn how.

Results from long-term studies are encouraging. Nearly 80,000 individuals in the United States are already past the century mark. Even if you don't achieve that, you'll likely get farther if you aim higher. Referred to as *The Generation C's,* half still live independently. Estimates are that by the year 2050 they will number well over a million.

Females do outnumber males eight to one in this group of Generation C's. Generation C males, however, tend to be healthier and have better cognition than their female counterparts.

Interested? Some will say "Of course!" Some, but not all.

Human beings have the marvelous and inalienable right to make choices about their lifestyle. You can choose to be among those who believe it's too much work or in the group who says *yes* to a Longevity Lifestyle.

It is pretty clear by now—or should be to those who have been staying abreast of emerging research in the areas of health and longevity—that physical health impacts brain function.

Conversely, mindset impacts physical and mental health. They go hand in glove, as Eastern medicine has known for eons and as Western medicine is now beginning to acknowledge and embrace.

This book is *not* an attempt to present yet another weight-loss or health-management program. Google those words and be amazed at the number of sites that pop up, each certain their program is the bees knees for those with a bit of willpower.

Neither is it an attempt to analyze current crash or fad diets, tweak an existing program, or offer yet another one.

Nor does it try to showcase the work of a few specific researchers, a great many of whom have made and are making important contributions to the science of high-level-wellness living. In some cases, their studies have pointed the way not only toward healthier lifestyles but also to bona fide longevity anti-aging strategies.

This book *is* designed to present relevant brain-function information in practical, easy-to-understand language. Keeping your brain, body, and weight in the game is the goal and it is doable. Actually, it's quite simple, although not always easy. The logic is basic and straightforward: create a Longevity Lifestyle and stick with it. It matters!

Those who are sports enthusiasts are familiar with a game playbook or at least know what it represents: a range of possible set plays or a notebook containing descriptions and diagrams of the plays that a team has practiced, especially a football team.

Metaphorically, think of this book as a *playbook* for a Longevity Lifestyle. It contains both a range of possible set plays that can be practically applied as well as descriptions of plays that others have practiced already and are practicing currently. Artist Seth Foley captured this concept in creating his book cover illustration: the brain, lungs, stomach, and heart studying the #12 diagram in the playbook in order to help keep them in the game. Again, metaphorically, the #12 diagram is a play on one of the components of a Longevity Lifestyle.

Chapters 1 to 26 contain narrative about real people, real questions, and real life experiences discussed with their wellness coach. The human brain tends to remember stories more easily than just a list of facts. The stories present information in a practical, informative, and easy-to-understand way, offering tips for creating and maintaining a Longevity Lifestyle. They also point out unhelpful myths and traps into which you can easily stumble if unaware. Challenges can derail progress, so forewarned is forearmed.

The Appendix is divided into five sections:

1. **Longevity Lifestyle Components**: summary of the big picture in a nutshell. Each of the thirteen components already has herein been addressed in some way.

2. **The Mediterranean Way**: key aspects of traditional cuisine and way of life. Recommendations—personalized to each brain and body—are believed to be beneficial to long-term health.

3. **Shopping and Eating Reminders**: tips loosely based on the Mediterranean Way. Post them in the kitchen. Carry a copy in your car. Use the tips to help keep you on the path to better health.

4. **The 12 Steps of a Longevity Lifestyle:** strategies for dealing with unhealthy habits. Worldwide, twelve-step programs have been shown effective in dealing more successfully with a variety of addictive behaviors. Since some foods have been discovered to compete with alcohol and other drugs of abuse for the same brain receptor molecules, Twelve Steps seem appropriate.

5. **Obesity Pandemic:** obesity is turning into a pandemic and is going global. Obesity is linked with more than 50 diseases—including type 2 diabetes, heart disease, some forms of cancer, and dementia. A decrease in the amount of physical activity in the lives of many individuals is believed a contributor to the obesity pandemic. To stop this pandemic, each person must "be the change" he or she would like to see in the world.

The Selected Bibliography contains additional resources as does the Authors and Resources section in case you want to delve more deeply into this topic on your own.

Take advantage of the companion *Longevity Lifestyle Matters—Companion Notebook*, designed to help you utilize the information from your reading, personalize it into knowledge, and practically apply it in a way that works for you. Each brain and body differs. There is no one size fits all. There are principles of health and longevity that can apply to all in some way or other.

If you are reading this book, it is highly likely that you are making the choice to increase your knowledge about health and longevity and practically apply researched principles in ways that work for your brain and body. As the years go by, you'll be glad you did. There is no easy fix, however, no genie that smokes or snakes out of the lamp when you rub it, no magic or miracle reversal potion.

Keeping your brain, body, and weight in the game requires information, knowledge, choice, practical application, and vigilance for the rest of your life—and it is doable. In about 12 weeks, a motivated individual—*motivated* is key—can create and implement a Longevity Lifestyle.

Success involves identifying unhealthy (often automatic) habits and replacing them with healthier habits, which can then become automatic. It requires the practical application of strategies that have been shown to be effective, while avoiding those that don't. It demands daily vigilance along with a lifetime commitment. In the end you may choose to apply these concepts in your own life to reach health goals and avoid preventable pitfalls. You do stand to increase your chances for looking and feeling younger, for adding life to your years, maybe even adding years to your life, for preventing what can be prevented.

And when you begin feeling better, looking better, thinking better, role-modeling better health, and as you discover you have more energy to accomplish some of your cherished goals—you will be glad you stepped up to a Longevity Lifestyle.

Does a Longevity Lifestyle guarantee that you will avoid or prevent every negative health issue? Unfortunately, no. But as Leigh Hunt put it, the groundwork for all happiness is good health. What you can avoid or prevent will be solid gold in your life bank. Go for the gold!

It's time to get your brain, body, and weight *in the game!* In the end, you stand to come out ahead. Dig in. Get started!

Turn the page and meet Edna and Allen in Chapter 1.

—The Authors

The secret of getting ahead
is getting started.
The secret of getting started
is breaking your complex
overwhelming tasks into
small manageable tasks and
starting on the first one.
—Mark Twain

Club 122 Longevity

Chapter 1

"This looks like the place," said Edna, hesitantly, glancing at her husband and taking a deep breath. Together, they stood and surveyed the gold lettering on the frosted-glass door.

Club 122 Longevity
Keeping Your Brain, Body, and Weight in the Game
Welcome!

"Well," said Edna, drawing out the word. "Nothing ventured, nothing gained. I guess."

"I have nothing to lose," her husband replied. "I've already had one heart by pass surgery and, according to the surgeon, I'm close to needing another—if I don't have a heart attack first."

"Don't say that!" exclaimed Edna, pushing open the door into a pleasant waiting room. Within minutes the receptionist ushered them to a well-appointed office where they met the wellness coach.

"I'm Edna and this is my husband, Allen. His surgeon referred us," the woman said, her face wrinkled with worry and anxiety mixed with outright apprehension. Allen stood motionless, wary.

After a moment he cleared his throat. "My surgeon said you could help me develop a Longevity Lifestyle. One that might help to keep me alive for a few more years." His voice sounded skeptical.

Before the coach could comment, Edna said. "The sign on your door says 'Club 122 Longevity.' What is that?"

"It's a club for people who have embraced a Longevity Lifestyle with the goal of living to be at least 122 years old," said the wellness coach. "According to Guinness World Records, one of the oldest verified ages in recent history is that of Jeanne Louise Calment of Arles, France. Born on the 21st of February 1875, she lived until the 4th of August, 1997. That's 122 years, 164 days."

"Oh, my!" exclaimed Edna. "Did you say 122 years? That's a very long time,"

"I didn't realize it was even possible to live that long," said Allen. "Me? I'd just like to live to see my first grandchild."

Allen paused and sighed. "So far my body isn't cooperating. Adopting a Longevity Lifestyle appears to be my last hope."

"Although there are no magic fixes, research has demonstrated doable strategies that can reduce your risk for obesity, heart disease, type 2 diabetes, dementia, cancer, and other undesirable conditions—which may also increase longevity. It all starts and ends in the brain. Yours. There is also a close connection between you and your heart.

"Am I to understand that you are interested in doing everything possible to implement clear recommendations based on emerging data and commit to a Longevity Lifestyle?"

"Well, maybe, if..." Allen began. "Okay, are there any guarantees that this will work for me?"

"Are you are asking whether assurances exist that a Longevity Lifestyle will prevent all illness and disease, keep you in the same size clothing you wore at your most fit, and result in health, happiness, success, and longevity?

"If you are—the answer is no. There are no such guarantees. None implied and none given. Life is far too capricious. The preponderance of evidence, however, leans toward the perspective that everyone can do something—and it's far better to do something than nothing."

"I'll do it with you," pleaded Edna, turning to look at Allen. "I like the thought that doing something is better than doing nothing. What do we have to lose? Let's give it a shot. Let's at least try, if only for a couple of weeks"

"A couple of weeks won't do it," said their coach. "It takes time. I reiterate, there is no instant fix. It takes the body a long time to fall out of balance, and it will take a while to return to homeostasis. After all, you didn't acquire your current state of health in a few days, and it will take more than a couple of weeks to realize improvements.

"In about twelve weeks, however, those who are motivated—and the key word is *motivated*—can create and implement a Longevity Lifestyle, something they will embrace for as long as they live and that may help them lower their health risks through practical applications and daily vigilance.

"This is neither a flash-in-the pan nor an intermittent solution. Some estimate it could take a month for every year in which you lived unhealthfully. If you plan to be alive for the foreseeable future, however, it's doable. You can accomplish many health-related goals without debt-building financial expenditures or daily sessions with high-priced doctors, trainers, exercise physiologists, or nutritionists—if you are willing to develop healthier replacement habits; create and consistently maintain a Longevity Lifestyle."

"And if you are willing to keep your brain, body, and weight in the game for the rest of your life. But you do need to get started."

"It sounds like you're describing individuals who live in so-called *Blue Zones*," said Allen. "I've read that they live significantly longer than most people."

"Researchers have found that Blue-Zone individuals share some common lifestyle characteristics that are believed to contribute to their longevity.

"These include recommendations for:

- Embracing a vegetarian diet that focuses on fruits, vegetables, nuts, and whole grains
- Avoiding alcohol, tobacco, and mind-altering drugs
- Promoting "pure water, fresh air, and sunlight" as part of a good-living formula

"In a sense, think of Blue-Zone individuals as having embraced a type of Longevity Lifestyle."

"Could you explain briefly what a Longevity Lifestyle looks like?" asked Edna. "What would we need to do?"

"Yes," Allen added. "I want the bottom line before I decide whether or not to commit to this, because I sense it would involve making some changes in the way we have been living."

"We've talked about getting off our treadmill existence for several years now, but so far it's only been talk," said Edna, frowning.

The wellness coach took two sheets of paper from a drawer and handed one to Allen and the other to Edna.

"This list briefly outlines components of a Longevity Lifestyle. You're welcome to take these with you. Read them over. Talk about them. Matter of fact, read them aloud to each other."

"Read them aloud?" asked Edna. "I've not read aloud since our children were little. Is there a reason you suggest that?"

"Reading aloud is much more stimulating to the brain than reading silently, so much so that it is now considered an anti-aging strategy. You stimulate the three main sensory systems when you read out loud. You see the words, feel with tongue and teeth and mouth as you articulate them, and hear yourself making the sounds."

"Oh," said Edna, smiling. "We can do that. We'll take turns reading aloud so both of us get some brain stimulation."

"As to your comment about a treadmill existence, some talk about health and longevity but fail to walk the walk. Others don't even talk the talk. A Longevity Lifestyle requires you to talk the talk as you walk the walk. It's the best option for potential grandparents who are hoping to see at least their first grandchild!"

"Do you think this is doable for someone who's already had one bypass surgery and potentially is facing another?" asked Allen. "I thought it might be impossible for someone in my state of health."

"None better," said their wellness coach, smiling. "Unfortunately it sometimes takes bypass surgery, heart attack, stroke, or some other rather catastrophic event to knock people off the frenetic treadmill of life and get them to stop long enough to seriously contemplate a different way to live. A Longevity Lifestyle is really quite simple, although not always easy."

"Perhaps the best news is that good health requires neither Herculean endeavors nor Olympic efforts that consume your entire day in focused practice. But it will take some time, effort, follow-through, and commitment."

"At work, Allen has spent most of his career putting in really long hours, juggling multiple priorities, putting out proverbial fires of one type of another, and mentoring younger executives," Edna began.

"Plus we purchased a fixer-upper on half an acre at the edge of town—we being the fixer-upper," said Allen, jumping into the conversation. "In retrospect, that might not have been our wisest choice, seeing as our eldest son was in college and the twins were both entering high school. You know what books and tuition cost.

"At the time, of course, it seemed like the thing to do. But several years have passed and the remodeling is never-ending. There's really no finished room in which to relax. We've been eating quick, fast, and probably relatively unhealthy meals because the kitchen is still in such an uproar. We've managed with only a hotplate for several months …"

"You are describing a great deal of long-term stress that likely has flooded your body with stress hormones," said their coach. "Add to that the years of unhealthy eating and an environment that is not conducive to relaxation and you have a recipe for heart disease."

"Although my job may be less stressful in some ways than Allen's, I've still felt stretched between working, remodeling, and trying to support the twins in their school endeavors, They've just started their freshman year of college. Most of our weekends are consumed with projects on the house or the property, and those that aren't are spent traveling back and forth to the college." Edna sighed audibly.

"She's right," agreed Allen. "Dustin is gifted musically. Very gifted. We like to encourage and support him by attending all his musical programs, but it does make for a lot of driving."

"Denay, on the other hand," said Edna, "is captain of the school's freshman basketball team. A good player, she's beyond passionate about the game. To be fair we like to attend as many of her games as possible, too. Unfortunately, the musical programs and basketball games don't always fall on the same weekend."

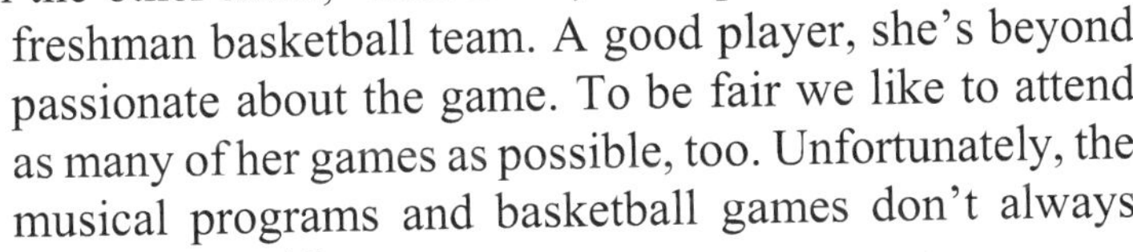

"Between Dustin's music and Denay's basketball," said Allen, "we've been burning the proverbial candles at both ends—on top of the house remodeling and landscaping, with no moss growing beneath our feet or our wheels."

"Let me be clear about this," said their coach. "Stressful jobs, ongoing remodeling, two kids in college, less-than-optimum eating habits, and it would appear a sleep deficit exacerbated by all the traveling. My brain's opinion is that you both look pretty good for the condition you're in."

Allen and Edna burst out laughing.

"But seriously, if you want to see your grandchildren, you will need to make some significant changes in the way you're living. Embracing a Longevity Lifestyle for the rest of your life increases the likelihood that this can happen. There's no better plan for two people who can't wait to meet and greet their future grandchildren—assuming your offspring cooperate by producing some."

Edna laughed again.

Allen rolled his eyes.

"So, where to from here?" he asked, finally.

"Where you go from here will depend on you. It will require that you learn and practically apply some solid principles on a daily basis. Stress management, for example. But how, when, and where will be up to you."

"In addition, you will need to pay attention to your brain. After all, you are where you are today because of how your brain has functioned in the past and the choices you have made. Everything starts and ends in the brain, you know. I like to describe good health as merely the slowest possible rate at which you can die, while still remaining in relatively good shape."

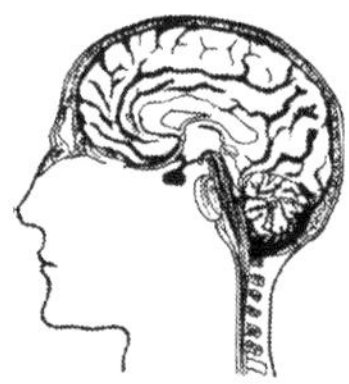

"Oh, that's good," said Edna. "Okay. In for a penny, in for a pound. I joining *Club 122 Longevity* and I want a lifetime membership!"

Allen nodded. "Count me in, too. This is the first ray of hope I've had for a long time. It's *Club 122 Longevity* all the way—for both of us."

"I believe that's a good choice," said their coach. "It certainly has been for me. Just go to www.club122longevity.com and sign up.

"Because every brain is unique, the Longevity Lifestyle you create will—of necessity—be unique, as well. It needs to fit you. This makes it easier to maintain it for your lifetime. Please know that I am willing to work with you to accomplish your goals."

The couple left, smiling, their facial expressions looking very different from when they had arrived at the office.

In Chapter 2, meet Stephen and the *peter-out* mindset that he'd had since he was the pudgiest kid in the sixth grade.

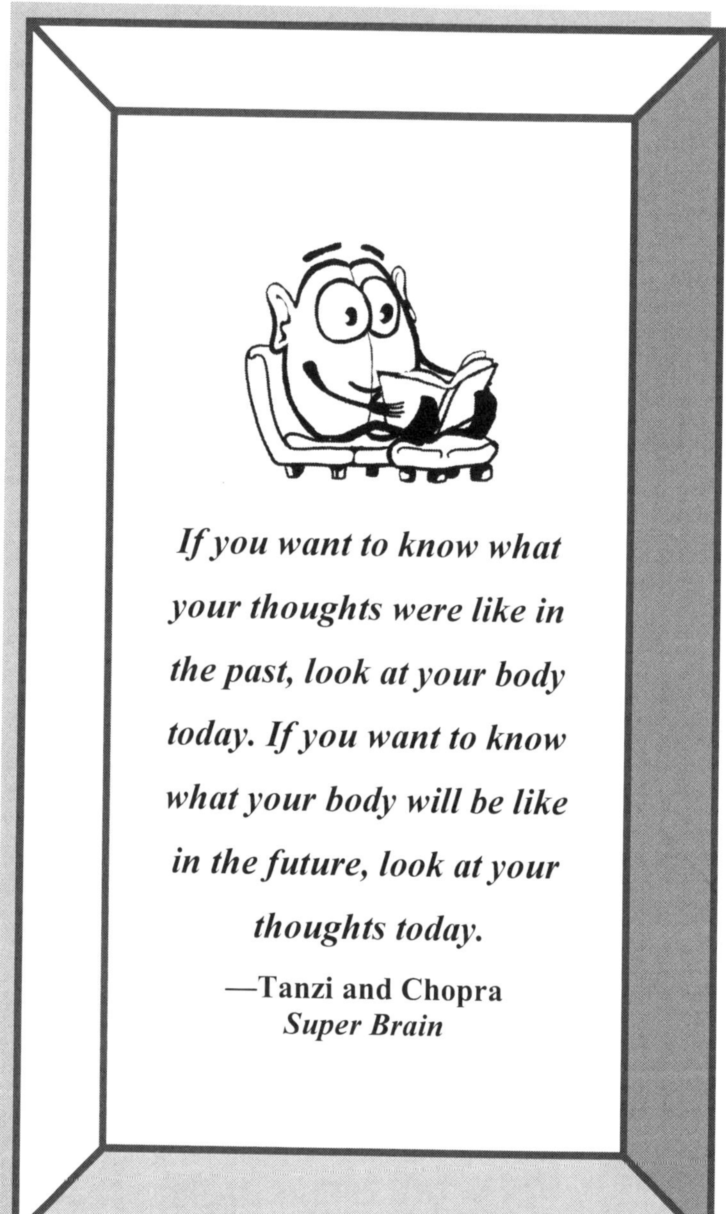

If you want to know what your thoughts were like in the past, look at your body today. If you want to know what your body will be like in the future, look at your thoughts today.

—Tanzi and Chopra
Super Brain

All about You

Chapter 2

"I've never exercised in my life," Stephen said, settling his considerable bulk into the chair. It creaked. The chair, not his bulk, and his wellness coach winced. "Not on purpose, that is. I supposed you're going to tell me I need to start adding more physical activity to my life but frankly it's not my cup of tea. Never has been. Actually, I don't think I can do it."

"If you don't think you can do it, you likely won't do it," said his wellness coach. "It reminds me of a quote from *Peter Pan* by J. M. Barrie: *The moment you doubt whether you can fly, you cease for ever to be able to do it.* When it comes to exercise, mindset is paramount to getting you up off the proverbial couch—and moving. It appears you've already made up your mind that exercise is not your cup of tea." Stephen shifted and the chair creaked, again.

"There's the mindset that thinks, '*Let's not rush into anything. You usually peter out pretty fast when it comes to exercise. You don't like to exercise. Just bide your time and you'll be back on the couch before you know it.'*

"And there's the mindset that thinks: *'You are doing this.'* "Remember that old expression 'the nose knows?' Well, your brain knows what you think, how you feel, and what your track record has been."

"The *peter-out* mindset has been the story of my life since I was the pudgiest kid in sixth grade." Stephen paused, remembering. "I think I was afraid I couldn't be successful, what with my family's weight problems and all, so I didn't even try. Guess it's time I faced up to the fact that I took the way of least resistance."

"That describes many people on this planet," said his coach. "What did you mean by your 'family's weight problems'?"

I'd be willing to bet that if you added up just what my father and his three brothers weighed, the total would give a ton more than a run for its money!" exclaimed Stephen. "My mother and her sisters wouldn't be far behind; maybe even slightly ahead."

"Then you come by your weight honestly. Nevertheless, whether or not you continue at your present weight is really up to you. Compare your brain to a giant iceberg, most of which is hidden beneath the surface of the water. Think of your conscious mind as being the smaller portion of the iceberg that sticks up out of the water and your subconscious mind as the far larger portion submerged beneath the surface. That massive subconscious mind has an uncanny sense of whether or not you mean business. No metaphor is perfect, but you get the idea. If you mean business, if you think you can, the brain mobilizes its considerable resources to help you create a Longevity Lifestyle that includes exercise.

"The reverse is true also. If you are not serious and think you can't, your brain won't help you. The authors of *Super Brain* point out that your brain cannot do what it thinks it cannot do. Bottom line: If you think you can or you think you can't, you're right."

"And if I think I can't, then what?" asked Stephen.

"Then your subconscious just floats along, relatively in neutral—patiently waiting until you return to your old habits and routines."

"I fear I have no brain software for exercising," said Stephen. "Well, that's not precisely true. I exercise hand-to-mouth with snacks, and walking to the fridge, freezer, or cupboard for refills. I also exercise when I finally push myself away from the table, and so on."

"What a sense of humor," said his coach, laughing. "You have brain software programs for those types of body movements—basically avoiding regular exercise. Now you need to create software for actually exercising on a regular basis."

"I may be a slow starter," said Stephen, "but I'm beginning to realize that what I choose to delete from my life is only decimating my brain-body health anyway. And what I add, like exercise, can make me healthier and happier."

"Exactly," said his coach. "As you start living a more balanced life, your brain and body will get back into a homeostatic condition. Then you may be surprised at what you used to think you had to have. If you have not been exercising regularly, it's always a good idea to check with your doctor before beginning an exercise program."

"I've already scheduled an appointment with my doctor. He's going to faint when I ask him about exercising." Stephen laughed at the thought. "He'll likely be speechless for a minute or two, at least. I'm also going to stop by the store and purchase a set of bathroom scales," he added, "so I can weigh morning and evening. If I am going to do this, I want to KNOW when I've lost weight."

"Weight measurements are helpful if you don't get too attached to them. Once a week is likely a better option. That allows for fluid fluctuations that can occur on a daily basis. Weigh at the same time every week. Pick a day. Any day."

"Say you decide to weigh every Wednesday morning—and morning is better than evening. Go to the bathroom first thing in the morning to get rid of the urine that has collected during the night. Wear similar clothing for your weekly weigh-ins. I suggest you remove your shoes as they can weigh one or two pounds. You can gauge your progress by how your clothing fits, too, and some find that equally helpful."

"Ah, yes," said Stephen. "I remember that volume can change as you strengthen muscle tissue and shrink fat cells. It reminds me of an old trick question from childhood: 'Which is lighter, a pound of muscle or a pound of feathers?' We loved it when someone answered, 'Feathers, of course.'"

"I know," agreed his coach. "Pound for pound, they weigh the same. Muscle tissue is denser, however, and consequently occupies less space—a difference by *volume*, although not by *weight*. If you have a quart-sized container of fat cells and a quart-sized container of muscle tissue, the muscle tissue would weight more because of its density. Strategies of a Longevity Lifestyle do include shrinking fat cells and strengthening muscle tissue, which help sculpt your body."

Stephen pinched a thick fold of skin around his waist. "Talk about *pinching an inch*. I can pinch double or triple that. Easily."

"Visceral fat cells that congregate around one's middle, do far more than just impact the way clothes fit. They can disrupt hormonal secretions and the metabolism of fats and proteins that, in turn, can impact appetite, blood sugar levels, cholesterol, blood pressure, and insulin sensitivity. A larger waist measurement has been found to increase one's risk for type 2 diabetes, asthma, and some forms of heart disease and cancer, as well as cancer reoccurrence. People with high amounts of belly fat are more than three times as likely to develop memory loss and dementia later in life. There is also a correlation between belly fat and lowered levels of testosterone."

"What?" asked Stephen. "Lowered levels of testosterone? How so?"

"Testosterone plays a vital role in how the body balances glucose, insulin, and fat metabolism. Evidence developed over the past few years now shows that, while obesity does cause low testosterone, low testosterone causes obesity. A 2008 epidemiological study of 1,822 men by the New England Research Institutes (NERI) concluded that a man's waist circumference is the single strongest predictor of low testosterone levels. And in women, studies have shown that in the presence of abdominal visceral obesity the usual low-level processes of androgen (testosterone) conversion seen in fat cells is turned off."

His coach paused, then asked, "Do you know your waist measurement?"

"Nope," said Stephen, shaking his head. "It's just big."

"Then I suggest you pick up a flexible measuring tape. I have one here you can use for now." The coach took a tape measure from the drawer and handed it to Stephen. "It's important to do the measuring

correctly. First, place the tape measure around your waist over skin, making sure it lays just above your hip bones and slightly above your belly button. Avoid sucking in your stomach. Pull the tape snug but not tight. Then read the measurement."

Stephen heaved himself out of the chair. Taking the tape measure he removed his sports coat and placed the tape around his waist. "It's a good thing this is a 60-inch tape measure," Stephen said, ruefully. "Otherwise I'd need to tie a couple 36 inchers together." He maneuvered the tape measure, put his glasses on, and looked at the number. "I suppose you want to know?"

"Only if you want to tell me. It's your waist and your number. I encourage you to discuss it with your doctor, however."

"What should the measurement be?" asked Stephen

"For adult males, waist measurement should be 40 inches or less. Estimates are that more than half of adult males in the USA have a waist measurement greater than 40 inches. For adult females the measurement should be 35 inches or less. The majority of women between the ages of 50 and 79 are believed to have a waist measurement greater than 35 inches."

"I'll make you a deal," said Stephen. "When my waist measurement reaches 40 inches, I'll tell you what it was today."

"Deal," said his coach, rolling up the tape and putting it away.

"Now, let's figure out your Body Mass Index (BMI). It is a measure of body fat based on height and weight that applies to average adult men and women. It is often used to *screen* for weight categories that may lead to health problems (although it may not apply in cases of severe anorexia or for serious athletes and body builders.) Once you know your BMI, you can compare that number with general categories for an idea of your health risks.

"You're not alone, you know, with your weight issues. According to recent World Health Organization (WHO) global estimates, in 2014 more than 1.9 billion adults were overweight and 600 million of those were obese. That means about 13% of the world's adult population (11% of men and 15% of women) were obese. Overall, the worldwide prevalence of obesity more than doubled between 1980 and 2014."

"You used the terms 'overweight' and 'obese.' Is being overweight different from being obese?" asked Stephen.

"It's partly a matter of degree," his coach explained. "The WHO defines the average adult with a BMI greater than or equal to 25 as being overweight. Those with a BMI greater than or equal to 30 are considered obese."

"When I look in the mirror, I never think I look as big as my sister says I do," said Stephen. "Okay, okay, I know I could stand to lose some weight but I do not want to go hungry and I am *not into starving!* By the way, I've noticed that you haven't mentioned food or dieting—yet. I suppose that'll be next."

"Not likely," said his coach. Stephen raised an eyebrow. "A Longevity Lifestyle is not about deprivation or dieting, which cannot be sustained over time in any healthy way. It is about what happens in your brain and how you *live*. Make no mistake: good nutrition is important. Many people eat large quantities of low-quality refined and processed *empty* calories in the form of non-nutritious foods and drinks. All of which propels them toward weight gain and disease states. 'The key to a Longevity Lifestyle is to ingest sufficient amounts of high–quality unrefined and unprocessed *nutritious* food on a daily basis, drink adequate amounts of water, obtain enough sleep, and keep moving. It is not about dieting and deprivation."

"Ah, yes. The part about 'moving.' I'm sure that means exercise," said Stephen. "Treadmill, weights. I'm tired just thinking about it."

"Spending long amounts of time on a treadmill or jogging or running—while providing some cardio benefits—may not be all that helpful for the average person. Those activities may actually accelerate the aging process by increasing free radical production, to say nothing of joint wear and tear. Take heart. Appropriate physical activity and exercise are components of a Longevity Lifestyle but need not involve sweating on a treadmill for hours at a time."

"Many roads lead to Rome, as the old saying goes. Undoubtedly there's a way to get moving in a style that works for you. Truth is, with few exceptions almost everyone can do something. The key is to avoid focusing on what you cannot do and concentrate instead on what you *can* do."

"I've always viewed exercise in terms of just strengthening my muscles," said Stephen.

"That is a common perception. Many people think of exercise primarily in terms of sculpting their muscles, but it does much more than that. According to studies published in the journal *Diabetes Care* (2013), a combination of aerobic and resistance physical activities are vital to improving body fat distribution and glucose control.

"Sitting appears to have an immediate effect on the way your body metabolizes glucose and can contribute to the development of insulin resistance and may increase your risk for diabetes. Those who sit after eating have 24 percent higher blood glucose (sugar) levels than individuals who walk slowly after a meal. As a contributor to obesity, inactivity is right up there with poor nutrition and smoking as proven root causes of disease.

"According to *Super Brain*," his coach continued, "leaving aside medical issues, obesity is caused by the many small choices people make on a daily basis; choices to sit instead of move; to consume an average of 150 pounds of sugar and drink 57 gallons of sodas and sugar drinks per person annually. Some people consume less sugar than the average, which means, of course, that others are ingesting far more than the estimated averages. These eating patterns contribute not only to obesity but also to diseases linked with it."

"Sure would have been better if I'd dumped my *peter-out* mindset ages ago." Stephen waived his hand and added. "I know. Better late than never. Still …"

His coach smiled. "Fortunately, it is rarely too late to embark on a journey toward better health. Get rid of those negative thoughts. Stop thinking and talking about what you no longer want to do. Tell yourself you like your new habits and focus on the myriad benefits that will accrue to your brain and body. Get off your duff and move!"

"Remember to thank your brain when it helps you accomplish a piece of your goal," added his coach. "Say aloud, 'I appreciate your assistance. Let's do this—together.' Think of yourself as being in partnership with your brain."

"Okay, I'm rephrasing," said Stephen, standing up as he said the words. "*You are off the couch! You are walking. You know you can do it and you are doing it!* Based on your last comment, I guess I should add, 'and thank you for doing this with me.'"

The coach could hear Stephen chuckling, even after he had left the room and started down the hall.

In Chapter 3 you'll find out what George and mice had in common. And it may surprise you.

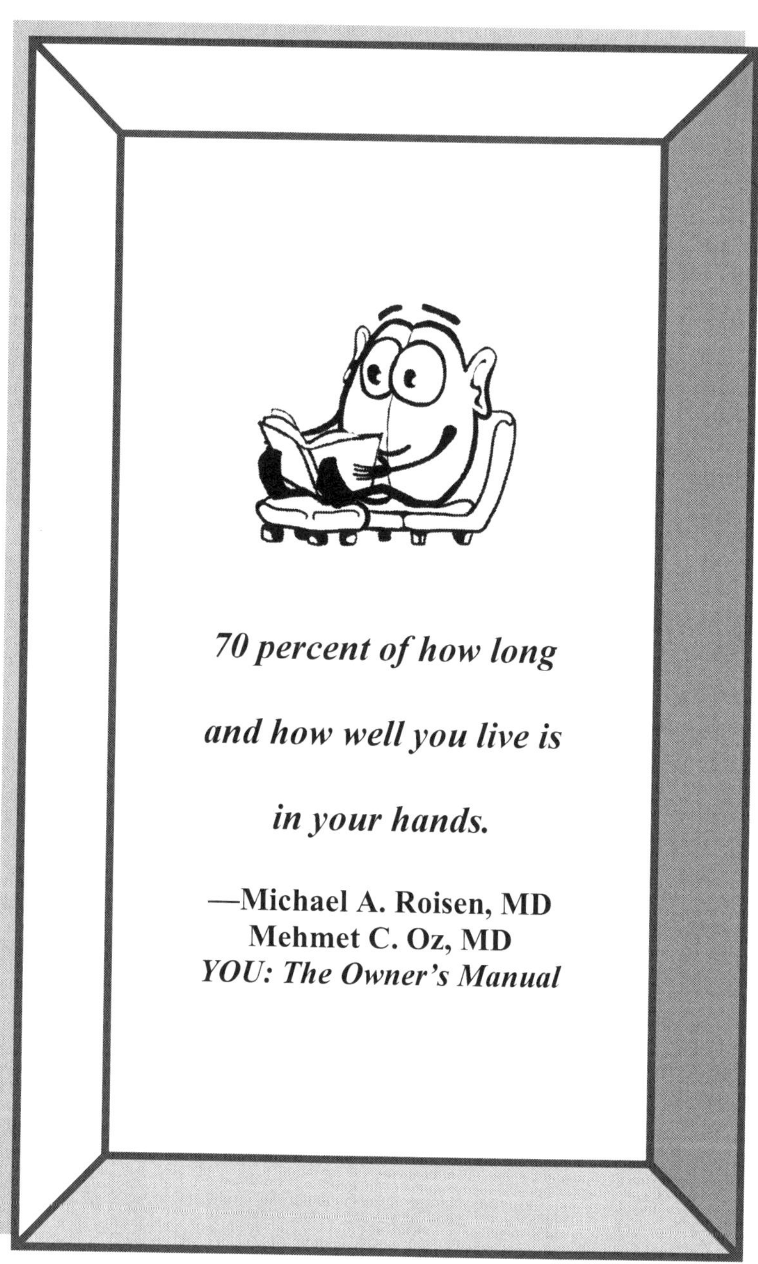

70 percent of how long and how well you live is in your hands.

—Michael A. Roisen, MD
Mehmet C. Oz, MD
YOU: The Owner's Manual

PAC for Success

Chapter 3

"I'm not sure about this," said George, shaking his head. "This stuff about a Longevity Lifestyle. I'm willing to try it, you understand, but quite frankly I'm not certain that I can do it. It seems like a very big chunk to bite off, to say nothing of chew!"

"Hmm," said his wellness coach. "I suspect you know how to bite and chew." George guffawed loudly.

"First of all, realize that there's a huge difference between trying and doing. Many *try*, while doubting success. *Trying* rarely achieves your goal. *Doing* often does because it means actually taking steps designed to increase your likelihood of success. The brain knows when you are serious and gets on board only when it senses you mean business. When it perceives you are in this only half-heartedly—in for a penny but not in for a pound—it fails metaphorically to put its shoulder to the wheel and just sits back waiting for you to resume your old habits."

"Based on that distinction it's pretty clear I've been *trying* more than *doing,*" said George, chuckling ruefully. "Actually, it's all my doctor's fault." George squirmed in his chair. "It's my doctor who's on my case about the risks of obesity. Every time I see him he blathers on about healthier long-term rewards. *Healthier long-term rewards.*"

"Can you guess the reason your doctor keeps *blathering* on about long-term rewards, as you put it?'

"Yeah," said George, having the good grace to look slightly sheepish. "We've known each other for decades, and he'd like me to trim off some of this excess weight. So would I, but to be perfectly honest, I like munching a double cheeseburger while I watch the sports channel every night. I usually pick one up on my way home from work. And when I've chowed down on that, if I'm still hungry I can always get a block of cheddar from the fridge. Sometimes I like the cheese even more than the cheeseburger. Cheese makes me feel really good."

"Of course it does. No mystery there. Mice like it, too. Probably for the same reason. Cheese contains an amphetamine-like chemical phenylethylamine or PEA. It's the same chemical that is secreted in your brain and body when you experience romantic love."

"You can't be serious!" exclaimed George. "Eating cheese gives my brain the same type of *chemical hit* as being *in love?"*

His coach nodded. "And with cheese, you don't even have to invest any time or energy in a romantic relationship. You just eat. In addition, during digestion, cheese breaks apart releasing opiates known as casomorphins, which not only help you feel good but also can trigger the release of histamine, a compound involved in the body's immune responses."

"No wonder I love cheese," said George, shaking his head. "Full of opiate-like compounds? "Who knew?"

"It's not rocket science—on the other hand, maybe it is when you think about the complexity of the human brain. It has been referred to as the most complicated kilo of matter in the universe and the last, and greatest, scientific frontier."

"Healthier long-term rewards," mused George, sighing. "That illusive pot of gold at the end of the rainbow. I want it all. Seriously; the short-term reward *and* the long-term healthier-life reward."

"I applaud you for recognizing that," said his coach. "Many have not even identified their want-it-all mindset."

"Mindset," said George. "Could you define that for me?"

"A mindset is the mental attitude or disposition that predetermines your responses; a set of opinions about something that strongly influences your inclinations. Everything starts in the brain and it begins with a mindset—yours.

"No one can ever have it all. There is no *free lunch*, per se. In life, you always give up something to get something. Actually, you gave up something to be here today. I have no idea what, but I know it was something."

"You're right. I gave up a movie, at least one double cheeseburger, a giant Coke, and a big tub of popcorn with extra butter. Hey, I gave up some of that *PEA* stuff." His grunt turned into a laugh.

"So, you could sprawl on the couch and munch a double cheeseburger, or you could take a walk and eat an apple. But not both at the same time. Success involves the ability to defer short-term gratification for a larger long-term benefit. It begins with mindset, and in the words of your doctor, for *healthier long-term rewards*."

"Mindset," repeated George. "I've never been very good at deferring much of anything that I really want," said George, snorting. "I seem to go for short-term rewards, which keep my weight and blood pressure high and my spirits and energy low. If I'd done differently, I wouldn't be in this mess!" He shifted his hefty self in the chair.

"*What-ifs* typically are unhelpful because it is impossible to go back," said his coach. "Most people do the best they can at the time with what they know. Now that you know better, you can choose to do better. Hone your ability to delay immediate gratification. Focus on the positive actions you are taking and learn to weigh short-term rewards against long-term healthier benefits." His coach paused for a moment and then added: "Ask yourself: 'What do I want more?' Then go for it."

"I know that intellectually," said George. "My feelings are something else again."

"Your conscious and subconscious thoughts are connected with your feelings. As Dr. Wayne Dyer once put it, you can't have a feeling without first having a thought. Studies have shown that your subconscious mind may have been thinking a thought for 7 to 10 seconds before you consciously became aware of it."

George studied a rather complex-appearing wrist watch and counted off 7 seconds. "If my subconscious mind has been thinking thoughts for 7 to 10 seconds, how am I responsible for my thoughts and feelings?"

"You are not responsible for every thought that crosses your mind," said his coach. "Once you become aware of a thought consciously, my brain's opinion is that you are responsible for either hanging onto the thought (and perhaps taking action based upon it) or choosing to think another thought. When you become aware of a feeling, a thought preceded it. If you want to change the way you feel, then consciously change your thoughts."

"Tell me more about this," said George. "It's interesting."

"What you put into your brain can trigger thoughts and feelings follow thoughts. You do have a choice about what goes into your brain by what you watch, listen to, read, say, observe, and so on."

His coach continued. "You certainly can't control everything by any stretch of the imagination, but you make many small choices every day. You are responsible for those choices because what goes into your brain can return in the form of thoughts, which then can trigger feelings.

"Once you become consciously aware of your thoughts, you decide if you want to nurture them or replace them. Although you're not responsible for every thought that crosses your mind, you *are* largely responsible for those you choose to ponder. In fact, some believe that is the essence of free will—making decisions, once you consciously become aware of your thoughts.

"You also choose whether or not to take action based on your thoughts and feelings. If you decide to take action, you must decide the action to take and the behavior to exhibit. Unless there is something seriously wrong with your brain, you are responsible for those actions and their consequences. Thoughts can travel across neuron pathways at rates of 400 feet per second or 200 miles per hour, which means that 7 to 10 seconds is quite a chunk of time neurochemically.

"That points out the benefit of taking a deep breath and thinking a few seconds before saying or doing something that might be an overreaction and which could create a mess that will need to be cleaned up later on. For example, if you choose to drive intoxicated, in the eyes of the law you are responsible for the crash that results—because you chose to drink and then drive."

"That helps to explain something I've always wondered about," said George. "Copy-cat murders. You know, the ones that often occur after a particularly grizzly crime is splashed around on the news. Scary, those. I just figured that obviously something was seriously wrong with the perpetrator's brain! "

“There likely was something a bit *off* in their thought processing, certainly,” said his coach. “And if they focused on replaying the reported criminal information in their brains, the information was converted to pictures that they followed in action.”

“Mindset,” said George, shaking his head. “That’s really what you’re talking about, isn’t it? I’m beginning to think my mindset is far more important than I would have credited it.”

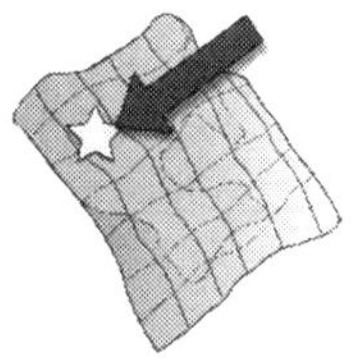

“Your mindset establishes your direction. Tells you where you are headed on the map of your life. It gets your brain on board (or not). Each day you make many small decisions that cumulatively move you toward or away from a Longevity Lifestyle.”

“A map for my brain. Actually a map *in* my brain,” said George. “I like that. I’ve always been pretty good at directions. I just need to create that *map* and then *visualize* it every day to help keep me on my Longevity Lifestyle journey. I can do that.”

“I have come to the conclusion that success in life involves an ongoing continuum of miniscule decisions. ‘Will I do this or will I do that?’ The eventual consequences you experience result from their cumulative effect. Make each small choice with an awareness of the potential long-term result of that decision. And it all goes back to mindset. Yours,” said his coach, smiling. “Henry Ford put it very well in these words:

If you think you can do a thing or think you can’t do a thing, you’re right.

“Like a double cheeseburger and a block of cheddar cheese,” said George. “I’ve never really considered how those little choices can and do add up. You’ve just given me more to think about. I can see how if I alter my small daily decisions, down the line …” His voice trailed off.

"I just remembered part of a little verse from grade school. Something like tiny drops of water and tiny grains of sand, make a mighty ocean and a pleasant land." George chuckled.

"Maya Angelou has been quoted as saying:

> *Life likes to be taken by the lapel and told, I'm with you kid. Let's go.*

"That's a good description of a positive mindset. A successful Longevity Lifestyle requires the development of a *PAC* Mindset. PAC is an acronym. Each letter stands for one of three main components."

His coach briefly explained each of the three components.

- **'P' stands for developing a POSITIVE can-do attitude**

  Think and speak in positives. Tell your brain: *you can, you choose, you are.* Think and talk about what you are doing as if it's all already in place. Avoid thinking and talking about what you no longer want to do. When you recognize a negative thought, it is absolutely essential to change it; rephrase it into a positive thought.

  This is not a Pollyanna approach, pretending that bad things don't happen, but it does mean that once you acknowledge the issue, you immediately move to gratitude for the good things. You learn from your mistakes and use that experiential knowledge to make different decisions in the future.

  Think *plenty* instead of privation and *abundance* rather than scarcity. Dump can't do and think *can do*."

- **'A' stands for making ACTIVE mental pictures**

  Actively picture in your mind's eye what you are doing every day to embrace a Longevity Lifestyle. Picture the various behaviors you are exhibiting in order to be successful. Think of the pictures as a collage of desirable behaviors that you can choose from for the rest of your life, behaviors that will help you achieve desirable outcomes. Of course you can tweak and improve them as you go along, developing new ones as needed.

  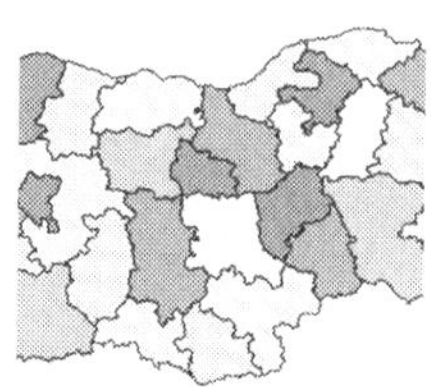

  If you need to be at a healthier weight, visualize what you will look like when you achieve your goal —and then follow through on your plan to realize that goal.

"Positive and Active," said George. "I need to work on both of those."

His coach continued with a brief explanation of the third component.

- **'C' stands for identifying CREATIVE options and alternatives**

  A Longevity Lifestyle needs to work for each brain—and each brain is unique. Learn the general principles, then apply strategies that incorporate those general guidelines in ways that fit you and your brain. That will increase your likelihood of following them for the rest of your life. Be realistic in your expectations and strive to keep your life in balance, homeostasis. Your goal is to keep life in your years and to live as many healthy years as possible. Years that keep brain and body active. Years that include high levels of at least mental, emotional, physical, spiritual, and social function.

"I can see that I need to *pack* my *PAC Mindset*, and take it with me everywhere. Fortunately, it's inside my brain!" George smiled.

"It is," his coach agreed. "Everything starts and ends in the brain. Creating and maintaining a Longevity Lifestyle is first and foremost about mindset, about what goes on inside your brain and your mind. You simply need to access it to help you be successful. Once you truly get that, you are light years ahead of most people on this planet, who, if they think about it at all, tend to believe that old phrase: *The devil made me do it.*

"Even though everything starts and ends in the brain, there are continual and complex interactions between brain and body. Your weight, for example, results from a combination of brain-body interactions. In turn, a weight that is too low (think anorexia) or a weight that is too high (think overweight or obese) can adversely impact both brain and body. The deleterious effects on your brain of being overweight or obese can increase your risk for any number of disease processes and illnesses, including dementia."

"For the first time in my life, I am grasping what it means to live a Longevity Lifestyle. Quite frankly," said George, seriously, "I think I'm light years ahead of myself in terms of where I was even last week!"

"The secret of getting ahead is getting started—you've started!" said his coach, smiling. "Now you just need to keep on keeping on."

"Yes, I have started," said George. "And I intend to keep on keeping on!"

Turn to Chapter 4 and meet Tom, who identified two energy-eaters.

Having a growth mindset doesn't force you to pursue something. It just tells you that you can develop your skills—it's still up to you whether you want to.

—Carol S. Dweck, PhD

Eavesdropping on the Brain

Chapter 4

"How was your week, Tom?" asked the wellness coach.

"Honestly?" replied the large man, heaving a big sigh as he slumped into his chair. "I may be a total failure at creating a Longevity Lifestyle. I thought it would be easier. Maybe I need to lower my expectations."

"Sounds like you had a challenging week," his coach said. "Low expectations tend to get low results, however. High expectations tend to give higher results."

Tom sat up straighter in his chair. "Hmmm."

"Dr. Carol Dweck points out in *Mindset* that your brain is always eavesdropping on your thoughts. As it listens, it learns. *Thinking* you are a failure will contribute to you *feeling* like a failure. Your brain cannot do what it thinks it cannot do. If it does not perceive and expect success it will perceive and expect failure.

"Dweck also wrote about two different types of people and two differing mindsets: fixed and growth. Those with a *fixed* mindset believe that who they are is carved in stone. When they perceive failure, they feel worthless, unlucky, and often give up. Those with a *growth* mindset, on the other hand, believe they can change and improve through application and experience."

"Even though they face challenges, growth-mindset people refrain from putting themselves down or throwing in the proverbial towel. They just keep on building their skills and practicing."

"Fixed mindset or growth mindset. I need an example."

"I don't know what was so challenging about last week," said his coach, "but let's imagine that several unexpected events occurred. You ran out of gas on the freeway, and by the time help arrived, you were already late for an important meeting. In your rush, you parked improperly and later found a ticket on your windshield, to say nothing of your pounding headache from missing lunch and snacking on sugar cookies. And when you called home, your wife was not particularly sympathetic."

Tom laughed. "That's pretty close. What are you, a mind reader?"

His coach continued. "A *fixed* mindset would say: 'I'm beyond unlucky. Why me? My life is pitiful. Things are so frustrating. I feel like everyone else is better off than I am. Maybe smarter, too. I feel like just giving up. There's nothing I can do to change things. Maybe I should just cash it all in.' A *fixed* mindset would push you to eat chocolate or ice cream or drink too much wine with dinner in an attempt to feel better. Or maybe it would tempt you to act out your frustration: pick a fight with your wife or throw something at the wall or kick the dog or veg out in front of the TV and lose sleep.

"A *growth* mindset would more likely think: '*This is a good reminder to keep the gas tank at least half full. Next time I'll be more careful when parking the car. And a nutritious lunch would be a much better choice than eight sugar cookies. There's certainly no point in taking this out on others.*' A *growth* mindset would not enjoy the frustrating events, but neither would it use pejorative labels or fail to eat and sleep properly or throw up its hands in abject helplessness or be unkind to others. It looks for the lesson in what happened and learns from it."

"I'm pretty sure I grew up with a negative fixed mindset," said Tom. "My whole family, too. It's like the way we thought about things was locked somehow. I want to unlock my brain and become more positive and flexible."

"I think that those who are creating a Longevity Lifestyle—with the view to maintaining it as long as they live—need to develop a positive mindset along with positive self-talk, a positive communication style, and flexibility of thinking. Even your body's energy levels are closely connected with your mindset, thoughts, self-talk, and the internal mental pictures they create.

"Positive thoughts and feelings add energy to your system, while negative thoughts and feelings deplete your energy. Anxiety and anger are energy eaters. A negative mindset and thinking style, can turn into a vicious cycle and drag you down. That's partly because the brain tends to pursue congruity. When in the grip of a strong emotion, the brain tends to trigger recall of past situations that involved a similar emotion in order to promote congruity."

"How do you define brain congruity?" asked Tom.

"The brain wants everything to match, to be in cinque," his coach replied. "It's quite simple, really. Only one main idea at a time can fill the brain's working memory. If you are fearful or thinking negatively, that is what will be in working memory. Negativity triggers the recall of negative thoughts and memories. The stress response itself can be extended by dwelling on the negative aspects of an event.

"On the other hand, positively tends to trigger the recall of positive thoughts and memories. If you think of something for which to be grateful, that will be the focus of your brain's working memory. Studies have indicated that fear and gratitude cannot co-exist simultaneously in the brain. In other words, gratitude trumps fear."

"That puts a different spin on a lot of things," said Tom. "For starters, I had no idea that changing the way I think could be so powerful."

"Affirmation is the label for a style of thinking that emphasizes using positive words to communicate with yourself and others. The power of positive is very strong. Jean Marie Stine has pointed out that mental states are particular susceptible to affirmation, which is the mind's programming language."

"That sounds a bit like Pollyanna," said Tom.

"Learning to think positively is not a Pollyanna mindset. Bad things do happen to good people. Developing an affirming communication pattern *is* a way of responding to life with a sense of gratitude and happiness, thinking and speaking in an empowering, can-do style. Jean Marie Stine has pointed out that mental states are particular susceptible to affirmation, the mind's programming language."

"Think energy, Tom. Positive emotional states create coherence within the human system. The word coherence comes from a Latin word meaning *to stick together.* I think of it as a cousin to congruence. When all components of a system are operating in positive congruence or coherence, virtually no energy is wasted."

"That certainly is a new way to think of energy," said Tom, shifting in his chair. "It's amazing to think of the body generating energy. Reminds me of electricity generated by hydropower as well as by the wind using new types of windmills on wind farms."

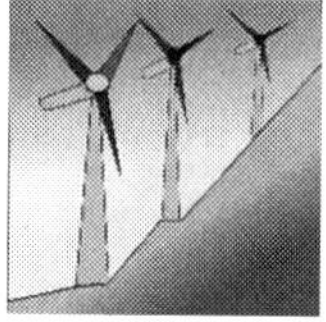

"Jon Gordon, author of books such as *Energy Addict* and *The Energy Bus,* points out that when you think positively about the day ahead, you increase the levels of both your mental and physical energy. And that can impact how you perceive and respond to the events of the day."

"Wondering if I need to lower my expectations likely falls into the category of unhelpful thoughts," said Tom. "Those types of thoughts won't increase my energy." He laughed.

"I'll repeat my earlier comment: low expectations tend to get low results while higher expectations tend to produce higher results. Creating and maintaining a Longevity Lifestyle is about liking and caring for your body because it's the only one that will be with you for your whole life. A Longevity Lifestyle can result in a decrease in the amount of excess fat you pack around on a daily basis, and a more optimum weight is associated with:

- Better blood flow
- Lower blood pressure
- A healthier vascular system.

"Oh my," said Tom, rising and pacing. "That's probably one reason I'm a widower. My wife was a wonderful woman: capable, articulate, funny, a fabulous cook. We fell in love and married right out of high school. Katie was a bit overweight even as a child and she carried that weight, and added to it, her entire life. When she died at age fifty-seven, she weighed close to three hundred pounds and didn't know a cauliflower from a computer. I didn't think much about it. From this vantage point, however, if we'd known back then what we know now, things might have been different. For both of us."

"You can only do what you know," said his coach. "Information about how to live healthier for longer seems to be coming into its own in the age of the brain. Unfortunately, women may be even more susceptible to obesity. And adult female obesity is more likely to lead to brain atrophy, a phenomenon that increases the risk for brain damage and dementia. Females who are obese throughout life may be at even higher risk for losing brain tissue. And loss of brain tissue, of course, has been linked to cognitive decline."

"What about obesity and brain function in males?" asked Tom, patting the *spare tire* wrapped around his middle. "I assume there are some general risks associated with obesity regardless of gender. By the way, I'm finding these topics much more interesting that I ever thought they'd be."

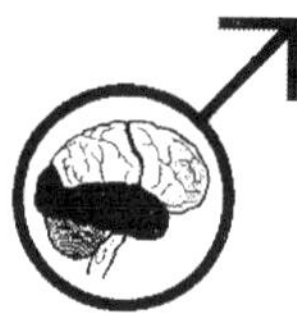

"I'm glad you are, Tom, and you're correct. Obesity is not good for any brain at any age, male or female."

His coach mentioned a few examples.

- Those who are overweight tend to live unbalanced lives. Often they find ways to work around their obesity, adapting to it and perpetuating the vicious cycle.

- Obesity appears to be associated with degeneration of the white matter (myelin) that wraps around and insulates neuronal axons.

- Obesity increases the risk of brain damage to the temporal lobes, largely responsible for language, memory, and hearing.

- Obesity can be fueled by unconscious behaviors such as automatically putting snack foods into the mouth without stopping until the entire bag or bowl is completely empty.

"You might want to do your own internet search on obesity and exercise your brain at the same time," said his coach. "You may be surprised at the number of study reports that pop up. Some of them are quite fascinating. The good news is that you are doing something about creating healthier habit patterns now."

"As I said, too bad we didn't understand a Longevity Lifestyle earlier in our marriage." Tom resumed his seat.

"Unfortunately, our three kids are quite heavy, too. Maybe I need to tell them what they should start doing."

"Do your children live nearby?" Tom nodded.

"Children watch their parents all the time and at every age. Your best bet may be to lead by example. They'll notice your Longevity Lifestyle and may ask questions. Be ready with brief answers, pointing them to resources they can study for themselves. That's often more successful."

"That gives me something to think about … still wish we'd done it differently," said Tom, shaking his head. "It's a sad past, it is."

"Does the name Johan Cruyff ring a bell, by any chance?" asked his coach.

"Sure does," replied Tom quickly. "Dutch ex-footballer. Cruyff may be one of the best players in the entire history of the sport; started the Cruyff Institute for Sport Studies. He's also famous for his quirky use of the Dutch language. His so-called *Cruyffisms* like 'You can't score if you don't shoot.'"

"I enjoy reading them myself," said his coach. "A recent airline magazine included several of them. One of my favorites is: *There is no future without a past.* So be glad you have a past, Tom, because that gives you the option of a future. Although it's impossible to go back and redo anything, it is possible to move forward and create a healthier future for yourself. Focus on the positive actions you are taking. Evaluate your expectations carefully. Select those that are realistic and that *you* want to meet. Create options, alternatives, and strategies that work for *you*. And enjoy maintaining a Longevity Lifestyle.

"I definitely want to be around for my children," said Tom.

"Do you by any chance have grandchildren?" his coach asked.

Tom nodded. "A boy and a girl. They are something else, those two. I'd like to help them avoid packing on pounds in the first place. That reminds me. My doctor mentioned *adrenal exhaustion*. What exactly is that?"

"Adrenal exhaustion can occur when things get out of balance. The adrenal glands become tired from pumping out stress hormones, likely from the combination of a high-stress career, a sedentary lifestyle, and far too high an intake of sugar and caffeine.

"In his book *The Brain and Emotional Intelligence* Dr. Daniel Goleman uses the term *allostatic load* when referring to a situation when the damaging effects of stress hormones predominate. They can create a variety of imbalances in the immune and nervous systems. These stress hormones can also harm the hippocampus (your brain's search engine), impair memory, increase insulin resistance, degrade or deteriorate the myelin sheath (think fiber optics) around nerve axons, and increase one's risk for diabetes, heart disease, and artery blockages."

His coach handed Tom a list of potential symptoms that may point to adrenal exhaustion.

They included:

- Decreased ability to withstand stress
- Poor memory and difficulty concentrating
- Low libido, fatigue, and a lack of stamina
- Abdominal fat that doesn't seem to go away
- Craving for sweets or salty foods
- High blood pressure, rapid heartbeat, dizziness
- Recurring infections and poor wound healing
- Signs of premature aging

"Okay, that does it," said Tom, determinedly. "I don't have all those symptoms, but I have some of them. And if I'm really honest, I believe I thought that losing weight would somehow take care of other problems in my life."

His coach chuckled. "In his book *Self Matters* Dr. Phil McGraw points out:

> '*You can never, ever, use weight loss to solve* problems *that are not related to your weight. At your goal weight or not, you still have to live with yourself and deal with your problems. You will still have the same husband, the same job, the same kids, and the same life. Losing weight is not a cure for life.*'"

Tom sat quietly for several minutes, staring at his hands. Finally he said, "All this has given me a new perspective, a different view of things, a vision for creating and implementing a Longevity Lifestyle. I'm serious. I intend to set the best example I can for my offspring. Better late than never."

Smiling, Tom was on his way, a new gleam of purpose in his eye.

Chapter 5 is next. Meet David, who was taught that self-talk could get a person locked up.

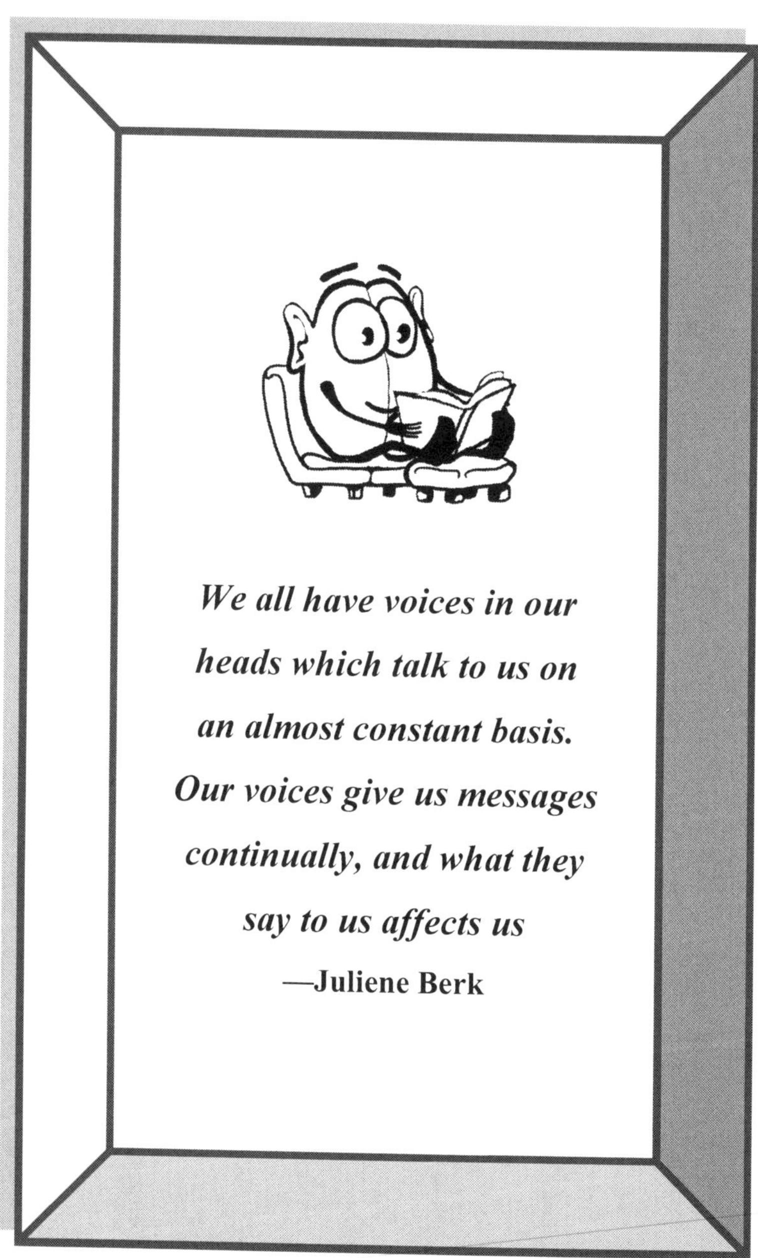
We all have voices in our
heads which talk to us on
an almost constant basis.
Our voices give us messages
continually, and what they
say to us affects us
—Juliene Berk

White Bear Phenomenon

Chapter 5

"What's this I hear about self-talk?" asked David. "Me, I don't believe in it. My dad thought talking to oneself was a symptom of mental illness. He'd say, 'It's bad enough to mutter aloud occasionally; it's quite another to answer. That can get you locked up!'"

"All human beings talk to themselves," said his wellness coach, "although some seem to be unaware of that. Self-talk is just a label for what you tell yourself. And what you tell yourself makes all the difference in the world. Many people talk to themselves in unhelpful ways, speaking negatively instead of positively. It's important to listen in on your own conversations and develop a communication style that helps program your brain for success."

"In fact," continued his coach, "you're talking to yourself right now, holding a private conversation with yourself, although I don't know what you're saying."

"Well, I'll be a ..." David cleared his throat, "ah-h-h a monkey's uncle. I *was* talking to myself, saying, 'I wonder what my coach will spring on me today.' And then you come up with self-talk!" His eyebrows raised half-way to his hairline.

"That's what thoughts are," said his coach. "Personal, internal, private conversations with yourself."

"Fortunately, most of us have some type of *governer* that prevents us from blurting out every word of our private internal conversations, every thought that crosses our minds. But when that governer fails momentarily . . ."

"Been there, done that," said David, "and then asked myself, 'Did I really say that aloud? So what's so important about self-talk that puts it up there with mindset?"

"When twins are delivered, one baby is born first, if only by a few seconds. Think of mindset and self-talk as a set of twins. Mindset influences self-talk and together they impact behaviors.

"John Lembo stated it like this: *Every waking moment we talk to ourselves about the things we experience. Our self-talk, the thoughts we communicate to ourselves, control the way we feel and act.*

"Thoughts and words create internal mental pictures in the neocortex or 3rd brain layer, the portion that contains conscious thought. Think of this process as creating a map for your brain to follow. The 1st and 2nd subconscious brain layers do not use language per se, but they can perceive the pictures (map) that filter down to them. Your subconscious mind follows the pictures and usually does its best to push you toward them.

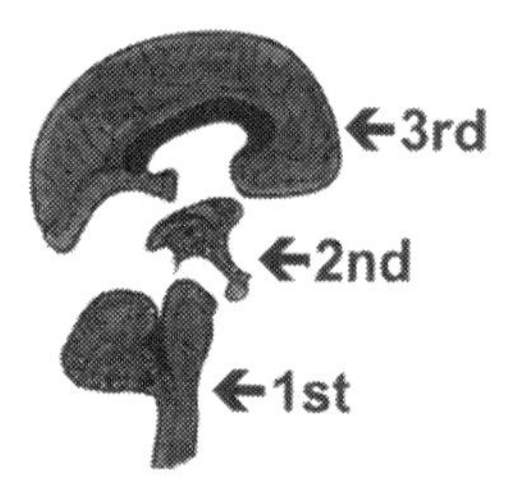

"The kicker is that the brain deals easily with positives, a one-step process. What you say and think forms the picture you create in your brain. Negatives on the other hand are a two-step process—which often creates a challenge for the brain. When the brain perceives the words, (thoughts, self-talk, spoken, read, or heard) it creates a picture from the words. The word *don't* indicates that the brain is not to follow the picture it just created, so the brain must figure out how to alter the picture, which it may or may not convert accurately."

"And if it misses the word *don't* altogether, the brain may just continue to follow the first picture it created."

"Oh, my!" exclaimed David. "When I told my kids, 'Don't touch the stove' their brains first created a picture of touching the stove. It would have been more helpful to say, 'Keep your hand away from the stove.'"

"Correct," said his coach. "That's a one-step process, so the brain has nothing to convert."

Which means, of course, we also should have said things like, 'Remember your homework' or 'It's time to practice your trumpet,' or 'Play outdoors for an hour before you play a video game.'"

"Exactly. Dr. Daniel Wegner refers to this as the *white bear phenomenon.* When you say, 'Don't think about the white bear,' a representation of a white bear goes into your brain's working memory and that becomes all you tend to think about. In a similar way, if you say 'I don't want to eat a big dinner late at night,' your brain initially pictures eating a big dinner late at night and may miss the 'don't.'"

"A negative instruction tells you what *not* to do but rarely tells you what *to* do, which, of course, is relatively unhelpful. Are you supposed to eat large dinners early in the evening or small dinners late at night or no dinner at all? The brain has no clue because you were not specific. It is usually much more helpful to say something like, 'You eat a small dinner before six o'clock. You eat slowly and feel satisfied.' By any chance did you ever read *The Adventures of Tom Sawyer?"* David nodded. "Mark Twain must have understood the white bear phenomenon at some level because he has one of the characters say: "To promise not to do a thing is the surest way in the world to make a body want to go and do that very thing."

"I even remember that," said David, chuckling. "By the way, earlier you used the word 'you' when scripting some self-talk examples. Isn't it better to say 'I'?"

"You may choose to use 'I'," said his coach. "Some believe that in that case you'd need to say, 'I, David,' to make sure your brain knows exactly about whom you are speaking. Others think it may be more effective to speak about yourself using the pronoun *you*. It depersonalizes things slightly and emphasizes that *you* are collaborating with *your* brain and mind and giving the directions. In a sense you, your brain, and your mind are separate entities. It's like the 'me, myself, and I' jargon. Most people have little concept of how they can cooperate with their brain and mind to be more successful.

"Currently, there is no complete consensus about how the brain and the mind interact or coexist. There is debate and controversy. Some think the physical brain develops first and then somehow creates the mind. Other scientists suggest that the mind may create the brain, rather than the other way around. What appears to be quite certain is that they can impact each other. Metaphorically, consider traffic: vehicles create traffic, which then can either facilitate or impede vehicles. In much the same way, the brain directs what goes on in the body. And what goes on in the body can facilitate or impede functions of the brain."

"It seems to me that the mind and brain must be two separate but interactive entities," said David. "Which do you think came first?"

"That's the old *chicken or the egg* controversy. I sometimes wonder if the brain and mind develop somewhat simultaneously and help each other along. The brain is beginning to develop within a few weeks after conception—maybe even by the fourth day."

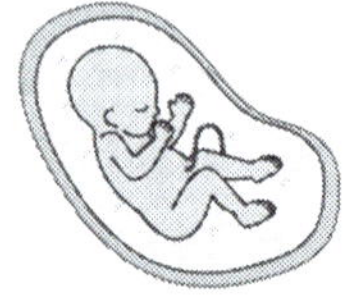

"Studies suggest that sound may be the first sensory system to develop during gestation. Once the baby is born, it is able to recognize sounds and songs that were heard repeatedly during pregnancy. The auditory system of the brain is obviously involved with hearing sounds and decoding them, but the conscious mind is also involved in recognizing the melodies.

"Interestingly enough, studies also suggest that sound is the last sensory system to go at the end of one's life. The brain is amazingly complex. And who knows? Brain research may have just scratched the surface. What is being discovered, however, is marvelous. And when it is practically applied, it can be life changing. You'll just need to stay tuned."

"I've not thought much about my brain or my mind," said David. "Learning about them is quite interesting. And I now realize that I *do* talk to myself! In the past I just thought of that as *thinking*, if I thought about it at all."

"Clearly, all human beings talk to themselves much of the time, regardless of what they call it." His coach smiled.

"I want to be more positive in the way I think and speak to myself," said David. "Correction. I need to say that differently. *You* are creating a Longevity Lifestyle and maintaining it every day. *Your* blood pressure is lower." David stuck out his chin and added: "*You* and I feel better already!" They both laughed.

"Thoughts are more important than most people believe. Everything begins with a thought—a precursor to words, actions, feelings, and all communication with yourself and others. In order to feel, do, and communicate, you must first have a thought, even though you aren't consciously aware of having had the thought.

"I'm learning to be more aware of what I'm thinking—at the time I'm thinking it," said David. "Mindful awareness, as you put it."

"Glad to know that," said his coach. "You're the only person on this planet who can change the way you think or the way you communicate with yourself and with others."

David nodded. "Some of my relatives tell me regularly how awful I look at this weight. It makes me feel bad about myself so I try to avoid even seeing them."

"In general, human beings tend to communicate with others in the style they use with themselves. When individuals speak negatively, that's likely the style they use with themselves. Their brains must be tired and discouraged from being spoken to so negatively—to say nothing about the brains of the people to whom those individuals speak. It's sad, really. Perhaps they think they are helping. Maybe not.

"The bottom line is, take a look at your life now and compare it with how you want your life to be. You know what you need to do in order to move toward a Longevity Lifestyle. Ask yourself, 'Of the new habits I want to create, which one would be of most benefit?' Once you have selected one new behavior, decide what is realistic for you to achieve. Avoid being afraid to start small, especially with exercise and weight-management goals."

"Oh," said David. "You mean heading for the gym tomorrow for a three-hour workout might not be my best option right off the bat?"

"Likely not," said his coach, laughing. "Especially if you've been relatively inactive for months—or even years."

"I've already stopped guzzling soft drinks," said David, "and my drop-dead bed time is eleven o'clock. The first few days without soft drinks were rather difficult. I'll admit I was a bit surprised by that, but in retrospect it wasn't all that bad. Neither is going to bed by eleven at night."

"So what are you tackling next?" asked his coach. David shrugged.

"You might consider this idea," said his coach. "Go home, think about it, and write down one measurable goal for yourself. Picture in your mind's eye what that will look like when it has been accomplished. Say aloud what you plan to do as if it's already accomplished, and frame it in a positive style."

David steepled his fingers. "I don't need to go home and think about it," he said. "I can set a goal now. Let me see: *You* are walking for fifteen minutes after dinner. *You* are dropping half a pound this week. *Your* pants are looser. Good for *YOU!*"

"That's a good start," said his coach. "What specific small steps can you build into your daily routine to maintain the daily walk?"

"How about these?" David asked.

"Set the equipment to record my favorite talk show. That will give me something to look forward to at the end of my walk.

"Change into my walking clothes before I eat dinner. That way I can walk immediately after the meal.

"When I finish eating, get up from the table, head directly out the front door, and start walking."

"Good," said his coach. "Breaking a large goal into smaller specific steps can help you be more successful."

"Give me a recap of that mindset stuff again," said David, pausing with his hand on the doorknob. "Matter of fact, let me record it on my cell phone so I'll have it handy."

"PAC Mindset. Remember, PAC is an acronym:

- **'P'** stands for developing a POSITIVE can-do attitude

- **'A'** stands for making ACTIVE mental pictures

- **'C'** stands for CREATIVE options and alternatives

"Self-talk follows mindset. Develop a PAC Mindset and take it with you everywhere.

- "Think and speak in positives. Stop telling your brain what you do not want to do. Always tell your brain what you *are* doing as if it's already a done deal. Talk to yourself using the pronoun *you*.

- "Develop a map for your brain to follow by actively picturing in your mind's eye how you will look as you achieve your goals.

- "Be flexible and creative. If it's too hot to walk, swim. If there is nowhere to swim, go to the gym. If there is no gym, walk in an indoor mall. If you like cucumbers but none are available, try celery.

- "Remember: both a negative mindset and a positive mindset are self-fulfilling. If you think you can or you think you can't, you're right. What you tell yourself makes all the difference in the world."

David nodded. "Got it. Thanks." And he was out the door.

Chapter 6 is where you'll meet Josh and his besotted brain. That's right. *Besotted* brain.

Take Charge!
If you don't deal with your
fears, distress, anger,
or sadness—
comfort food will.
—Laura Pawlak, PhD

Besotted Brain

Chapter 6

"At one time or another over the last 25 years, I've been addicted to at least booze, cigarettes, sex, and overeating." Josh moved from the chair to the office love seat. It better suited his size.

"In that order?" asked his wellness coach.

"Not exactly," Josh replied. "At one point I became so besotted with sex that my wife finally got fed up and said she was out of there if I didn't get a handle on it. I went to an addiction recovery program and reduced my *besottedness* for sex. But then my smoking went from two to four packs a day. My doctor climbed my frame; said I was showing signs of emphysema, and if I didn't want to be in for a world of hurt I'd better quit. Next I attended a Smoke-Free Life program and ditched the tobacco. But then I started drinking heavily, to the point that my boss threatened to cut me free to look for another job. I'd thought I'd been *sneaking* nips at work, but evidently I hadn't been all that clever. So I went to yet another program and dried out. That was when food took over. I'd always been an overeater but I cranked it up a notch, taking it from an avocation to a vocation. My doctor pulled me up short; told me to put a lid on the calories or my wife might as well start planning my funeral."

"Pour in its drug of choice and the brain is momentarily happy," said his wellness coach. "But there are usually negative consequences for the *besotted* brain"

"I know," exclaimed Josh. "Look at me for heaven's sake. I look like a plump penguin. A very plump penguin to put it bluntly."

"You might want to change the way you are describing yourself, Josh. Ralph Waldo Trine is very clear when he says *Never affirm or repeat about your health what you do not wish to be true.* And, by the way, I see quite a handsome face."

"Maybe ten years ago, before I added a couple hundred pounds." Josh waved his hand dismissively. "What's handsome about a double chin? What's attractive about a spare tire? They may look good on some cars, but not around my waist."

"Some primates seem to go for them. The spare tires, not the cars."

"Good one," laughed George. "Your sense of humor is killing me."

"Actually, a good sense of humor and laughter are good for both brain and body. On the other hand, your weight likely is—slowly, stealthily, insidiously, inexorably killing you."

"I was afraid you might say that," Josh mumbled. "So what are my options? Bariatric surgery to get my stomach stapled?"

"That is an option but it's a drastic surgery, and many people gain their weight back. That's the problem with a besotted brain. With your history, no doubt you know already that the biggest cure for one addictive behavior is another addictive behavior. That's because it's all about what happens in the brain reward system. Perhaps you need to take a long hard look at your habit patterns around self-medication."

"But I can't live without food," said Josh, turning pale. "I found I could live without tobacco and alcohol and without sex three times a day—but food? I cannot live without food!"

"You're right. You cannot live without food. In all likelihood you can live without overeating; without ingesting poor quality foods and beverages; without using food to self-medicate."

"*Self-medicate*," said Josh. "What does that mean?

"It's a term that describes what humans do to help themselves feel better. Everyone does it. The issue is whether or not a person's habits of self-medication result in desirable or undesirable outcomes. For example, tobacco, alcohol, sex, and some foods impact the brain in much the same way. They release a cascade of substances that trigger the brain reward center and can make you want more and more."

"Guess I just have an addictive personality," said Josh, shrugging. "My mother smoked, drank a bottle of booze a day, and pigged out on mac 'n cheese when she was pregnant with me. It's in my genes."

"Your biological inheritance plays a part, but estimates are that 70 percent of how long and how well you live is in your own hands. If your brain believes there is no problem with your lifestyle, it will continue to prompt you to do whatever triggers your brain reward system and makes you feel better in the present moment, in the *now*, giving little if any thought to how it will impact your future health and longevity."

"In spite of the fact that I'd like to be floating down the river of *de-nile* right now," said Josh, "what you're saying makes sense. When my counselors talked about *self-medicating*, I tuned out. Talk to me. This time I'm ready to pay attention and listen."

"Think of the brain, not as a pot of gold (although it is likely the ultimate pot of gold), but rather as both a pot of chemical stew and as a pharmacy. Metaphorically, think of yourself as both chef and pharmacist." Josh raised an eyebrow, questioningly.

"As chef, you alter *seasonings* by what you ingest or take in from the outside. This includes everything you eat and drink; prescribed medications; tobacco products in any form; and drugs that you drink, sniff, snort, inject, swallow, or rub on your skin (legal or illegal, over-the-counter or off-the-street).

"As pharmacist, you alter brain *chemistry* by engaging in behaviors or thoughts that trigger your internal pharmacy to release brain chemicals: activities such as risk taking; exposure to music, movies, and social media; strong emotions and feelings, video games, and sexual activities."

"Can you give me some specific examples?" asked Josh. "The chef part I get, but pharmacist? I've never thought of my brain as having its own built-in pharmacy much less my being a pharmacist!"

His coach described a few.

- Physical exercise triggers the release of endorphins, the brain's natural morphine. That's one reason exercise is an important part of a Longevity Lifestyle. Appropriate exercise helps to reduce aches and pains.

- When you maintain a negative mindset and think or speak negatively, serotonin levels can fall. This neurotransmitter influences your energy levels, your sleep, your ability to experience joy, and your outlook on life.

- Thoughts of hopelessness or helplessness are associated with a reduction in levels of norepinephrine, which influences your mood and your response to stressors.

- Mirthful laughter triggers the release of any number of internal substances and can strengthening immune system function.

- And then there's dopamine, a chemical related to your ability to experience pleasure. It also influences muscle steadiness and the way in which the pre-frontal lobes of the brain hold on to information. It has been linked with all manner of addictive behaviors. Dopamine levels tend to fall when you think you cannot cope.

"It is much more complex than that," said his coach, "but you get the idea. Every thought you think—*every* thought—is believed to alter your neurochemistry in some way. That's the reason mindset and self-talk are so critical to creating and maintaining a Longevity Lifestyle. Think of habits as pieces of brain software. You created your old habits by repeating behaviors that gave some type of reward. A payoff. Perhaps they helped you avoid boredom or relieved emotional or physical pain. Maybe they gave you pleasure or helped you experience a sense of wellbeing.

"In a sense, both a computer and your brain have hardware and software. On a computer you load the software and run the program. In your brain, you activate the habit and exhibit the behavior. Your brain's software programs become almost automatic with practice. Once developed, the habits are tenacious. That's the bad news and the good news. It can be a challenge to create new software to override the old habits that give you a reward but also negative or undesirable outcomes. The good news is that when you develop new or replacement habits with positive outcomes, you've got them. That's the reason you still know how to ride a bike even when you haven't ridden one for twenty years. Your bike-riding software is just hanging around in your brain in case you might want to use it again sometime."

"Can you see me on a bike?" asked Josh, in mock disbelief.

"Certainly," said his coach. "You might need to begin by using a reclining bike in the gym for awhile. But, yes, I can see you on a bike."

"I guess I can, too," said Josh, "when I'm a few pounds lighter. Actually, my old bike is still hanging on a big hook in the garage. I used to love going for bike rides. Well, I may do that again."

"You can free yourself from old habits that are giving you negative outcomes by creating replacement habits and using willpower to implement them, one at a time. With consistent practice, they can become even stronger than the old habits. But it takes constant vigilance. When your life gets out of balance, it's easier to fall back on an unhealthy behavior—one that altered your brain's chemical stew quickly and triggered the brain reward system. No surprise, *balance* is a key component of a Longevity Lifestyle."

"It takes a lot of work to alter brain software, as you put it," said Josh. "But I know what it takes. Boy, do I know!"

"You're right. But around the world millions do it every day. Smoking, for example, is reportedly one of the most difficult addictive behaviors to alter and a million people quit every year in America alone. You did."

"Yeah, and replaced it with something that's going to take a lot of work to replace with something else. That was a tad shortsighted."

"This time, replace overeating with a healthier behavior. One that gives you positive outcomes and for which you will not need to find another replacement—for the rest of your life. Dealing effectively with old behaviors requires dealing with the associated health issues and the routines that often trigger cravings for the old behaviors, which could lead to a relapse."

"I just heard about lawsuit that was filed against a fast food chain alleging that their food was responsible for a customer's obesity, which contributed to her developing diabetes." He laughed.

"Apparently the plaintiff claimed she'd become addicted to fast food. If I'm not mistaken, lawyers for the company executives supposedly pointed out—in their defense—that no one holds customers at gunpoint. If people choose to eat or overeat foods that are low in nutrition and high in fat and sugar, they only have themselves to blame. Are foods really addicting? I remind you, I have to eat to live. Food keeps me alive after all!"

"Yes, you do need to eat to live. *Eat to live.* That's the key. However, many seem to live to eat. Currently, food addiction is not a recognized medical diagnosis but that may change sooner than later because some foods have been found to trigger the same brain reward system as drugs, alcohol, tobacco, sex, and gambling. More and more evidence is pointing toward the fact that some foods are at least habituating and very likely trigger addictive-like behaviors. In the future, a defense such as the one put forward by the food industry may fail. But people do make choices, so it's anybody's guess as to the position a jury might take in future lawsuits."

"What foods trigger addictive-like behaviors?" asked Josh. "I mean, I ate—overate—a lot of different foods."

"Researchers have known for some time that sugar triggers the release of opiates in the brain, which make you feel better and, consequently, can urge you to eat. When people say they crave carbs, they are wanting foods that release sugars rapidly into the bloodstream and produce a *food high.* Many simple carbs, in the form of sugar, white bread, pasta, and refined white-flour, white-rice and products made with them (often combined with sugar, milk or cream, and fat) do this. Chocolate, for example."

"Oh, there's always chocolate," said Josh, laughing. "At one time I was eating a pound of chocolate a day in one form or another. Truffles, shakes, candy bars, syrup …"

"Chocolate contains a number of natural compounds that affect the brain. Its taste alone can trigger opiate-like effects in the brain. Supposedly, chocolate reaches its point of maximal irresistibility when it is made with a fifty-fifty mixture of sugar and fat," said his coach. Josh sighed audibly.

"Some meats and dairy cheeses also appear to fall into this category. A study by the Physicians Committee for Responsible Medicine found that study participants often had a harder time giving up dairy cheese than most other foods. During digestion the casein in cheese breaks apart. When this happens, large amounts of morphine-like compounds known as casomorphins are released. They act on the brain reward system and make you feel better. So you want to eat more. You crave more."

"Don't I know!" exclaimed Josh. "My life has been one long series of serious cravings—and my giving in to them."

"Picture a craving simply as your brain demanding some of the old *seasoning* it used to get. Just because your brain demands a specific reward doesn't mean you need to provide it. Who's the *parent* here? Who's the *adult*? Dig to discover the *payoff* from the old behavior. You can deal with something once you can label and describe it. In fact, how about craving a Longevity Lifestyle?" They both laughed.

"The results of a pilot study led by Thilo Deckersbach, PhD, of Harvard Medical School in Boston, demonstrated a reversal of obesity-related abnormalities in the brain reward system in response to food cues. This suggests that it is possible to rewire your brain reward system by changing your behaviors—mindfully and consistently. Using the *Yale Food Addiction Scale,* University of Michigan researchers ranked foods from 'most problematic' to 'least problematic' in terms of addictive-like behavior."

His coach pointed to a list of foods that were posted on the office bulletin board. The top 12 foods ranked as most problematic were, in order:

Pizza	Ice cream	Cake
Chocolate	French fries	Dairy cheese
Chips	Cheese burgers	Bacon
Cookies	Sodas	Chicken

"Well," said Josh. "My mission this week—and I choose to accept it—is to dig deep to discover the payoffs. So long, plump penguin." He started to leave, then turned back. "Give me the bottom-line steps to alter an old behavior."

1. Identify the behavior that is giving you negative outcomes and address the health / relationship issues related to them.

2. Select a healthier replacement behavior.

3. Develop a positive mindset and careful self-talk patterns.

4. Use willpower to implement the replacement behavior.

5. Alter routines and tweak environments that trigger cravings for the old behavior.

"Remember to reward yourself and your brain for your successes," said his coach. "You can do this."

"I am doing it," said Josh, smiling. "Longevity Lifestyle here I come."

Alba found out how an old fable is relevant to a Longevity Lifestyle. Turn to Chapter 7 to discover what she learned.

There are really only two requirements when it comes to exercise: one is that you do it; the other is that you continue to do it.

—Jennie Brand-Miller
The New Glucose Revolution for Diabetes

Slow and Steady Wins

Chapter 7

"The other day I asked my Auntie if she'd heard the latest news flash about good calories and bad calories," Alba said, placing her pocket book by her chair.

"And?" prompted her wellness coach.

"And she nearly took my head off, that's what. I don't get it. Auntie had told me she was starting a new diet because, to quote her, 'I know my eating habits are toxic.' After she loses a few pounds her plan is to eat more nutritional foods—but at her weight she has a lot to lose."

"The topic of nutrition is a hot button for some," said her wellness coach, smiling. "Just offer to touch on eating habits or favorite foods or dieting, and you may need a body guard! Indeed there are likely as many opinions about nutrition as there are brains considering the topic."

"Auntie is planning on doing three months of *deprivation duty* as she dubs it. It's not as if this is something new. It's a pattern with her. I've watched it for years. She goes on a three-week fast or takes a series of high-colonics or eats only raw foods or drinks only liquids or severely restricts the number of calories she eats. You name it; she's tried it," said Alba, shaking her head.

"The minute she loses a few pounds she's right back on her toxic eating habits. I love my Auntie and this isn't good for her!"

"I can see you care about your Auntie," said her coach. "And you're right. It isn't good for her, her crash dieting as well as her weight. In the words of Roland Sturm, Economist for the RAND Corporation, being obese is like being twenty years older than you really are. It does more damage to your quality of life, causes more chronic medical conditions, and incurs more healthcare expenditures than either smoking or alcohol abuse.

"Unfortunately, many people do think *deprivation* as soon as the topic of desirable or even optimum nutrition comes up. However, eating less is not the ticket. While eating fewer empty calories derived from dense, refined, and processed foods is important, eating less overall isn't. In fact, many people sabotage their Longevity Lifestyle by eating too little. It's a problem similar to that of crash diets that require severe calorie limitation. If you eat too little food for long enough, you'll soon be craving more food. Desperately. A recipe for bingeing.

"Imagine forcing yourself to breathe only five times a minute. Do that for long enough, and you'll soon be gasping for air. Focusing on severe caloric restriction puts mental images of deprivation in working memory—a temporary workspace in your brain that allows you to focus on moment-to-moment information. You tend to think about whatever is in working memory. *Can't-have* pictures push you to focus on *loss* instead of visualizing nutritious food that can energize your brain and body. Sooner or later, most people scrap the calorie restrictions and, if they don't binge on favorite foods right away, within a couple of years they've gained back the lost pounds—if not more. This process, especially when repeated, can do a number on the brain, allowing it (along with hormones and neurochemicals), to wobble wildly out of balance. The brain and body function best when everything is in balance. Let the brain get out of balance and the cascade effect can be less than positive."

"I once heard somebody comment that you never outrun your knife and fork," said Alba. "At the time I thought it was cute—maybe not so cute in real life. But to lose weight my auntie has to reduce calories, right? The coach working with my best female friend (BFF) has her counting calories all day long—and I'm talking every single calorie! It's a real bore when the two of us go out to eat. In fact, she jokes that she expends bunches of calories just by spending so much time counting them. Of course she hates it, the counting, so that eventually goes by the wayside and she's back to not outrunning her knife and fork."

"Current studies suggest it may be more beneficial to identify unhealthy versus healthier calories. David S. Ludwig, MD, PhD, a pediatrician and endocrinologist at Children's Hospital in Boston, points out that so-called high-glycemic foods may influence the brain in a way that entices some people to overeat. He advises those seeking healthier menus to take a closer look at *what* they eat, rather than just how *much* they eat. While it is important to be aware of total calories ingested and increase physical activity and exercise, the true secret, according to Ludwig and his colleagues, is to cut out refined carbohydrates.

"Simply tracking calories only appears to be misguided, at best. Focusing on what you choose to avoid (remember the White Bear Phenomenon) and obsessing about calories can be a major stressor in itself, and unmanaged stressors are a risk factor for obesity. Focus instead on building a Longevity Lifestyle in balance—one you'll maintain for the rest of your life. That way, once you reach your desired weight, you just keep on doing what you are already doing, which makes it more likely that you will avoid regaining the weight you lost."

"Wow! What a concept!" exclaimed Alba.

"It would be an unbelievable relief to concentrate on selecting healthier foods rather than obsessively counting calories. If my Auntie were here today, what suggestions would you give her?"

Alba's wellness coach thought for a few moments and then provided a few suggestions.

- Breathe. Smile. Take it a step at a time.

- Stop spending time, energy, and anxiety counting calories.

- Not all calories are created equal—a calorie is not a calorie is not a calorie. Some are *empty* and some are nutritious.

- Place less emphasis on counting calories and more on selecting foods that are lower on the Glycemic Index.

- Learn to eat based on physiological hunger. Make heathy choices and then enjoy what you eat. Eating nutritious food when you are truly hungry can be very satisfying.

- The choices you make are important and every choice has consequences. Veronica Roth said that one choice can transform you—or it can destroy you.

"Remember that the brain requires glucose to function at optimum levels," her coach continued. "That's one of the problems with many crash diets that severely limit carbohydrates. Complex unprocessed carbs provide an excellent source of quality glucose. Studies have provided some good news, too. Generally, eating unprocessed carbs as part of a healthy menu does not appear to influence weight gain."

"How do you define *unprocessed carbs*?" said Alba.

"They are simply foods in as natural state as possible," her coach replied

"The 'trick' (if you want to call it that) to effective weight management may simply be to reduce one's intake of refined and processed carbohydrates. These include white sugar, white rice, white bread, white flour—and products made with them."

"Can you give me some quick tips?" asked Alba.

Her coach summarized what Alba wanted to know.

- Eat high quality foods including healthy carbs that are high in healthful nutrients: fresh or frozen vegetables and fruits, nuts and seeds, legumes, and whole grains such as quinoa (instead of white bread, white sugar, white flour, and products made with them). The calories in these types of healthy carbohydrates provide the brain and body (including muscle tissues) with a good energy source, plus fiber, vitamins, minerals, and other micronutrients.

- Select foods that are low on the Glycemic Index (GI) and have a low Glycemic Load (GL). For example, use hummus (or peanut butter powder mixed in water) with celery or jicama rather than with regular nut butters, white pita bread, or deep-fried crackers and chips. Carrying a GI-GL chart to the grocery store a few times can help you identify and recall which foods have lower GI's and GL's.

- When shopping, learn to distinguish between high quality and poor quality foods. Select a raw apple versus apple pie or apple juice, raw or dry-roasted nuts instead of those that are salted and roasted in oil, steel-cut or old fashioned oats over instant oatmeal, carrots rather than carrot cake, fresh oranges (instead of orange juice), mixed-grain pasta instead of white semolina, and sweet potatoes rather than white potatoes or hash browns or French fries or potato chips.

- The key is to keep it simple and easy. Your best guideline is to eat foods in the most natural state possible, avoiding refined and processed foods, and drinking water over any other beverage (such as sodas, diet drinks, fruit juices, or sweetened juices and drinks).

"I get it," said Alba. "And I need to do this for myself, as well. My current weight is about 35 pounds higher than when I graduated from college. I want to avoid yo-yo routines and do this in a healthy manner."

"A Longevity Lifestyle is designed to help you return to an optimum weight range. Once your desired weight is achieved, the next goal is to maintain it. If you have developed healthier replacement behaviors for old patterns of unhealthy eating, drinking, and physical activity, maintaining your optimum weight will be much easier. Remember that it may take from several months to several years to achieve this."

"Several months? Several years? You've got to be kidding—that seems like forever!"

"Hardly forever," said her coach, chuckling. "You're planning to be alive for a lot longer than just *several years*, aren't you? Rein in your impatience. How long did it take you to arrive at your highest weight? Ten years? Fifteen? Rome wasn't built in a day.

"Factor that time in against the proposed length of time required for you to shed those pounds. Well, you no longer want them, do you? Give those pounds away. Picture yourself donating your excess poundage—to an elephant or a hippopotamus or a walrus or whatever. "

"What a good idea," said Alba, laughing. "I think I'll do just that. A walrus, I think. Yes. Definitely a walrus."

"Remember, you are crafting a Longevity Lifestyle. You are learning to live the way you will live for as long as you live. Even dropping half a pound a week will add up quite nicely over time, and you'll have an increased risk of keeping it off. Learning to delay gratification can apply to waiting patiently for that smaller clothing size." Alba nodded, her forehead wrinkled.

"Growing up, did you read Aesop's fable about the race between a tortoise and a hare?"

"I have a vague recollection of that," Alba replied, "but I fear I've forgotten most of the details. Fill me in."

"Okay, here's the scoop. I find the tale relevant to a Longevity Lifestyle."

Alba sat back and enjoyed the fairy tale.

Once upon a time, a long time ago, so the story goes, there was a hare who was in the habit of ridiculing a tortoise for moving so abysmally slow. At the speed of, well, a turtle. Eventually the slow-moving tortoise challenged the hare to a race.

The day came and, no surprise, the hare soon left the tortoise way behind. Eating the hare's dust, no less.

A little cocky because he was so-o-o-o supremely confident of winning, the hare took a nap midway through the agreed-upon course. When the hare awakened from his siesta, he discovered to his astonishment and complete consternation, that his competition, crawling slowly but steadily, had already crossed the finish line and had won the race.

"In the long term, slow and steady wins, Alba."

Alba nodded. "Maybe so, but I'd much rather get all the excess weight off and then get on with the business of living."

"I understand," said her coach. "Once you make the decision you want to get on with it as fast as possible. Remaining patient can be a challenge. Nevertheless, many health professionals recommend slow weight loss as the safest and most effective approach. You didn't pack on those pounds in a few weeks. Trying to take them off too quickly can sabotage your success. Gradual weight loss promotes long-term loss of body fat, not just water weight, which can be quickly regained."

Alba nodded.

"It also gives you time to build new patterns of eating and drinking and exercising and staying active, the ones you will practice for the rest of your life," her coach continued. "Slow and steady—in creating a Longevity Lifestyle—wins."

"Okay," said Alba finally. "Slow and steady wins. Actually, that that removes some of the pressure to hurry up and be successful, instantly."

"Be successful in the long term," her coach affirmed, smiling.

As the woman walked away down the hall, the coach could hear Alba's voice repeating: *slow and steady wins, slow and steady…*

Chapter 8 is up next. Find out what may be *killing* America.

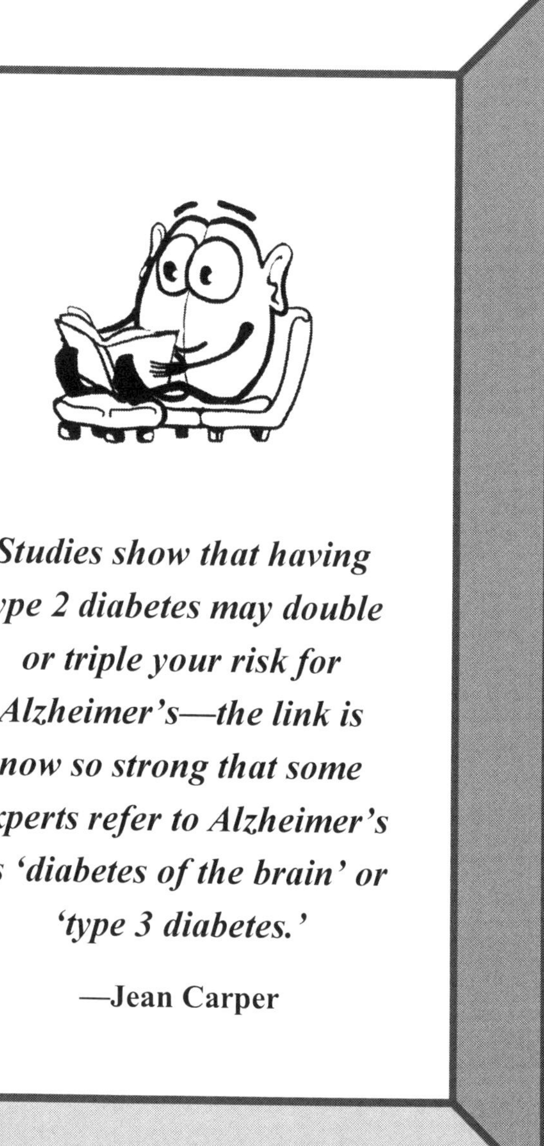

Studies show that having type 2 diabetes may double or triple your risk for Alzheimer's—the link is now so strong that some experts refer to Alzheimer's as 'diabetes of the brain' or 'type 3 diabetes.'

—Jean Carper

Death by Sitting

Chapter 8

"I just read an article reporting an interview with Michelle Obama," said Marie, entering the office. "She was quoted as saying that a sedentary lifestyle is killing Americans. That's what she said. *Sitting* is *killing* Americans." Marie kicked off her shoes.

"Killing Americans? That sounds deadly," said her wellness coach.

"Apparently it is! Deadly. Her solution was that people need to move more: cut their lawns, wash their cars, walk to the store or to school whenever possible, make their bed, scrub their dishes, and vacuum the floors. The theme was that Americans need to get active! To get outdoors and play games—baseball, tennis, croquet, golf, basketball, volleyball, badminton, horseshoes, and you-name-it. To ride bicycles, go for walks in nature, and take vacations where they can hike in national parks or run along beaches or kayak on lakes." Marie paused.

"You know, her comments have gotten me thinking differently about exercise. Instead of perceiving it as one more thing to add to my already busy lifestyle, I now think of it as just *moving more.* I even walked here today instead of cabbing it. It's only five blocks from my office."

"Walking is good exercise," said her coach. "In *20/20 Thinking* Dr. Maggie Greenwood-Robinson outlines several key benefits of walking. It increases the flow of oxygen to the brain and body, triggers the release of brain chemicals that can enhance creativity, and stimulates the right cerebral hemisphere."

Her coach listed some additional benefits.

Exercise can:

- Help to boot-up brain function
- Strengthen immune system function
- Increase HDL, the 'good' cholesterol
- Help to better control blood sugar
- Assist in weight management
- Improve lung function
- Decrease resting heart rate
- Lower blood pressure and decrease risk of heart disease

"Naturally there are safety recommendations, as well. Talk with your physician before starting an exercise program, especially if you've been very sedentary. Individuals with diabetes, hypertension, heart disease, arthritis, pulmonary conditions, or other health conditions may need additional safety guidelines for exercise. And if you were to develop symptoms during exercise such as unusual shortness of breath; tightness in your chest or shoulder or jaw, lightheadedness; dizziness; confusion; or joint pain, you should stop exercising immediately and contact your physician." Marie nodded.

"Ideally, a well-rounded exercise program includes several types of activities: general physical, aerobic, stamina-building, and flexibility, along with appropriate balance and strengthening exercises, and so on. The more variety, the more likely you are to stay on your program."

"I did some gymnastics in high school." Marie laughed. "Guess I better start going to the gym and exercising for ninety minutes, seven days a week."

"Caution! Caution!" said her coach, holding up both hands. "Behavioral scientists Maura Scott and Stephen Nowlis, writing in the *Journal of Consumer Research,* point out that people are more likely to actually achieve their goals on a long-term basis when those goals are set as a low-high range rather than as a hard-and-fast absolute rule."

"Boston Sports Clubs found that participants who exercised for twenty to thirty minutes did so more consistently than those involved in forty-five to sixty minute workout sessions. This suggests that you're more likely to stick to a shorter duration workout than a longer one. Being successful involves two important factors: how challenging and how attainable. You need to feel challenged enough to perceive a sense of accomplishment, but only to the extent that you think there is a realistic possibility of actual achievement. That's the beauty of setting low-high range goals; they are realistically challenging and flexible."

"Oh," said Marie. "Can you give me an example of a low-high range exercise goal?"

"Exercise four to six days a week, include a variety of physical activities, and visit the gym two to four times each week. Tape a calendar to your bathroom mirror with your low-high range goals written at the top. Mark each day you exercise and when you go to the gym."

"That keeps the bottom line of your flexible low-high range in front of you. If you do more, fine—as long as you keep your life in balance. If you fall off the wagon, the faster you climb right back on, the better. Your overall goal is to reduce sedentary activities and get you moving. Get up and move for thirty or sixty seconds every thirty minutes if you are doing sedentary work. If possible, do some of your work standing at a raised desk and alternate between sitting and standing.

"Rather than using a regular chair, some choose to sit on a large inflatable exercise (stay) ball, which not only burns more calories than sitting in a chair, but also helps with balance. Climb stairs instead of always taking the elevator. At home carry out the garbage, walk the pooch, swim, ride a bicycle (even a stationary bike), and so on. Leave the car parked in favor of walking to do errands whenever possible. It's all about staying physically active at every age.

"Michael R. Roizen, MD, in his book *Real Age*, connects physical activities with retarding the onset of symptoms of aging. That's just one more potential benefit."

"What's your take on aerobic exercises?" asked Marie.

"Aerobic exercises (also known as cardio exercises) are designed to stimulate and strengthen the heart and lungs, thereby improving the body's utilization of oxygen and, over time, one's stamina. To be effective, they require a minimum duration and frequency. And the benefits accrue when the exercises are done over the long term rather than just for the short term. The American Heart Association recommends a minimum of thirty minutes of some form of cardiovascular exercise at least five days per week. To improve cardio-respiratory fitness and help manage weight, the American College of Sports Medicine recommends that at least three thirty-minute sessions per week should be devoted to moderate to vigorous exercise."

"The good news," continued her coach, "is that physical exercise doesn't have to be done all at one time. Three ten-minute or two fifteen-minute walks would reach the recommended minimum guideline and burn the same number of calories as walking for the full thirty minutes at one time."

"Oh my," said Marie. "I have been limiting my options by thinking rigid hard-and-fast rules. I can easily get in ten minutes of brisk walking during my morning and afternoon breaks. And if I walk to a local salad bar and back at noon, there's another ten minutes. This is doable!"

"It's definitely doable," said her coach. "Many sports qualify as aerobic exercise, too. The sky is the limit, actually. There is usually something for everyone who can exercise."

Her coach listed several examples.

- Tennis
- Rollerblading
- Skiing
- Volleyball
- Cycling
- Step aerobics or using an elliptical trainer
- Doing sit-ups
- Pushups
- Hiking
- Kick boxing
- Jazzercise
- Jumping rope
- Rowing
- Swimming or diving
- Skateboarding
- Snowboarding
- Line dancing

"You didn't mention jogging," said Marie. "My neighbor jogged regularly until she developed joint problems and her doctor told her to stop."

"Jogging is getting mixed reviews in terms of exercise for the average person," said her coach. "You might want to do an internet search on the downsides. Reports are that jogging can compound cellulite and damage joints over time. You need exercise, but you also want to *do no harm.*

"Some are now recommending intensity training, believing this strengthens the heart muscle more effectively. For example, alternate a couple minutes of very fast walking with several minutes of more moderate walking. You could follow the same pattern on a rowing machine or stationary bicycle. Many people have no idea how important exercise is to brain function. The decision to exercise maybe one of the best decisions you ever make. Remember, in the words of E. A. Bucchianeri: 'we are the sum total of the decisions we have made.'"

"I've definitely made that decision," said Marie. "Matter of fact, I just purchased five-pound dumbbells. The package insert said strengthening exercises are designed to increase and maintain your muscle strength."

"That they are. Strong arm, thigh, abdominal, and back muscles are essential for doing everyday tasks, like lifting a twenty-pound toddler, putting away groceries, maintaining good sitting and standing posture, and placing your carry-ons in the plane's overhead bin. Exercising with dumbbells, lifting weights, or using other muscle-strengthening equipment can help. "Even those who are wheel-chair bound can often do simple exercises using dumbbells. The bottom line is to do what you can—safely, appropriately, and in balance. Stop worrying about what you are unable to do. Focus instead on what you can do. And then do it."

"Stretching exercises differ from strengthening ones, right?" asked Marie.

"Right," her coach replied. "They are different. Stretching exercises help improve flexibility and the ability to maintain good range of motion. The American College of Sports Medicine recommends stretching each of the major muscle groups at least two times a week for sixty seconds per exercise. Side stretches and yoga exercises are types of stretching. You can find more examples on the Internet.

"As people age, the tendency is to be less active, especially after retirement. Activities that involve movement, which can help with balance and decrease one's risk of falling, are gradually replaced with sedentary activities. Some have even referred to this phenomenon as *death by sitting*."

"Hmmm," said Marie, laughing. "That sounds like an Agatha Christie novel. If she'd written a book entitled *Death by Sitting*, I'll bet the story line would be interesting."

"That may be closer to the truth that you might realize," said her coach seriously. "Jacquelyn Kulinski, MD, cardiologist, and colleagues analyzed data from 2031 participants (ages 20-76) in the

Dallas Heart Study and concluded:

- Sitting for too long doubles the risk of diabetes.
- Each hour of sedentary time was associated with a ten percent higher odds of having coronary artery calcification.
- Each added hour spent sitting was associated with a fourteen percent increase in one's coronary artery calcium (CAC) score."

"The health consequences of being too sedentary may differ from those of not getting enough physical exercise. According to Dr. Kulinski, reducing daily sitting time by even one or two hours potentially could have a significant and positive impact on future cardiovascular health."

Eyes wide, Marie looked at her coach. "Oh my. I was making a joke! I spend a lot of time sitting at the computer. Last week I was told I could have something-or-other added to my desk, which would give me the option of doing some of my work standing up. I laughed and blew off the idea but I just changed my mind."

"In addition to strengthening the heart and bolstering the immune system, physical exercise boosts energy, relieves stress, and improves sleep. Regular physical exercise helps your body handle glucose more efficiently and is a good sugar stabilizer. It can bring high blood sugar levels down, and low levels up. On top of that, it can stimulate the release of substances in the brain and body that can help you feel more alive and energetic. Now add 'sitting less' and you may have a winning combination going for you."

"Such a deal," said Marie. "I'm committed to this Longevity Lifestyle plan. My doctor just told me I'm borderline for developing type 2 diabetes. By reducing body fat, increasing my activity levels, and decreasing my sitting, I'm hopeful I can avoid developing diabetes. It would be so worth it!"

"That it would!" said her coach. "Studies are showing that if you pack around extra weight, the long-term effect on both brain and body will be negative. Swedish researchers report that adult women who are obese have an increased risk of brain atrophy, which increases the risk for brain damage."

"It's not completely clear how brain atrophy leads to brain damage. It may be because obesity increases the risk of diabetes and high blood pressure, conditions that could cause brain damage and lead to a whole host of problems including memory loss and other forms of dementia."

"I'm on it," said Marie. "By the way, I forgot to tell you that what really started me *moving* was my neighbor asking me to walk her dog. Emily (my neighbor, not the dog) fell off a stool last week and broke her leg. She'll be on crutches for a couple of months. Once I got started, I realized I felt better, so I decided that's how I want to live my life. When Emily gets the cast off, I agreed to keep walking with her and her dog. The three of us will walk together."

"Well, there you have it," said her coach. "Good decision. I'm proud of you. Your good deed has turned into a good deal for you. By the time Emily is recovered, you'll be well on your way to having developed the habit of walking. As Lailah Gifty Akita put it:

> *You are the only person who can decide how you wish to live your life.*"

Meet Marge and discover what she learned about *booting up* her brain. Turn to Chapter 9.

Exercise is the single most powerful tool you have to optimize your brain function.

—Richard Restak, MD
Mozart's Brain and the Fighter Pilot

Booting up Your Brain

Chapter 9

"Exercise," said Marge. "I used to stand on my head when I was a girl. Not anymore! My doctor has been trying to get me to start exercising again but I'm so busy. At our last visit she reeled off several benefits of physical exercise but I had no way to write them down."

"Regular physical exercise can protect your brain cells against stress, improve your mood, and help slow mental decline, to name just a few," said her wellness coach.

"Okay. Today I have pen and paper so I can write down what you tell me," said Marge, opening her mini-iPad. "I'm ready."

Her coach summarizing the following research.

Twenty minutes of mild aerobic exercise at the beginning of the day can turn on fat-burning neuropeptides, the effects of which can last for hours. This can be critical in managing diseases such as obesity and diabetes. The value of exercise has less to do with building muscles or burning calories and more to do with getting the heart to pump faster and more efficiently, thereby increasing blood flow to nourish and cleanse the brain and body organs.

—Candace B. Pert, PhD
Molecules of Emotion: The Science behind Mind-Body Medicine (1999)

Physical exercise helps the brain to *boot up* efficiently, in much the same way as you would boot up a computer.

—Kenneth A. Giuffre, MD
The Care and Feeding of Your Brain (1999)

Aerobic exercise helps increase production of neurotrophins that stimulate the growth of nerve cells (i.e., stimulate the development of new synapses and support growth of the myelin sheath).

—Pierce J. Howard, PhD
The Owner's Manual for the Brain, 4th Edition (2014)

Exercise is the single most powerful tool you have to optimize your brain function. Individuals who are aerobically fit may also have an intellectual edge. Exercise can improve creativity, concentration, and problem-solving.

—Richard Restak, MD
Mozart's Brain and the Fighter Pilot

Regular physical activity can help you prevent or manage a wide range of health problems and concerns, including stroke, metabolic syndrome, type 2 diabetes, depression, arthritis, specific types of cancer, and falls. It can leave you feeling energized and looking better. It can lead to enhanced arousal for women and reduced risk of problems with erectile dysfunction in men.

—Healthy Lifestyle Fitness
Mayo Clinic

Exercise strengthens the heart, bolsters the immune system, boosts energy, relieves stress, and improves sleep.

—Mary O'Brien, MD
Successful Aging (2005)

Three basic types of physical activity can help retard the onset of aging symptoms: general physical activity, stamina-building activities, and strength and flexibility exercises. Exercise burns energy and reduces stress levels.

—Michael F. Roizen, MD
Real Age, are You as Young as You Can Be? (1999)

The benefits of regular physical exercise can:

- Strengthen your cardiovascular system
- Help to regulate glucose and insulin
- Combat stress by dissipating cortisol
- Improve your mood and enhance motivation
- Boost your immune system
- Strengthen your bones
- Foster neuroplasticity (the ability of the brain to change itself)

—John J. Ratey, MD, and Eric Hagerman
Spark: The Revolutionary New Science of Exercise and the Brain. (2008, 2010)

Aerobic exercise provides cardiovascular conditioning. The term aerobic actually means “with oxygen,” which means that breathing controls the amount of oxygen that can make it to the muscles to help them burn fuel and move. Your heart rate increases in direct correlation with the intensity of the exercise: by how hard you are working, what your goals are, what limitations you have, and your current fitness level.

—Stay Fit
Cleveland Clinic

Regular physical activity/exercise helps many of the body's systems function better, keeps heart disease, diabetes, and a host of other diseases at bay, and is an ingredient for losing weight. A sedentary lifestyle does the opposite, increasing the chances of becoming overweight and developing a number of chronic diseases. Despite all the good things going for it, only about 30 percent of adult Americans report regular physical activity during their leisure time—and about 40 percent admit that they get no leisure-time physical activity at all. Being a 'couch potato' may be harmful even for people who get regular exercise. A morning run or brisk lunchtime walk brings many health benefits—but these may not entirely make up for a day in front of the computer or an evening in front of the television. Cutting down on 'sit time' may be just as important as increasing 'fit time.'

—Benefits of Physical Activity
Harvard School of Public Health

Regular physical activity is one of the best things you can do for your health. It can:

- Reduce your risk of cardiovascular disease
- Reduce your risk of some cancers
- Strengthen your bones and muscles
- Improve your mental health and mood
- Manage your weight
- Help prevent falls
- Increase your chances of living longer

—*Physical Activity*
The Centers for Disease Control and Prevention (CDC)

"That's quite a list," said Marge. "Quite an impressive list! Is there any downside to exercising?"

"There's a downside to almost everything, especially when used inappropriately or to excess. For example, some get caught in the trap of 'If a little is good, a lot is better.' Some are careless when exercising so get injured.

"Researchers in Germany used PET (Positron Emission Tomography) scans to study the brains of ten athletes following a two-hour run. The scans confirmed that during the run, endorphins were released in parts of the brain known to be involved with the processing of emotions. Endorphins contribute to *runner's high*, along with released norepinephrine, serotonin, dopamine, and brain-derived neurotrophic factor. Since exercise increases levels of these substances, it's possible to become addicted to them. If this occurs, it can cause you to over exercise because you are craving these substances and the over-exercising triggers your brain's internal pharmacy to release them. While I doubt this will happen to you, it's still something to be aware of."

"I cannot imagine I'll ever become addicted to endorphins," said Marge, laughing. "But I'll keep it on my radar screen. Okay. How do I begin?"

"What did your physician recommend at your last office visit? The one that motivated you to embrace a Longevity Lifestyle?"

"She told me to start walking five minutes a day for the first week, then move it up to ten minutes the second week, and then increase to fifteen the third week. She also recommended setting an ultimate goal of about thirty minutes a day."

Her coach raised as eyebrow. "And?"

"Okay, okay. So far I've not done anything. But I have *thought* about it." Marge squirmed in her chair.

"Since everything begins and ends in the brain, thinking is a start. And it's a good idea to check with your doctor before you begin an exercise program, especially when regular physical exercise has not been your …"

"Habit," Marge said, finishing the sentence. "Let's be perfectly honest—I've never *ever* had an exercise program." Her eyes twinkled. "I'll start with the walking, although it isn't much."

"Five minutes is five minutes. Something is better than nothing. As John Wooden put it, 'Do not let what you cannot do interfere with what you can do.' Begin with your doctor's recommendation: five minutes. That's a realistic goal. Picture in your mind's eye exactly how achieving your goal will look, and be specific when you talk to yourself."

"Okay," said Marge. "How's this for an announcement?" She spoke as if she were addressing an audience. "'*You* are on board with exercising. *You* are walking for five minutes every day. Every day, mind you. *You* feel better and you already have more energy.'"

"That's a great start. Next, access willpower to make this happen. Before you know it, you'll be up to ten minutes, then fifteen. As little as ten to fifteen minutes of brisk walking can boost your attention and problem-solving skills. Eventually you'll be walking for twenty or thirty minutes a day. Just be careful to avoid turning exercise into a long, have-to drudgery."

"I know," said Marge. "I tend to like variety and hate routines. Any ideas or suggestions?"

"For some, individuals, breaking physical exercise up into two or three sections helps them stay consistent. For others, variety in exercise is the key. You might try alternating aerobic exercises with strengthening exercises, balance exercises, flexibility exercises, and so on. The pros of exercise clearly outweigh any cons—hands down. Do whatever you can on a regular basis, in balance."

"How could I have been so stupid and so completely short-sighted?" asked Marge. "Avoiding exercise and overeating? Dumb, dumb, dumb! Now look what I have to deal with!"

"When you know better you can do better. Now that you know better you can do better. Did you hear what you just said?"

"What, *stupid*, *short-sighted,* and *dumb*?" asked Marge.

Her coach nodded. "What you think and say create mental pictures, and your subconscious tends to follow those pictures. Think of the internal mental pictures that are created with words such as these:

- "You overeat all the time. You can't do anything right, so no point in trying.
- No one likes you at this weight. You let yourself and everyone else down. You aren't worth much.
- "You make really dumb, short-sighed decisions.
- "You can't do this. It's too difficult. You may as well just go out in the garden and eat worms!"

"I see pictures of failure," Marge said, when she had stopped giggling.

"Conversely, think of what type of mental pictures are created with the following words:

- You are exercising every day you have more energy. It feels great. You are definitely worth the work.
- "You eat two servings of vegetables every day, one raw, if possible.
- "You eat one serving of legumes and one of basmati brown rice, along with some chia seeds or sesame seeds. You enjoy the taste.
- "You eat at least one piece of fresh fruit every day.

"Success," said Marge. "Mine. I see in my mind's eye positive, empowering, can-do pictures of exactly what I need to do."

"There you have it. The power of positive self-talk. I like a quote attributed to Vishwas Chavan: *Who you are today is the outcome of the choices you have made in the past. Choices that you will make today, will shape your future.*

"I like it too," said Marge. "I did not realize how important positive self-talk is. I choose success. And I have some practicing to do, starting now!"

Turn to Chapter 10 and learn how a musical metaphor helped Ken understand macronutrients and micronutrients.

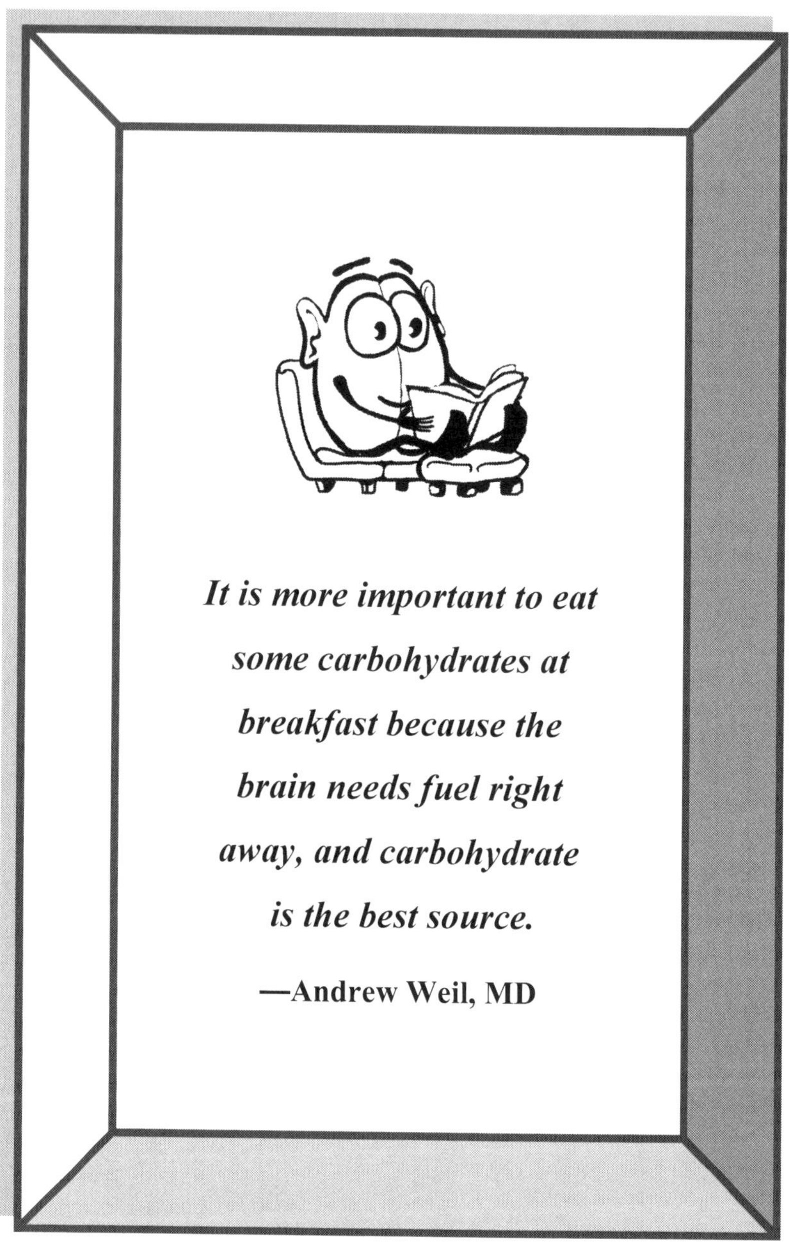

It is more important to eat some carbohydrates at breakfast because the brain needs fuel right away, and carbohydrate is the best source.

—Andrew Weil, MD

Counting Conundrum

Chapter 10

"I've been imagining this week, seeing things in my mind's eye," Ken said, settling himself in a wooden chair. "Imagining what a Longevity Lifestyle looks like in my life, especially in relation to nutrition."

"Good," said his wellness coach. "I suspect you have a good imagination. Anyone who has so skillfully avoided whatever he didn't want to do for more than half a century probably does." Ken's guffaw could be heard down the hall. "Tell you what. Let's exchange places—in imagination. What do you think I'd say to someone in your shoes?"

Steepling his fingers, Ken closed his eyes and pursed his lips. Clearing his throat, he began in a Soto-professor tone. "Mindset is paramount when dealing with lifestyle issues. Do you have a workable plan, or are you all over the proverbial map? Do you understand the benefits of optimum nutrition as well as appropriate exercise? Are you committed to creating and maintaining this way of living for the rest of your life?" Ken opened his eyes. "How did I do?" he asked, grinning.

"Bravo!" said his coach. "You've been doing your homework. Trying to take over my job, are you?"

Ken started to shake his head, then stopped. In a voice more serious than usual, he said, "Not yours, per se. But altering my lifestyle is helping save my skin. By this time next year—when I role model a more fit form—I'd like to volunteer, to help others move toward a Longevity Lifestyle."

"You're on, Ken. A real-life success story, yours, can be a powerful motivator." Ken smiled. "Now, what would you like to begin with today?"

"Some things about nutrition are rather muddy in my mind," he said. "And there are others that I don't understand at all. For example, I hear macro this and micro that."

"Let's start from the very beginning. A very good place to start," said his coach.

"*Sound of Music,*" Ken said immediately. "I like musicals and my kids loved that one—the version with Julie Andrews."

"Let's use that metaphor. Musicals have principal actors and supporting players. Think of macronutrients as principal actors—carbohydrates, proteins, and fats—foods that provide calories that the body uses in relatively large amounts. Micronutrients are supporting players, substances important to brain and body but needed in smaller amounts: vitamins, minerals, and enzymes. They contribute little in terms of calories. For example, the enzyme amylase helps break down carbohydrates into glucose—the main circulating sugar in human blood and the principal source of energy for cells that make up the human brain and body. For most living things, actually."

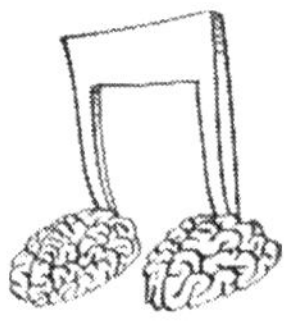

Ken nodded. "And I've heard the word *calorie*, but what it is remains a mystery. A black hole."

“A calorie is just the name for a unit of energy. By definition it’s the amount of energy required to raise the temperature of one gram of water one degree Celsius. Think of calories as providing fuel for energy.”

“My truck won’t run without diesel, my car won’t run without petrol. You’re saying I won’t run without calories?”

“Not for long, Ken,” said his coach. “Not for long. How do you select fuel for your car?”

“It runs better on higher-octane fuel. When I use inexpensive low-octane fuel, a variety of pings and pongs keep me company. Not so musical, either!”

“Think of calories as fuel. Each individual needs a specific number of calories. Too few and you lack energy to live a fulfilling and productive life. Too many and you will eventually gain weight.”

“I’ll bet you’re talking about those controversial *carbs*,” said Ken. “How really important are they?”

“Extremely important because they provide energy for the body, especially for the brain and nervous system. According to the McKinley Health Center at the University of Illinois, Urbana-Champaign, carbohydrates are the macronutrient needed in the largest amounts, because carbohydrates are:

- “The body’s main source of fuel and can be used easily for energy by all tissues and cells. They can be stored in the muscles and liver and later used for energy.

- “Necessary for the brain, central nervous system, kidneys, and muscles (including those of the heart) to function properly.

- "Important for gastrointestinal health and the timely and appropriate elimination of waste.

"And you're right. There has been (and continues to be) a great deal of controversy about the most beneficial types. Carbohydrates are not all created equal. "Just as differing types of gasoline have differing octane ratings, carbohydrates come in differing grades of quality. Bottom line? The *quality* of the carbohydrate is key."

"I get the difference-in-octane analogy but what exactly do you mean by *quality*?" asked Ken.

His coach explained. "Some carbohydrates are simply more nutritious than others. Period."

"Highly processed and refined foods are often referred to as *empty calories* because most of the nutrition has been removed. Refined sugar and white flour products, for example, along with alcohol and other highly processed foods. Eating too many empty calories is bad for your brain and contributes to obesity. In fact, some are saying that excessive consumption of sugar can lead to health problems similar to those that are caused by the excessive consumption of alcohol." Ken nodded.

"There are three main categories of carbohydrates: simple, complex, and fiber. The assigned classification depends on the chemical structure of the food itself and how quickly the sugar it contains is absorbed. Simple carbs contain one or two sugars. They are found in dairy products as galactose, as fructose in fruit, in high-fructose corn syrup, white flours, white rice, and in many refined and processed products. Double sugars such as maltose are in some vegetables, lactose in dairy, sucrose in refined table sugar and syrups, and in honey.

"Carbs containing three or more sugars are referred to as *complex* carbohydrates. Found in starchy vegetables, legumes, whole grains, and fruit they provide calories as well as vitamins, minerals, enzymes, and other micronutrients. The United States Department of Agriculture (USDA) Dietary Guidelines recommends 45 to 65 percent of one's total calories should come from carbohydrates—preferably from healthier complex carbs."

"Fiber refers to carbohydrates that the body cannot digest. It is the indigestible portion of plants that pass through the intestinal tract intact and help to move waste out of the body. It is not absorbed into the bloodstream, and provide no calories.

"Low-fiber eating patterns have been shown to trigger problems (e.g., constipation and hemorrhoids) and to increase the risk for certain types of cancers such as colon cancer. High-fiber eating patterns have been shown to lower cholesterol levels, decrease risks for heart disease and obesity, and may help prevent diabetes.

"There are two main types of fiber: soluble and insoluble fiber. They each play important roles, especially in relation to bowel function, but they act in different ways. Generally, people need to eat some of each type.

- "Soluble fiber absorbs liquid, forming a gel, which can help resolve diarrhea by removing excess fluid from the bowel. It can help lower blood cholesterol and glucose levels, too. Soluble fiber-rich foods include strawberries, blueberries, apples, avocado, dried figs and prunes, oranges, and mangos; veggies such as asparagus, edamame, broccoli, green beans and peas, carrots, plus legumes, oats, barley, psyllium, and peanuts—containing the highest soluble fiber per serving for nuts. Almonds, Brazil nuts, sesame and sunflower seeds are good sources, as well."

- "Insoluble fiber, on the other hand, passes through the intestines largely intact. It increases stool bulk, which can help resolve constipation. Whole grains top the list of insoluble fiber-rich foods, along with air-popped popcorn, zucchini, broccoli, cabbage, leafy greens, and root vegetables; plus legumes, most beans, raspberries, unpeeled apples and grapes, walnuts, almonds, and sunflower seeds.

"And there are some foods that contain both types of fiber: oats, legumes, mangos, almonds, avocados, cucumber, celery, and carrots, for example."

"I like all of those foods," said Ken. "Hmmm. Simple, complex, and fiber. So of the three categories of carbohydrates, I take it simple carbs are the problem. If I avoid simple carbs, I should be good to go, right?"

"Not so fast," his coach replied. "It depends on the *type* of simple carbs and their relative proportion to other foods that you are eating. The *problem* arises with using too many simple carbs in proportion to other foods you are eating: primarily fruits or too many *refined processed foods* in your menu. Sugars such as those found in candy, sodas, many pastries and desserts, along with highly refined foods like pastas and white breads, add calories but minimal nutrition. Consequently, it is wise to limit these. Instead, choose complex carbs in as natural a form as possible."

"Bread. I've never been a really big bread-eater," said Ken. "Of course burger and hot-dog buns. Other than that, when I do eat bread, I've always preferred real sourdough bread to regular commercial yeast breads." He paused. "But sourdough bread is typically made with white flour so maybe that isn't a good choice after all."

"I prefer sourdough bread myself," said his coach.

"Traditional sourdough (containing only wild-yeast sourdough starter) apparently has some real benefits. It is made through a process of fermentation, so it contains beneficial bacteria known as probiotics. When probiotics are present in the bread-making process, they help break down some of the gluten, so sourdough may actually be easier on the gut than commercial yeast-wheat breads. Probiotics may also lower your insulin response and make some nutrients more readily available for digestion. And, yes, as you mentioned, it typically is made from white flour so some nutritionists recommend eating only one or two slices a day. Selected bakeries are now making traditional sourdough using cracked wheat and/or a mixture of several grains and seeds."

"I'll look for that type," said Ken. "Mashing some avocado on a slice or two of sourdough toast would make me a good breakfast." His coach nodded.

"You know," Ken continued, "I got into the habit of grabbing simple carbs instead of taking responsibility for preparing nutritious meals," said Ken. "In fact, I think I might be addicted to simple carbs—well, to white sugar, anyway. Is that possible?"

"The answer appears to be 'yes.' Sugar and other refined carbohydrates are high on the list for being at least addictive-like because they create effects similar to those of alcohol. Refined foods, especially those containing sugars and white flours, can produce a temporary high through an increase in brain chemicals such as dopamine, serotonin, and norepinephrine. Sugar itself can act like a drug. As you decrease the amount consumed, you may experience withdrawal symptoms such as nausea, headaches, irritability, and anxiety."

"Hmm. I've had all those symptoms. And I guess …" Ken paused, his voice trailing off.

"I guess I've *self-medicated* by guzzling soft drinks and eating high-fat high-sugar snacks. To say nothing of huge favorite meals: four-egg omelets, hash browns loaded with bacon grease—plus the bacon, of course—and stacks of pancakes or waffles dripping both butter and syrup."

"Dr. Nora Volkow, Director of NIDA (National Institute on Drug Addiction), has found that some individuals have more difficulty controlling their eating habits than their narcotics," said his coach. "Some researchers suggest eliminating processed sugar in 'cold turkey' fashion. In most cases the symptoms last just a few days and then you begin to feel better."

"There's that mindset thing again," said Ken. "Do it now or drag it out. Reminds me of that quote by Ralph Waldo Emmerson: *The ancestor of every action is a thought."*

"With what research is uncovering about brain function, it would appear that Emmerson hit the nail squarely on the head," said his coach.

Ken stood, gathering his things. Hand on the door handle he paused a moment and then announced, "I think I'd prefer to go cold turkey with the sugar thing and get it over with." And with that, he was out the door. Whistling no less and with a spring in his step as he headed down the hall.

Allison had been taught to avoid waste, which was creating problems for her waist. Meet Allison in Chapter 11.

The reality for 76 million Baby Boomers will be an average life span in excess of 100 years, with unexpectedly good health—so much so, in fact, that you will scarcely be able to tell a fit and active 65-year old from a healthy and athletic 105-year-old.

—Ronald Katz, MD

Waste or Waist

Chapter 11

"But I really *do* want to be healthy," Alison wailed. "I'm drinking plenty of water—I have at least one very pale urine per day and sometimes two—and am moving toward a Mediterranean-style plant-based cuisine, eating more fruits and veggies every day. And I'm including some seeds and raw nuts and a variety of whole grains. But when they weighed me at the doctor's office today, I'd gained a pound. A whole *pound!* Go figure."

"We talked about the benefits of keeping a daily food journey for a week," said her wellness coach. "Several times, in fact." Alison nodded. "It has been shown to be a consistently helpful tool for many and can help sleuth out what is sabotaging your success. Beginning today I strongly recommend you do this."

"I really don't want to take the time to write everything down for a week," said Alison, "but neither do I want to gain another pound." She and her coach discussed the pros and cons. Finally Alison agreed to the recommendation. Reluctantly.

At her next visit, Alison brought seven days of food journaling, carefully documented. "Can't say I enjoyed doing this every day," she told her coach, "but I think I've got everything recorded. After doing the work, I certainly hope it means something to you."

Her coach reviewed the journal. Running a finger down the list, she paused at one entry. "Ice cream. Tell me about the ice cream. There is an entry for *two bowls* each day for seven days."

Oh, that," said Alison. "I like my ice cream in the evening. While I watch movies, you know. It reminds me of family. We often made ice cream at home and ate it together, in bowls or waffle cones or as banana splits or floats or you-name-it. That's how we expressed love."

"Some families do develop a 'love language,' so called," said the coach, "that revolves around food. I understand that when you eat ice cream you think of your family with affection. Ice cream has a high glycemic load, however, and is not on the list of recommended foods."

"Oh, I know that," said Alison, cheerfully. "But I'm just using it up."

"You're doing *what*?" asked her coach.

"You know. Just using it up. I have a freezer filled with ice cream. Bought it on sale a few months ago. The ice cream, not the freezer. I'm just using it up. When it's all gone, I won't buy any more, sale or no sale. I couldn't throw it out, could I? Why, that would be wasteful! Blame my mother. She always said, *Waste not—want not.*"

"Is your mother living with you now?" Alison shook her head. "Then you might take a page from a quote attributed to Steve Goodier: *An important decision I made was to resist playing the blame game. The day I realized that I am in charge of how I will approach problems in my life, that things will turn out better or worse because of me and nobody else, that was the day I knew I would be a happier and healthier person. And that was the day I knew I could truly build a life that matters.*"

"But I always add some bits of fruit or nuts to make the ice cream healthier," protested Alison.

"How important is your health?" asked her coach. "A freezer filled with ice cream is very *waist-full*—pun intended. Eaten, it will likely go straight to your middle, bits of fruit or nuts notwithstanding. Just like unmanaged emotions, an unmanaged environment can sabotage a Longevity Lifestyle."

"But the ice cream is not in my home, per se," said Alison. "It's in the garage!" At that, they both laughed.

"Your environment can either help or hinder you in being successful," said her coach. "It can work for you or against you. Make it work *for* you."

"What do you mean?" asked Alison, her forehead wrinkled in puzzlement. "How would I make my environment work *for* me?"

The coach summarized five suggestions while Alison took notes.

1. Bring into your home only what you have decided to eat and drink. Go through your house, garage, office, and car, and give away everything you have decided to remove from your menu. When those foods, beverages, candy, cookies, ice cream, and chips are no longer readily available, you will be less likely to ingest them. There's a big difference between opening the freezer to find ice cream readily available and having to drive to a grocery store to purchase some.

2. Give your brain plenty of time to register that you have had enough to eat (satiety). This typically takes at least fifteen minutes. Take a bite of food, chew slowly, and savor the flavor. Flavor intensity tends to fall after the second or third bites of the same food. After that, you're eating primarily from memory rather than from hunger or intensity of flavors.

Eat only two bites of the same food at a time. If you choose to have dessert, eat only two or three bites at most. Savor each bite and remind yourself: "*You* eat two bites and feel satisfied."

3. Stop thinking about or discussing stressful or unpleasant topics at mealtimes. Discuss discipline (if you have children), finances, or areas of disagreement at other times. Provide a calm, unhurried, and pleasing environment while you eat. Remember, serotonin levels are influenced by what you think and how you act. And serotonin levels impact not only your brain and nervous system, but also your digestive system.

4. If you are in a huge rush or in the midst of a stressful situation, consider deferring your meal. You can easily wolf down 1500 calories in under ten minutes when eating quickly and without mindful awareness. And if the situation is stressful, what you eat might just sit in the pit of your stomach, anyway, creating an unpleasant sensation. Sometimes it may be wise to just drink a glass of water and wait to eat until things are calmer. Or, eat lightly, choosing an apple or a salad with lemon juice as dressing or a bowl of soup.

5. Eat to live rather than live to eat. Schedule regular mealtimes; train your brain when to expect food. Remember, everything starts in your brain. Make mealtimes enjoyable. Whenever possible, sit down to eat. If you have the option, eat with family members and friends at the table. Enjoy conversing with them. Share jokes or humorous stories and choose to laugh, since laughter releases enzymes that help with digestion. Report on something interesting you saw or heard recently. If you live alone, do something enjoyable during meal time (e.g., listen to your favorite type of instrumental music or a favorite singer or humorist or author or an audio book).

"Those tips are helpful but I'm unwilling to give up my evening treat while I watch TV," Alison said stubbornly. "No one, no one," she repeated, "can make me give up my nightly treat!"

"No one is trying to *make* you do anything, Allison. You know the basic strategies and you need to implement them in ways that work for your brain. Half a cup of frozen yogurt is a healthier option."

"I suppose I could switch to frozen yogurt instead of ice cream," said Allison. "Especially high-calorie boutique ice cream, even though I love the taste. And I could eat half a cup instead of half a quart smothered in butterscotch syrup, candy-covered peanuts, and whipped cream."

Those two bowls of ice cream every night must have been something to see, thought her coach. *I can only imagine!*

"But don't call me!" Alison said abruptly, sticking out her chin rather dramatically. She was on a roll. "I'm not a person who wants other people bothering me under the guise of being supportive, helpful, encouraging, or you-name-it. Please know that although I appreciate the information, strategies, and tips, I'm doing this in my own way, in my own time, and on my own terms. And if we meet unexpectedly in town, do not ask me how I'm doing. Somehow that question always comes across as if the person expects me to fail. I'll call you. Maybe. Understood?"

"Understood," said her coach, smiling. "I'm glad you know yourself, Alison, and have identified what works for you and what doesn't. Of course I will honor your requests. No calls. No asking how you are doing. If you choose to give me an update at any time, however, I will be glad to hear from you."

Alison nodded, gathered up her belongings, and disappeared through the doorway.

Her coach sat quietly for a few minutes, elbows on the desk, lips pursed, hands folded. *That was interesting. Alison must have had some unfortunate experiences with coaching. That or she's decided that creating and implementing a Longevity Lifestyle is not that important or just too much work right now—or ever. Maybe she thinks I'd be disappointed to hear that news. Or perhaps she really does better on her own. Time will surely tell.* And with those thoughts, the wellness coach refocused attention on the next appointment.

Three months passed. Six months morphed into seven. Nine months headed toward ten and kept right on moving. Soon an entire year had passed with nothing from Alison. Not one word. Nada. Zip.

One morning, the office phone vibrated into life. The wellness coach answered to hear a voice say, "This is Alison. Do you remember me? I'm calling with an update."

"Of course I remember you." The coach was just on the point of asking "How are you?" when their previous conversation came to mind.

"Aren't you going to ask me how I'm doing?" asked Alison.

"No, I'm not. At our last visit I promised not to do that. I'm happy to listen to anything you want to share, however." There was a short pause.

"Ah, yes," said Alison. "I remember. I was very specific, wasn't I?" She paused, chuckling. "How about we start this conversation over? And this time be sure to ask me how I am doing."

"Okay. We'll start over."

"Hello. This is Alison. Do you remember me?" There was short pause. "I'm calling to give you an update."

"Of course I remember you, Alison," said the wellness coach. "I'm delighted you called. Tell me, how are you doing?"

"I hardly know where to begin," said Alison. "I am doing so well!" She reeled off half a dozen examples.

"First, I substituted a half cup of frozen yogurt as my evening treat, leaving off butterscotch syrup, candy-coated peanuts, and whipped cream. And I gave away my second freezer to an orphanage, along with all the ice cream.

"Next, I purchased a water filter because I don't like the way our tap water tastes." She laughed.

"Water has become my primary beverage of choice. Imagine! Water! And I'm much more active. Swimming two or three days a week at the gym, and walking at least two or three other days. At least once a week I remember to do balance and strengthening exercises."

"I've learned to like Mediterranean cuisine, including lots of fresh veggies, fruit, raw nuts, and legumes. Beans have actually become a favorite of mine, especially hummus. A year ago I wouldn't have believed that was possible. At first, some of my friends called beans the *musical food*."

"Musical food?" asked her coach.

"Yes. They go *toot-toot*," said Alison, laughing.

"That's a new one," said the coach. "Cute."

"Being more active and avoiding late-night meals have helped me sleep less fitfully. Most nights I get eight hours (not five or six) and wake up feeling refreshed and energetic.

"And last—but certainly not least—my body is changings. Slowly but surely. Nearly 37 pounds have disappeared over the last year. I don't know what that works out to per week, but it's at least three pounds a month. Do you know what it feels like to lose thirty-seven pounds and have your clothing no longer feel painted on?"

"Not personally," said her coach, "but I certainly have seen the relief, excitement, and gratitude expressed by others who have gotten serious about creating and maintaining a Longevity Lifestyle."

"Well, I'm here to tell you that it is beyond wonderful," said Alison. "I have more energy than I've had at any time since high school. And with the swimming and walking, my muscles have firmed up just like you promised. That in itself has impacted the way my clothing fits."

Altogether it was a very rewarding conversation. It reminded the coach that one cannot read another's mind, that one never knows for sure the decisions people will make or who will choose to create a Longevity Lifestyle and make it work for them on a daily basis.

Chapter 12 is next. You'll meet Roger who was confused about weight being "all in your head."

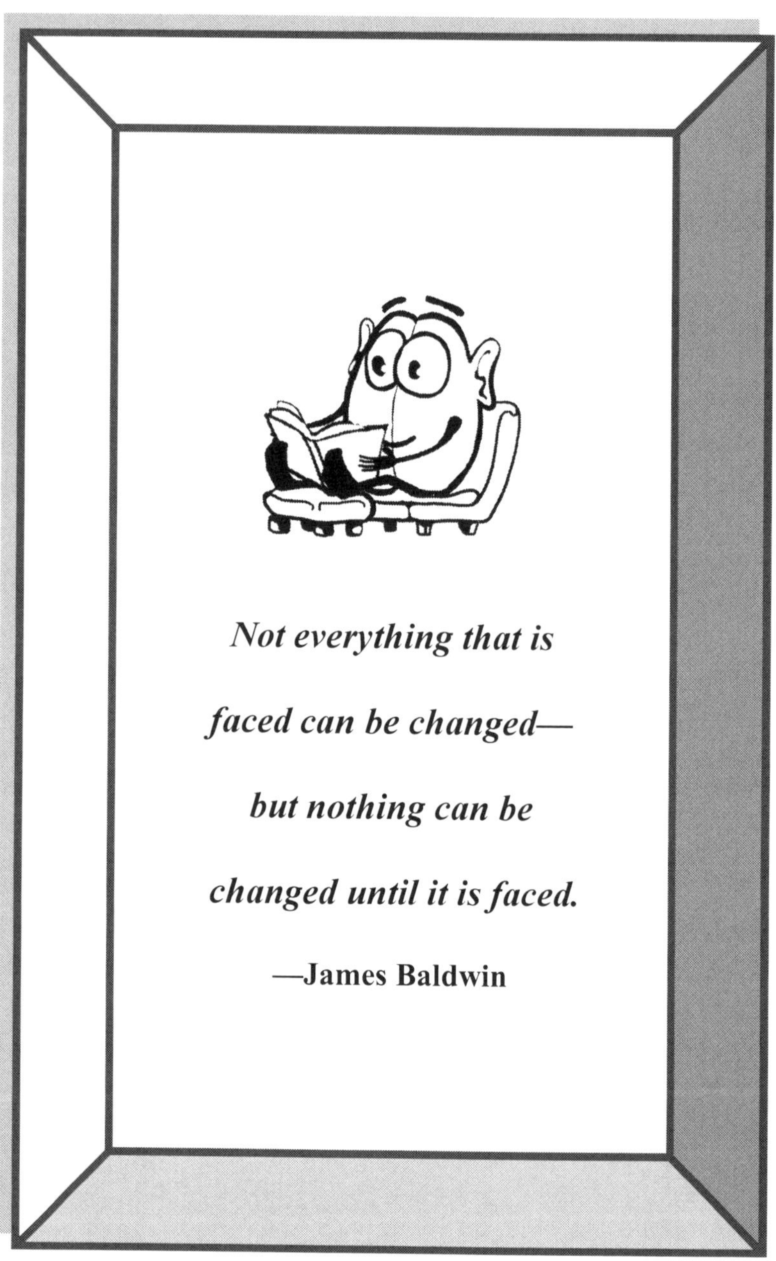
Not everything that is
faced can be changed—
but nothing can be
changed until it is faced.
—James Baldwin

Ultimate in Competition

Chapter 12

"I have a pattern of overeating," said Roger. "Serious overeating. Go figure!"

"Many people have that problem," said his wellness coach. "Studies have shown that the brain can be altered by repeated exposure to large amounts of favorite foods in the same way that addictive drugs can alter the brain. These favorite foods, often high in fat and simple carbs, stimulate the release of the master molecule of addiction: *dopamine*. Because dopamine helps you feel better and experience pleasure, it's easy to eat more of the foods that stimulate its release.

"This can dull the dopamine system, gradually requiring larger quantities of food or more frequent eating to experience the same level of pleasure. It's often referred to as *developing tolerance* and is one reason addictive behaviors eventually escalate. Overeating can also result in the brain becoming *centrally resistant* to hormones such as leptin and insulin. This, in effect, turns the brain into one hungry machine and the normal *brakes*, which signal you have eaten a sufficient amount, become impaired."

"I've heard that your weight is all in your head, but I thought obesity and type 2 diabetes had to do with insulin," said Roger. "And insulin has to do with the pancreas, right? Last time I checked, my pancreas was nowhere near my head!"

"Good. You know something about anatomy," said his coach. "The explanation has a lot to with hormones."

"Am I going to be able to understand hormones? Some explanations are so complicated they slide right past my brain and . . ." Roger's voice trailed off.

"I am confident you'll understand. If at any time you don't, just stop me and I'll back up."

Roger nodded.

"Hormones are chemical messengers secreted by a gland or tissue and sent out through the blood stream. Quite powerful, only a tiny amount is required to alter cell metabolism. Some hormonal effects last from mere minutes to hours, like adrenalin. Others, such as testosterone, last for days to months. Hormones play a major role in keeping the brain and body in balance and help to direct and control the regulation of your internal environment.

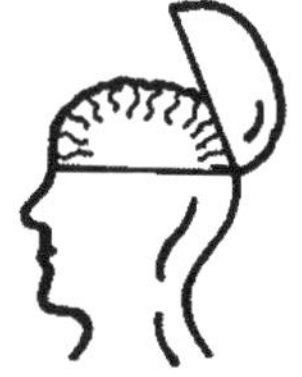

Adequate amounts of hormones—in balance—are essential for maintaining optimal brain-body health. Regardless of where in the body hormones are secreted, most make their way to the brain. That's the reason some say that your weight is all in your head."

"Ah-ha," said Roger. "I take it then, that insulin is a hormone that makes its way to the brain."

"Exactly," said his coach. "Insulin is a powerful and very important peptide hormone produced and released by beta cells in the Islet of Langerhans, part of the pancreas. As you may know, the pancreas is a cone-shaped spongy organ about twelve inches long that is located behind the stomach and attached to the first part of the small intestine or duodenum."

"I read somewhere that human beings cannot live without insulin," said Roger. "Is that really true?"

His coach nodded. "Insulin plays a major role in metabolism, the way your cells use digested food for energy. Insulin is the key that unlocks the door to the fat cell to let energy enter and subsequently be stored as fat. When blood glucose levels rise too high, insulin can stimulate the liver, muscle tissue, and fat cells to store excess glucose in the form of glycogen."

"On the other hand, if blood glucose levels fall below a certain point, insulin can reverse that process and help the body convert glycogen back into glucose. When inadequate amounts of insulin are available, individuals must take insulin injections (often several times each day) in order to stay alive. Sometimes people with insulin resistance must take insulin injections, as well."

"My cousin just told me she's been diagnosed with insulin resistance and type 2 diabetes. What exactly is insulin resistance?" asked Roger.

"Insulin resistance means that although the body produces enough insulin, it does not use it effectively. Rather, it allows glucose to build up in the blood stream rather than being absorbed by the cells. Muscle insulin resistance is the earliest detectable abnormality of type 2 diabetes. Factors such as genetics, obesity, and sedentary lifestyle can increase one's risk for muscle insulin resistance.

"In response to muscle insulin resistance, the pancreas may try to compensate by increasing its production of insulin, which triggers hyperinsulinemia (too much insulin). In turn, this expedites the accumulation of fat within the liver, a condition that occurs only when your total daily intake of calories exceeds the number you expend—day after day and year after year."

"As more and more fat is stored in the liver, that body organ becomes insulin resistant. Glucose production in the liver is disregulated, causing blood sugar levels to rise."

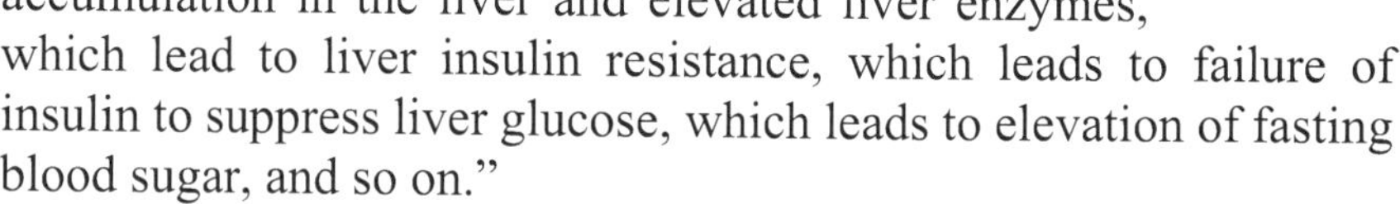

"You're talking a cascade effect," said Roger. "Like the pot fountain in my back patio."

"That's right. Excess calories ingested (typically as fats and refined foods) plus insulin resistance, lead to fat accumulation in the liver and elevated liver enzymes, which lead to liver insulin resistance, which leads to failure of insulin to suppress liver glucose, which leads to elevation of fasting blood sugar, and so on."

"I get it. One thing leads to another," said Roger. "It's mind-boggling. That's what."

"Central insulin resistance can contribute to cognitive decline in the brain, a condition now becoming known as type 3 diabetes. By the way, do you know about leptin and ghrelin, two other powerful hormones that impact weight?"

Roger shook his head. "Never heard of 'em."

"The average person has never heard of leptin or its cousin ghrelin, for that matter. The word *leptin* comes from the Greek word l*eptos* meaning thin. Known as the *satiety* hormone and made by fat cells, leptin regulates the amount of fat stored in the body. It does this by adjusting both the sensation of hunger *and* energy expenditures. A brake pedal, if you will.

"Hunger is inhibited (satiety) when the amount of fat stored reaches a certain level. Leptin is then secreted and circulates through the body, eventually activating leptin receptors in the hypothalamus. The good news is that physical exercise improves leptin signaling and helps with weight control."

"Ghrelin has an opposite effect. Ghrelin is known as the *hunger* hormone. Ghrelin receptors are located on the same brain cells as leptin receptors, so these cells receive competing satiety and hunger signals. Ghrelin is secreted when the stomach is empty. Think of Ghrelin as the accelerator pedal, if you will. Ghrelin acts on cells in your brain's hypothalamus both to increase a sensation of hunger and to increase gastric acid secretion and gastrointestinal motility to prepare the body for receiving an intake of food.

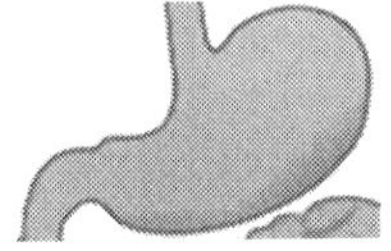

"When the stomach is stretched, ghrelin secretion stops. That's one reason for drinking a big glass of water 15-20 minutes before you plan to eat. The water helps stretch the stomach."

"That seems clear enough," said Roger. "It's a sophisticated energy system: pedal-to-the metal—full steam ahead; put on the brakes—slow down, take it easy."

His coach smiled. "Enter visceral fat cells that congregate around your middle. They do far more than just impact how your clothing fits. Visceral fat cells can disrupt hormonal secretions and the digestion of fats and proteins, which in turn influence appetite, blood pressure, blood sugar levels, cholesterol, and insulin sensitivity. This disruption can increase one's risk for type 2 diabetes."

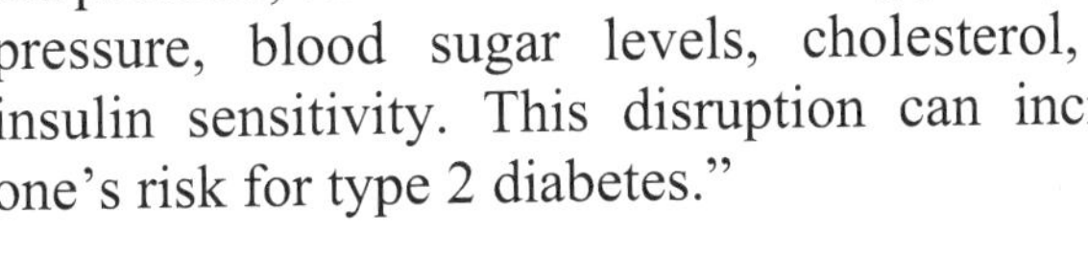

"More cascade effect," said Roger.

"A Longevity Lifestyle is designed to help rebalance these hormones. For example, an increase in fiber (soluble and insoluble) preferably from whole, intact foods, can improve regularity."

"In other words, it helps prevent constipation," said Roger.

His coach nodded and listed some other benefits of fiber.

Fiber can:

- Slow glucose absorption, which reduces insulin release
- Reduce the rate at which fructose is absorbed and delivered to the liver
- Delay stomach emptying, creating a sense of fullness (soluble fiber)

"Refined carbohydrates stimulate insulin secretion, promote overeating, and favor fat accumulation," said his coach. "Foods with a high Glycemic Load promote the over secretion of insulin—and insulin loves to tuck fat into cells. Minimizing refined carbs can help prevent these consequences from occurring."

"I get the reason now for avoiding *empty* calories. They tend to put on weight but add little, if any, nutritional value."

"Exactly." The coach looked straight at Roger. "Unfortunately, many individuals have not a clue that they are insulin resistant until diagnosed with some form of diabetes: type 2 diabetes, type 3 diabetes, or diabetes mellitus."

"So overeating, especially of poor quality foods such as high fat, high sugar, and refined foods can trigger hormonal imbalances including insulin resistance," said Roger, thoughtfully. "This is the first time I've really understood the links between insulin and refined foods and type diabetes and weight gain, and the links between exercise and hormones and weight gain. Amazing really. It appears more than worth my time to do whatever I can in the way of prevention."

"If people learn they have insulin resistance early on, the good news is that they can often delay or reduce the likelihood of developing diabetes by making changes."

“In addition to an impact on hormones, physical exercise helps to maintain energy balance, and appears to be critical for maintaining optimum weight over the long term.”

“I need to tell my cousin about a Longevity Lifestyle,” said Roger. “And that regular physical exercise may improve both glucose tolerance and insulin sensitivity. It could help her health. What am I saying? It could save her life!”

“Share, by all means,” encouraged his coach.

“What about fat cells themselves? I know they exist—I can pinch an inch of them on my body.” Roger smiled ruefully. “But I don’t know much about them.”

“There are several types of fat cells, or adipocytes, as they are called: white, beige, brown, and pink. They specialize in storing energy in the form of fat. As a rule, adipocytes in the body merely gain or lose fat content to facilitate changes in weight. However, if adipocytes reach their maximum fat capacity, they may replicate to allow additional fat storage. Once made, fat cells are very happy to be filled,” said his coach, laughing.

“So what happens to these fat cells, adipocytes, when I lose weight?”

“The fat cells shrink,” said his coach. “But even after marked weight loss, the body appears not to lose the adipocytes (fat cells) themselves. According to the World Health Organization, the fundamental cause of obesity is simple. It tends to occur when the number of calories in foods and beverages consumed exceed the energy expended. People either ingest too much food or are too sedentary and get insufficient amounts of exercise, or both.”

Roger looked thoughtfully at his *spare tire*.

"There is also the emerging understanding that overeating poor quality calories—high fat, high simple carbs, refined and processed foods, and fast foods—can result in inflammatory changes in the brain itself. The hypothalamus, a small but critically important organ deep in the brain, is highly sensitive to inflammation. And, unfortunately, inflammation is also linked with Alzheimer's disease."

"You said I'd understand, and I do," said Roger. "I wonder . . ." He paused.

"Yes?" his coached encouraged.

"I have one sister who is very heavy, obese really, and drinks much less wine than her twin, who is only mildly overweight but drinks several classes of wine every night. It's a puzzle."

"Women who have a family history of alcoholism have almost double the odds of becoming obese compared to those without a family history. However, obese individuals themselves generally show lower rates of alcohol, nicotine, and marijuana abuse than non-obese individuals. Some researchers suggest that's because poor quality foods—especially when overeaten—may compete with alcohol and other drugs for the same receptor cells in the brain reward system. How's that for the ultimate in competition? Fierce competition, all going on in your brain, hidden from view."

His coach paused for a moment and then added, "The bottom line is that if you continue to do what you've always done—you'll continue to get what you've always gotten."

"I get it," said Roger, chuckling. "I think my brain is full for today, but it's a good kind of full. Not the inflammation kind. And I'm committed to a Longevity Lifestyle. Understanding the reasons for living this way—the science behind mindset, self-talk, nutrition, exercise, and obesity—is going to help me maintain it, too, for the rest of my life."

Chapter 13 introduces Marjorie, who feared her brain was shot.

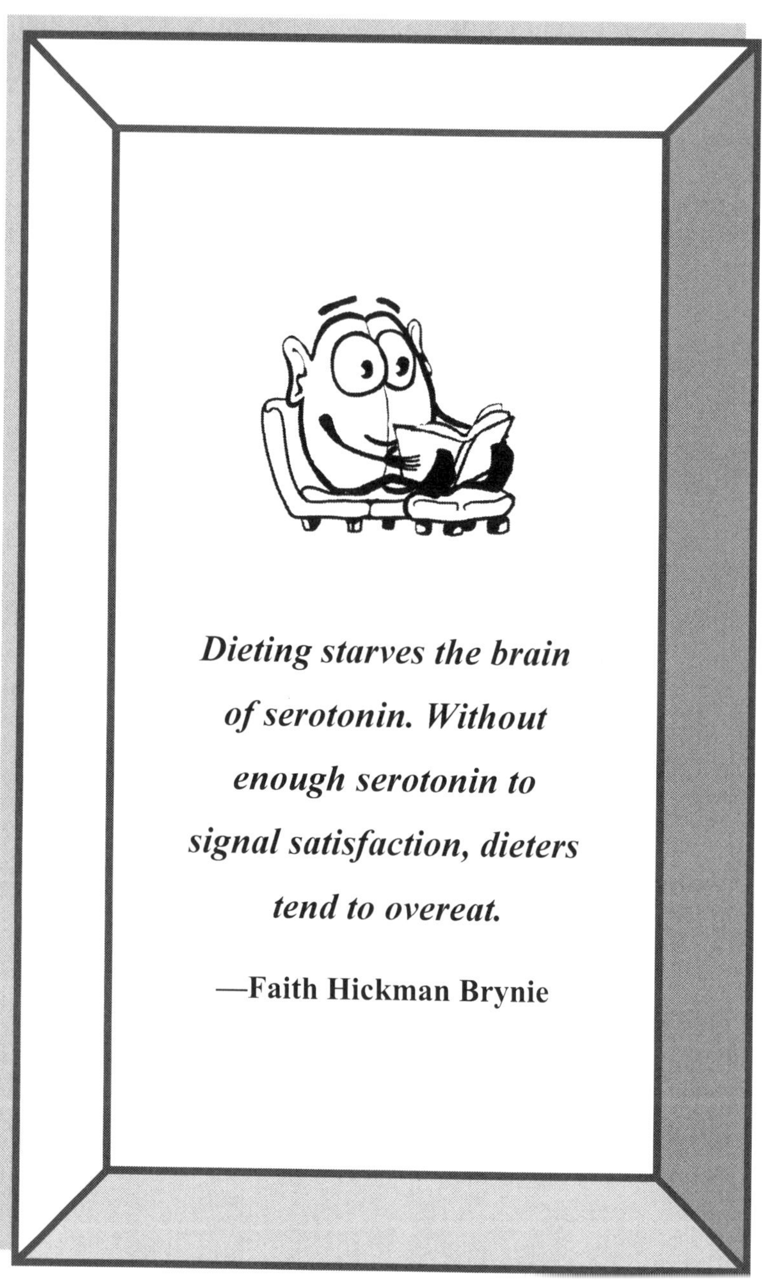
Dieting starves the brain of serotonin. Without enough serotonin to signal satisfaction, dieters tend to overeat.
—Faith Hickman Brynie

Food Wise and Fat Smart

Chapter 13

"I'm quite sure I've tried every fad, crash, and you-name-it diet in the world," said Marjorie. "And I mean in the world! Sure, each time I lost weight. But each time I eventually gained it all back—often more. Is my brain shot?"

"I doubt your brain is shot," said her wellness coach, "although repeated dieting can have serious side effects. Dieting, especially crash diets, may trigger some weight loss in the short term but rarely in the long term, because it doesn't result in consistent lifestyle changes. When you stop *dieting*, you return to your old eating patterns."

"I spent a small fortune on exercise equipment, too, but that never seemed to help, at least not with the weight. Are you saying losing weight is hopeless?" asked Marjorie, her eyes wide.

"Just the opposite," her coach responded. "Although fad and crash diets are not recommended, creating and implementing a Longevity Lifestyle on a consistent basis *is*. It can help keep your brain and immune organs—the most powerful healing system in the world—in homeostasis, in balance. This will help maintain life in your years—maybe even add years to your life. And, in the process, your weight can gradually return to an optimum range for your height and body build."

"I used to think there was something wrong with *me* because my dieting didn't work," said Marjorie. "But even when I'm not on a diet, I have food cravings. I love pie, especially cherry pie. I tell myself: *I can't have cherry pie, I won't have cherry pie. I'm not going to eat any cherry pie.* But after a few weeks my resolve flies right out the proverbial window. Then, I tend to binge. I've been known to scarf down a cherry pie at one sitting. Not a piece of cherry pie, you understand. An entire cherry pie!"

"What you resist persists. In most cases, depriving yourself of something that gives your brain a reward eventually will lead to bingeing. Stop telling your brain what you are not going to give it. Instead, remind your brain what you *are* giving it. Delay gratification by focusing on what you are doing—not on what you are no longer doing. Tell your brain 'You are eating _________' as if it's already a done deal."

"Dieting is my elephant in the room," said Marjorie. "Now that I see that, what do I do?"

"You might begin by removing the word *dieting* from your vocabulary. Dieting creates a picture of deprivation and no brain wants to be deprived. While you're at it, also get rid of the word *can't*. If the brain thinks it *can't*, it usually *doesn't*. Instead, focus your thoughts on your healthier replacement behaviors. I reiterate," said her coach, "stop talking about what you are no longer doing; think and talk about what you are doing. Consistently repeat your healthier replacement behaviors and soon they'll become habits."

"Consider it done," said Marjorie. "I am seeing the word *dieting* in my mind's eye and watching it fade from view. But cravings?"

"Picture cravings as your brain demanding a reward, something that you used to give it that made you feel better. Just because it wants something doesn't mean you must acquiesce."

"It isn't as if your brain is holding a weapon to your head and forcing you to eat—at gunpoint. When you become aware of a craving, acknowledge it and avoid thinking 'deprivation' and 'can't'. Instead, try a positive self-talk sequence." Her coach suggested several sample phrases.

> *So, you're craving cherry pie. You can have a piece if you choose to do so. Right now, however, you're choosing some fresh cherries (or a glass of water).*

"I need to change my self-talk!" exclaimed Marjorie. "I'll work on this this week. New topic. I need help understanding fats. I'm not even sure what fats do in the body."

"Fats are essential to many body processes," her coach explained. "These include helping to absorb fat-soluble vitamins, maintaining the integrity of cell and skin membranes, and assisting with proper brain function. But not all fats are created equal."

"I've heard there are unhealthy fats and healthier fats, but which is which?" asked Marjorie.

"Edible fats are found in both plant and animal foods. Unhealthy fats tend to come primarily from animal products that generally have a higher proportion of saturated fatty acids (except for seafood). Saturated fats usually are solid at room temperature, can raise cholesterol levels, and are linked with heart disease.

"Healthier fats from plant sources and fish generally are liquid at room temperature and contain a higher proportion of unsaturated fatty acids (except for tropical oils such as coconut, palm, and palm kernel oil). Most unprocessed nuts and seeds, olives, and avocados are considered examples of healthier monounsaturated fats. Walnuts, flaxseed, and some fish are examples of polyunsaturated fats, as are omega-3 and omega-6 fatty acids."

"Oh, yeah, those omega things," said Marjorie, laughing.

"Omega-3 and omega-6 are necessary for good health although they are not manufactured by the body. Omega-6, usually found in the food you eat, can help in reducing symptoms of diabetic neuropathy. Omega-3, needed for cardiovascular health, is found in fish or fish oils and in some supplements. Although healthier, unsaturated fats still need to be used in moderation because they're so calorie-dense. Fats contain 9 calories per gram. In comparison, alcohol has 7 calories per gram, while both proteins and carbohydrates have 4 calories per gram. A higher intake of even healthier fats often means an increased risk of gaining weight."

"There is a lot to learn, isn't there? It's fun though. I've already decided to use cold-pressed olive oil," said Marjorie. "I've read that it's extracted from olives without the use of heat and solvents, a process that can generate free radicals. How much fat do I need?"

"Some estimate you need 10-35 percent of your daily caloric intake in healthier fats. Unfortunately, many consume 40-50 percent of their daily intake through fat because it's contained in so many of their favorite foods: steaks, French fries, processed foods, dairy, cheeses, desserts, milk shakes, and so on. Too much fat, especially unhealthy fat, is linked with type 2 diabetes, heart disease, cancer, and expanding waist lines."

"How do trans fats figure into a Longevity Lifestyle?"

"They don't," said her coach. "Trans fats are not recommended as part of a Longevity Lifestyle. They may be the worst type of fat for the human brain and body. Consuming trans-fatty acids can raise the levels of undesirable LDL cholesterol. *Dietary Guidelines for Americans 2010* along with the Institute of Medicine, recommend keeping your consumption of trans fat as low as possible."

"You can do this by limiting your intake of solid fats from fatty parts of meat and dairy products, and artificial trans fats found in processed foods that contain hydrogenated or partially-hydrogenated oils. Adding hydrogen to liquid oils turns them into inexpensive, solid, trans fats that help increase shelf life of processed foods. Estimates are that the average American consumes 1.3 grams of artificial trans fats daily. Major contributors include fried and deep-fried foods, some microwave popcorn, frozen pizzas, margarines and spreads, ready-to-use frostings, cakes, coffee creamers, cookies, pies, doughnuts, and many commercial desserts.

"Even products advertised as being trans-fat free can contain up to 0.5 grams per serving. That can add up quickly. The Centers for Disease Control and Prevention website provides information on the different types of fats, including trans fats, along with their sources."

"That reminds me of the four food groups—designed to make meals quick, easy, and tasty—*fast, fatty, fried,* and *frozen.*" Marjorie and her coach laughed.

"Do you know that human taste buds likely do not register fat directly, at least not as they do for sweet, sour, salt, bitter, and umami?" Marjorie shook her head. "Fat may be more about mouth texture. Gina Willett, PhD, RD, points out there's a gooey, creamy smooth *mouth feel* to fats that trigeminal nerves pick up from lips, mouth, tongue, and teeth, sending pleasurable messages to the brain.

"Michael Moss, author of *Salt, Sugar, Fat: How the Food Giants Hooked Us,* explains that fat doesn't blast away at your mouth like sugar does. Fat is somewhat sly and secretive. Consequently, it can be much more alluring. As a component of highly processed foods, fat may be even more powerful than sugar. For this reason, binge foods are often high in fat and sugar, which makes them a challenge to resist. Too high a sugar content in a food and you may reject it for being *too sweet*. There seems to be no limit to the bliss factor of fat. And when mixed with chocolate, dairy, and sugar …"

"Don't I know!" exclaimed Marjorie, smiling ruefully. "Cakes, cookies, brownies, doughnuts, and pies. Bagels loaded with cream cheese. Cheese blintzes with sour cream. High-fat and soft ice creams. Let's face it, fats have been a challenge for me. And for most of my life I just ate them and never gave a thought to what they might be doing to my brain and body."

"You, along with a host of others," said her coach. Marjorie nodded. "Delaine Robins put it this way:

> *We pick and choose because of our power of choice. We sometimes pick and choose while never really considering the consequences.*

"In a *Journal of Nutrition* article, Nicole M. Avena and coauthors suggest that fat and sugar play collaborative roles. The sugar may largely be responsible for producing the addictive-like behaviors exhibited by susceptible individuals who eat poor quality, high-fat and high-sugar foods, while the fat promotes weight gain.

"No surprise, the food industry loves fat for giving baked goods a firmer texture and more bulk, plus it makes food more desirable by promoting the release of fat-enhancing chemicals that help to blend flavors. Fat also extends the shelf life of processed foods that can stay in your pantry for months at a time, to say nothing of the grocery store. And when used in frying and deep-frying, fats help provide that crispy, crunchy experience."

"I'm sure you can give me some tips on lowering my fat intake," said Marjorie. "I'd really like to do that."

Her coach provided several examples:

- Experiment with salad dressings. Using them is often more a habit than a necessity. Mix your own, substituting water for oil. Some salads may not need any dressing at all. Or try lemon juice or balsamic vinegar.

- When baking, use far less oil than the recipe calls for. Sometimes you can leave it out altogether. Sometimes you can substitute applesauce for at least half the oil to reduce fat calories.

- Limit refined and processed foods. Avoid fried and deep-fried foods. Spray a frying pan with coconut oil for stir-frying or making pancakes rather than pouring in oil.

- Dip a corn tortilla in cold water, place it in a pre-heated frying pan sprayed with coconut oil and steam first one side, then the other.

- Be careful about eating desserts, even so-called healthier ones. When you do choose a dessert, eat only two or three bites. Remember, flavor intensity registered by your taste buds falls off after two or three bites of the same food. After that you're eating primarily from *memory*. Save the calories for more nutritious foods.

- Even if you're not a vegetarian, choose to eat a vegetarian meal several times a week. Include legumes, unprocessed seeds and nuts, fresh and frozen fruits and vegetables, and healthy grains. Meat and animal products take longer for the body to digest, so going vegetarian even part time can give your gastrointestinal tract a break. Plus it can often help to lower your food budget, allowing you to put more in your piggy bank.

- If you choose to use dairy products, select non-fat or low-fat types and use them sparingly. Minimize the use of dairy cheeses, selecting white rather than colored and fresh rather than aged. Use them as a condiment rather than a main dish. Remember, it's easy to become habituated to dairy cheeses because they contain substances that can make you want to eat them often.

- Include moderate amounts of healthier unsaturated fats, primarily from plant sources.

- Fats contain a mixture of different types of fatty acids. While it is important to be careful of your total fat intake, the types of fatty acids you consume are likely more important in terms of risks for chronic diseases than just the total amount. Avoid saturated animal fats, hydrogenated and partially-hydrogenated fats, and all trans fats.

"These tips are doable," Marjorie said. "And here I thought this might be quite complex, if not a bit of a downer. As you say, *in life you always give up something to get something*. There are a few recipes I'll probably stop preparing altogether, but many of them I can tweak using these guidelines. You can be sure I'll be experimenting—starting this week. I'm on the up and up!" She and her coach hi-fived as Marjorie left.

Chapter 14 is next. Belle was desperate to reduce her risk for type 2 diabetes. Find out what her coach recommended.

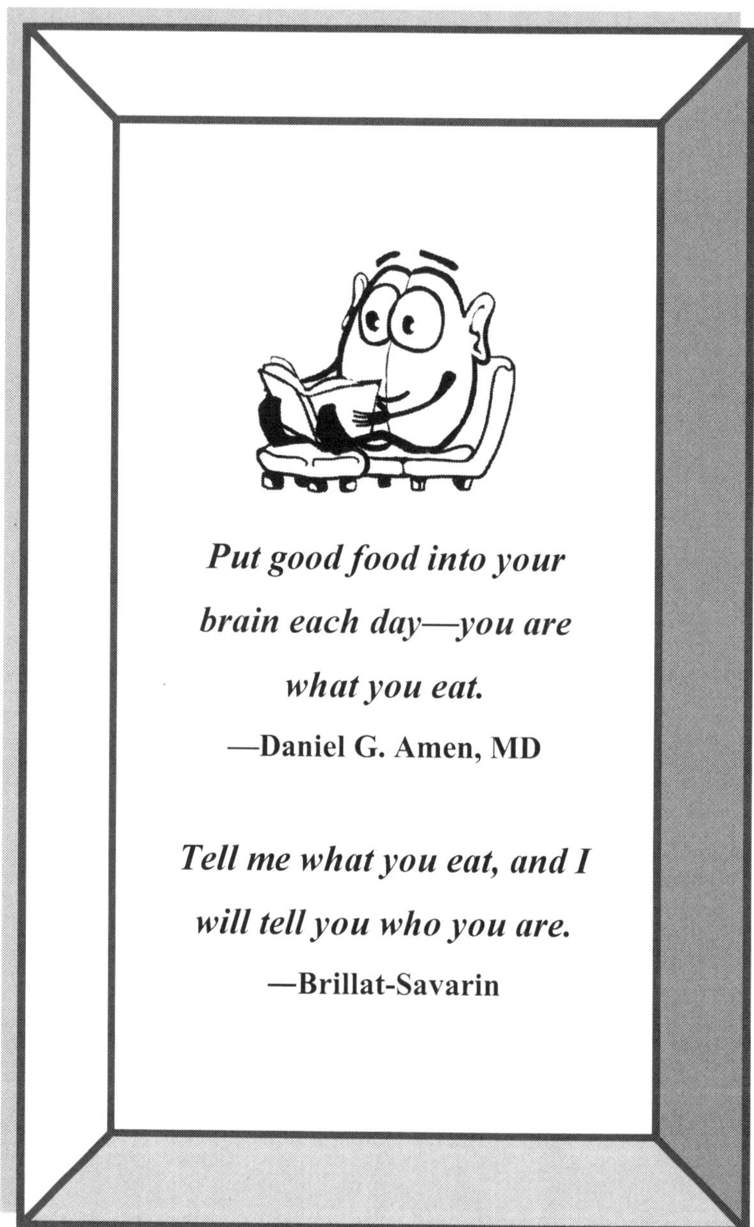
Put good food into your brain each day—you are what you eat.
—Daniel G. Amen, MD
Tell me what you eat, and I will tell you who you are.
—Brillat-Savarin

GI, GL, and G-Willie-Willikers

Chapter 14

"Type 2 diabetes runs in my family," said Belle, removing her coat. "And I've been told that having type 2 diabetes increases the risk of developing other types of health challenges. Just the thought of that stresses me out. I really would like to avoid developing type 2 diabetes!"

"That's a worthy goal," her wellness coach agreed. "Studies have shown that people with type 2 diabetes do have more than twice the risk of dying from heart conditions and stroke compared to individuals without diabetes."

"Is there any evidence that a Longevity Lifestyle could lower my risk for type 2 diabetes?"

"Dr. David Katz, director of the Yale University Prevention Research Center, points out that an impressive array of research findings spanning populations and decades have established that *lifestyle is the best medicine*. Causal as well as protective factors for all prevalent chronic diseases appear to be interrelated. This means that the same eating and activity patterns that help prevent cardiovascular disease could likely do the same for type 2 diabetes."

"That's excellent news," said Belle, relief in her voice. "You have no idea what that means to me!"

"Guangwei Li, MD, at the China-Japan Friendship Hospital in Beijing and David Katz, MD, MPH, of Yale University followed several hundred Chinese with high blood sugar levels for 29 years," continued her coach. "For the study, Dr. Li's group randomly assigned 438 individuals to the exercise and better-eating program, and another 138 patients (who maintained their regular lifestyle) to a control group."

"Interesting," said Belle. "I'm all ears."

"The program was designed to produce weight loss in overweight or obese participants, reduce the intake of simple carbs and alcohol in people of normal weight, and increase the physical activity of participants during their leisure time. The 438 individuals followed a nutrition and exercise program for 6 years and then were tracked for an additional 23 years. The results were reported in *The Lancet Diabetes & Endocrinology.*

"The incidence of death from cardiovascular disease in the control group who did not change their lifestyles was nearly 20 percent, compared with only 12 percent in the study group. Death from any cause was about 38 percent in the control group but only 28 percent in the study group. According to Dr. Li, 'These findings provide yet further justification to implement lifestyle interventions in people with high blood sugar, as clinical and public health measures to control the long-term consequences of diabetes.'"

"I want to lower my risk of developing type 2 diabetes, to say nothing of strokes and heart disease," said Belle. "Definitely I do!"

"That's what a Longevity Lifestyle is all about. Follow it to the best of your ability, for as long as you live. Little by little your risk should diminish and your life get back into better balance."

"What can I do to speed up the process?" asked Belle. "Like how many hours a day can I exercise?"

"Over-exercising is like dieting," her coach replied. "Eventually, you won't be able to maintain that excessive level. Appropriate physical activity and physical exercise are components of a *balanced* Longevity Lifestyle. Exercise can strengthen your muscles, sculpt your body, and assist you to stay toned as you move toward a desirable weight. It definitely can be of help in maintaining an optimum weight over the long term."

"Are you saying that exercising more won't melt off pounds *now*?" asked Belle, slumping in her chair. "So what's the point?"

"The *point*," said her coach, "is that physical activity and exercise offer more benefits than we would have time to discuss during the rest of this appointment. And once you have regained an optimum weight, exercise has been shown to help you maintain that weight."

"I guess I lost sight of the benefits," said Belle. "I think I was so frightened about the potential consequences of type 2 diabetes that everything else blew right by me. Please remind me."

So her coach reeled off nearly a dozen benefits from exercise:

1. Improves body composition, i.e., builds muscle tissue that burns four times as many calories as fat tissue.

2. Increases glucose tolerance.

3. Lowers blood pressure.

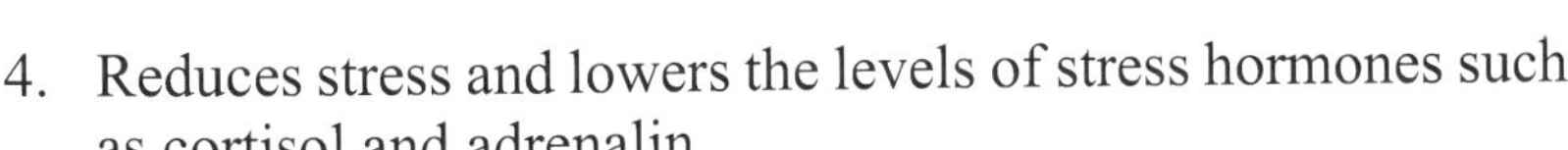

4. Reduces stress and lowers the levels of stress hormones such as cortisol and adrenalin.

5. Promotes the release of endorphins, the brain's natural opiate, i.e., morphine.

6. Increases brain sensitivity to both insulin and leptin, two critical hormones.

7. Likely impacts the brain's central regulation of food intake.

8. Creates new receptors for dopamine, the feel-better chemical and part of the brain reward system.

9. Appears to be the most effective approach to preventing excessive weight gain during pregnancy (along with eating nutritious, quality foods), which can lower the long-term risk of obesity for two generations.

10. Decreases the risk for heart and vascular diseases.

11. Lowers the risk for the development of prediabetes…

"Oh my!" exclaimed Belle, interrupting. "I've been focusing on weight loss, not on a balanced Longevity Lifestyle. I think I lost sight of the important part that physical exercise plays."

"It's easy to do. Especially when you're excited about dropping clothing sizes. Nevertheless, balance is critical to long-term success," her coach said.

"Another thing," said Belle. "My doctor talked about GI and GL, but it's all G-Willie-Willikers to me, as my mother used to say."

Her coach explained. "The Glycemic Index or GI was invented in 1981 by Doctors Wolever and Jenkins. GI measures how quickly foods break down into sugar in your bloodstream. High glycemic foods break down quickly and spike blood sugar levels."

"Sustained spikes in blood sugar and insulin levels may lead to increased risk for diabetes. Blood sugar spikes do not improve brain function, either. Table sugar or white bread has a GI of 100.

"The Shanghai Women's Health Study concluded that women whose menus had the highest GI ratings were 21 percent more likely to develop type 2 diabetes than women whose menus had the lowest GI ratings. Similar findings were reported in the Black Women's Health Study."

"So desserts have a high GI and most veggies, fruits, and nuts have a lower GI, right?"

"You're on the right track. Just remember that not all foods affect blood glucose levels the same way. Raw celery, green beans, almonds, and walnuts, have a GI of close to zero; white potatoes, parsnips, and raw carrots have GI ratings climbing up toward that of table sugar." Belle whistled.

"A GI greater than 70 is considered high; a GI between 56 and 69 is medium; while a GI of 55 or less is considered low. Knowing the GI rating of different foods can help you plan your meals more effectively. In general, it's the GI of the *meal,* rather than just one food that's important.

"Got it," said Belle. "So what's GL?"

"The Glycemic Load or GL was created by Harvard researchers. A similar concept, it measures the amount of carbohydrate in a specific serving size. Glycemic Load appears to be especially beneficial in dietary programs that target diabetes prevention as well as diabetes treatment, and in weight management. Foods with a GL of 10 or less fall in the low range and are typically healthier choices. Those with a GL between 11 and 19 are in the medium range. Foods with a GL of 20 or higher tend to cause spikes in blood sugar and insulin. These high-GL foods should be eaten very sparingly."

"Foods with a low GL in a typical serving size almost always have a relatively low GI."

"I take it there must be a GI-GL list and, if so, how would I read the numbers?" asked Belle.

"Yes, there are lists. Here's one example." Her coach handed Belle a sheet of paper. "How would knowing the GL and the GI for the foods listed help you decide what to select for your meal?"

Belle studied the list. "Let me see. A corn tortilla would be a better choice than a white bagel."

"That's it," said her coach, nodding encouragingly. "What else?"

Food	**GI**	**Serving (grams)**	**GL**
Bagel, white	72	70	25
Corn Tortilla	52	50	12
Brown Rice	50	150	16
White Rice	89	150	43
Apple	39	120	6
Banana	62	120	16
Green Peas	51	80	4
Lentils	29	150	5
Hummus	6	30	0
Oatmeal, old fashioned	55	250	13
Oatmeal, instant or quick	83	250	30

"Hmmm," said Belle, continuing to look at the list. "I'd select brown rice over white rice. And an apple has a lower GL than a banana. Should I be eating apples instead of bananas?"

"Variety is important," said her coach. "Avoid eating only apples just because they have a lower GI and GL. It's the general Glycemic Index and Glycemic Load of the meal that is important. Bananas are a good source of potassium, which may help your sodium-potassium balance. Just remember that the riper the banana, the more glucose it contains and the higher the GI."

"Oh, hummus!" exclaimed Belle. "It has a GI of 6 and GL of 0. I love hummus. This is great. Okay. My aim is to select a majority of foods that have a GI below 55 and a GL of 10 or less. I'll use a few foods in the moderate range, while avoiding those with a high GI and GL whenever possible."

"The way in which food is prepared can impact its Glycemic Load, as well," said her coach. "For example, the GI of pasta cooked 'al dente' (there's a slight resistance in the center when the pasta is chewed) is lower than when it is cooked longer."

"So how does knowing the serving in grams help me?" asked Belle.

"Good question. Lists often show servings in grams, which measure weight. Ounces measure volume, so converting grams to ounces can look like a challenge. Nevertheless, when you realize that one ounce is roughly equivalent to 28 or 30 grams, then you get the sense that 100 grams is almost half a cup. That makes it easier to get a general idea of serving size as well as GI-GL values.

"It's also possible to calculate the GL for any size serving of a food, an entire meal, or an entire day's meals if you want to. The formula is to take the number of grams in the serving, multiply by the Glycemic Index, and divide by 100."

"I can see the potential value of that but it sounds a bit intimidating," said Belle. "Math was not my favorite subject . . ."

"You may never have occasion to use that formula," said her coach. "Just know it exists. Information about Glycemic Index and Glycemic Load is designed to be general guide. Avoid agonizing about the numbers and look at the comparison picture."

"I can definitely do that," said Belle. "And here I thought this was going to be difficult, if not a bit of a drag. This is so doable."

"It is doable," agreed her coach. "Once you do this a few times you'll quickly get the general idea. Increase your intake of foods that are in as natural state as possible, especially green vegetables and legumes that have a relatively low Glycemic Load. Eating more of these foods will serve as a signal to your brain that there is an abundance to eat and you are not starving."

"I'm having fun with this, too. Do you remember telling me that if I could find a way to have fun, that could predispose me to keep living like this for the rest of my life?" Her coach nodded.

"I am having fun," said Belle, smiling. "Now, where do I find out more about GL and GI?" asked Belle.

"Entire books have been written on the topic," said her coach. "The Internet is another resource. A list of the Glycemic Index and Glycemic Load for more than 1,000 foods can be found in an article entitled 'International tables of glycemic index and glycemic load values: 2008.' Google those words. Do an Internet search and stimulate your brain at the same time."

"I will," said Belle. "I'll start by printing a list from the Internet, and I may get a book, too. Choices, choices. I like choices." She left the office, smiling.

Turn the page to Chapter 15. Meet Harry who was confused about the difference between a *feeling* and the physiological sensation of hunger.

Given the recent evidence on the addictive properties of certain foods, it looks like Ronald McDonald may have more in common with Joe Camel than anyone dares admit.
—Neal D. Barnard, MD

Ecstasy Excess

Chapter 15

"I need a pick-me-up," said Harry, breezing into the office. "I feel *really* hungry for some fried chicken, that's what. A Kentucky Fried Chicken special from the world's most popular chicken restaurant chain."

"Harry!" said his wellness coach, "hungry for some chicken is not a feeling. There is a big difference between being physiologically hungry because your body needs fuel and eating to help yourself *feel* better. The latter is often referred to as *emotional* eating."

"There's a difference?" asked Harry, honestly.

"Definitely," said his coach, "although many don't realize that, so they use food to help themselves feel better, often without even being aware of what they are doing. Studies have shown that people sometimes choose specific foods depending on whether they feel happy or sad, content or anxious, glad or mad. Emotional eating typically involves gravitating toward *comfort* foods when you feel down and other types of food (sometimes healthier, sometimes not) when you feel up." At that, Harry's eyebrows went up.

"You can only manage what you can label and describe. Have you identified your *comfort* foods, for instance? What foods do you gravitate toward when you are *blue* or upset or need a pick-me-up, as you put it?" There was no answer from Harry.

"Is it chicken, pasta, mashed potatoes and gravy, meatloaf, mac 'n cheese, chips, and surgery snacks? What do you love to eat when you want to celebrate something or feel excited? Is it ice cream and cake? What did you love during childhood?" asked his coach.

"In childhood? Why I liked everything, and I mean everything. For example, on my fifth birthday when I got my first dog, I was so excited. I remember seeing a huge loganberry cobbler sitting on the kitchen counter, still warm from the oven. Made from our own berries, too. I climbed onto a stool, dug in, and ate the whole thing. In hog heaven, as they say! My mother was mad. But my mouth waters now just thinking about it. Comfort foods. Hmmm."

"Harry! What you just described was enough cobbler to feed ten people! No wonder your mother was less than enthusiastic."

"I know," said Harry, sheepishly. "The year I turned ten my mother suffered a miscarriage, and a pall fell over the entire household. I recall eating an entire casserole of mac 'n cheese in one sitting." He paused, thinking.

"And there was the time when my granny fell and broke both hips. That day I felt really bad and so I wolfed down eight big franks smothered in cheese. On the other hand, the day my mare birthed a colt I felt wonderful, so elated that I have no idea how many bowls of home-made ice cream I ate. A lot! I remember feelings so good, almost *high,* as kids say today.

"Over the years I've downed entire pies, whole roasted chickens, enough mashed potatoes and gravy to feed a small threshing crew, casseroles of you-name-it, and entire loaves of bread fresh from the oven, dripping in butter, of course. In between, I ate quite sensibly. But you can see how difficult it is to say what my *comfort* foods are. I fear that I learned some really unfortunate behaviors in childhood. Probably developed some habits that have impacted my life rather negatively, too. I know I did."

"Many people do, Harry. You are not alone," said his coach kindly. "Dr. Lissa Rankin points out in her book Mind over Medicine how Scientists now believe that external signals—things like nutrition, the environment in which we live, even thoughts and emotions—can influence regulatory proteins that determine how and even whether DNA gets expressed in certain ways. In other words, it's not as cut and dried as we once thought. There's more and more science coming out about the physiology of what happens when you believe you will get well versus when you believe you will be sick. Yet, for many people, their thoughts about health stem from childhood, when negative thoughts about their health may have been programmed into their minds, sometimes even against their will.

Harry paused, a far-away look in his eye. "You know, maybe it's less the types of food and more the *amount* of food that did it for me, does it for me—the ecstasy of excess."

"That's a catchy phrase," his coach responded. "The ecstasy of excess. Pretty well sums it up, I'd say. In today's vernacular, eating huge amounts of food at one sitting would be referred to as binge eating. No doubt several factors combined to give you the sensation of ecstasy."

His coach listed a few possibilities:

- When you saw the food and anticipated an eating pleasure, your brain was already releasing dopamine, the feel-better chemical.

- Simple carbs, especially fat and sugar, along with casein in some dairy products, would have triggered the release of a number of substances, several of which act much in the same way as do amphetamines and opiates.

- Although you may not have noticed any pain, as your stomach was stretched to capacity, your body would have released endorphins, your brain's natural morphine.

- The excitement of eating might also have increased adrenalin levels, which would have caused dopamine levels to rise even higher.

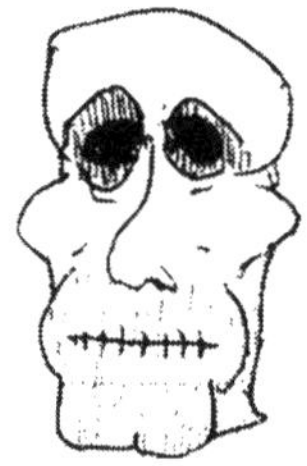

"Whoa. It sounds a bit like something out of Victor Frankenstein's laboratory instead of just my brain and body," said Harry.

"Harry, the complexity of your brain and body have it all over Frankenstein's lab. When you overfill your car's gas tank with fuel, you waste what spills out. When you overfill your body with food, you 'waist' it, too. You store it as fat and gain weight. That's where a simple food journal—hard copy or electronic comes in. It's a proven strategy to help you identify real-time eating patterns correlated with your present emotions. Don your *Sherlock Holmes* hat and become your own personal sleuth."

"Waist it!" said Harry, laughing. "I can don a *Holmes* hat."

"When you experience what you think are hunger pangs or you're tempted to binge, ask yourself: *Do you really need food or are you just in the habit of eating more food than you really need? If you are not physiologically hungry, are emotions and feelings driving your urge to eat?*

"Learn to recognize when your brain and body *need* food, as opposed to emotional eating. If it's been four or five hours since you ate a healthy balanced meal, your body may actually need food. If it's only been a couple of hours, something else may be triggering what initially appear to be hunger pangs. You may be thirsty rather than hungry." Harry nodded.

"Drink a glass of water, then wait 15-20 minutes and see if that satisfies your brain and body. Perhaps you're bored or just in the habit of grazing. Distract yourself: read a book, take a short walk, do your favorite hobby, or work some brain-aerobic exercises.

"If you're anxious about something, identify the issue and take steps to resolve it. You might want to take a page from recovery programs that often use the acronym HALT: the times when you are most likely to deviate from your Longevity Lifestyle are when you are Hungry, Angry, Lonely, or Tired. Eat only when you are physiologically hungry."

"I'm not sure I've ever been physiologically hungry," said Harry. "I've pretty much grazed all day, every day, most of my life."

"Nutritious food can taste even better when your body actually needs it. Eat to live rather than living to eat. When you do eat, select healthy foods and beverages, then sit down, eat slowly, and enjoy what you are eating. Being hungry and then eating nutritious food in pleasant surroundings makes for good company and a happy brain and body. Avoid skipping meals, which will increase your risk for overeating when you do have a meal. Think abundance, not deprivation."

"If I stopped grazing all day," said Harry, "maybe I'd be physiologically hungry at mealtimes. That sure would be something different."

"Keep a variety of healthier foods on hand. If you do choose to snack, make it a small, healthy one." His coach listed a few suggestions.

- A couple sticks of celery with a teaspoon of almond butter, or natural peanut butter or peanut butter powder mixed with a little water.

- A poker-chip size serving of hummus with some raw veggies (celery, broccoli, or jicama).
- A fourth of an avocado with a few multi-grain baked crackers or an apple with six raw almonds.

His coach went on to mention several other strategies for Harry to consider.

- Learn to be mindfully aware of your body, your thoughts, and your feelings. Pause periodically for thirty or sixty seconds during your meal and pay attention to your body and emotions. Focus your attention on what the food looks like, how it tastes, what the odors are like, and how the texture feels in your mouth. Take your time and savor it. How do you feel after eating it?

- Eat slowly, chew your food thoroughly, and pay attention to how your stomach feels. Since it takes at least fifteen minutes for the brain to register a feeling of fullness, you are more likely to overeat if you continue eating quickly until you feel completely full. Learn to tune into your body's cues—clues that tell you *I'm hungry* versus those that alert you to *I've had enough.* Try stopping when you're 80 percent full and pay attention to how your body feels. You can always eat a little more if you need to.

- Ignoring your emotions and feelings or trying to stuff them by stuffing yourself with food and beverages often contributes to weight gain. If you find yourself overeating, avoid putting yourself down. Instead, figure out the message behind that behavior. Do you need some self-nurturing and self-appreciation? Are you worried or anxious about something that you don't want to think about?

"Ouch," said Henry. "Some of those hit pretty close to home. Maybe even all of them! Okay. Whenever I have what I think are hunger pangs this week, I'll stop and ask myself if my body really needs food or if I'm just thirsty, bored, lonely, worried, indulging my grazing habit, or trying to feel better emotionally."

"Good self-care is a learned skill," said his coach. "One that provides many rewards."

"Speaking of self-care," said Henry, "I've always wanted to learn to fence so I've hired a tutor. I'm fencing to help increase my physical activity. Last week my instructor, who now is also my dueling partner, mentioned something about *intermittent fasting*. Is that something I should be doing?"

His coach smiled. "In all likelihood you're doing it already. While you sleep, you are, in effect, fasting during those hours. The term breakfast means that you are *breaking your fast.* If the last food you eat is at 6:00 pm and the first food you eat again is at 7:00 am, you have fasted, for eleven hours. Intermittent fasting is a technique whereby you periodically extend that fasting period for just a few more hours.

"Animal studies have shown that limiting daily calories can extend the life of the test rodents—sometimes by a third or more of the creature's usual life span. Research with humans is, of course, more anecdotal. Many people, however, use up valuable energy digesting unneeded food, which means the energy isn't available for other things. Plus the extra calories contribute to obesity.

"Some have suggested that as the body ages, cutting calories by about 10 percent can be helpful—as long as people are careful to avoid going below the recommended daily minimum caloric intake for males and females. *Intermittent fasting* is one way to do that and give your digestive system a rest at the same time."

"I'll bet that's what my fencing tutor was referring to. If the last food I eat is at 1:00 pm and breakfast is at 7:00 am, I would be fasting for eighteen hours instead of eleven. So, that would be considered *intermittent fasting.* I get it."

"That's right," said his coach. "Some people choose to do that once a week. Others decide they only need two meals a day on one of the weekend days."

"I think I'll consider that intermittent fasting idea. You know," Harry added, "it's always a rush to get to the gym from work anyway. I could start by just drinking water on the way to my lesson that one night a week and see how I do."

"Be careful," cautioned his coach. "If you expend a lot of energy in *dueling* practice you might tend to overeat afterwards."

"Oh, good point," said Harry, laughing, "And no pun intended. Actually, I'm usually ravenous after a fencing session."

"Think ahead and take an apple with you in the car or a few celery sticks. If you feel hungry, you'll already have a healthy snack on hand. You may want to try skipping dinner on an evening other than your dueling night or eat brunch and an early dinner on Sundays. And while you are enjoying learning to fence, also hone the skill of knowing the difference between emotional hunger and physiological hunger. That takes, practice, too. Eat when your body needs the food, rather than to change the way you feel."

"I've been resisting the food-journal idea but I think I'll start one today," said Harry. "I like the idea of being my own sleuth. I'll let you know what I discover. I'm also going to pick up some healthier snacks on my way home tonight, too. Gotta run. See you next week."

"Carol Dweck points out in *Mindset* that the view you adopt for yourself profoundly affects the way you lead your life. It's obvious your view is changing."

"For the better," said Harry.

What do a pack of playing cards, a hockey puck, and a poker chip have in common? The answer in Chapter 16 may surprise you.

Studies show that having type 2 diabetes may double or triple your risk for Alzheimer's—the link is now so strong that some experts refer to Alzheimer's as 'diabetes of the brain' or 'type 3 diabetes.'

—Jean Carper

When Smaller Is Better

Chapter 16

"We need help with size," said Juliette firmly, seating down beside her twin sister.

"We definitely need help with size," echoed Jeanette. "But me… according to my doctor I'm bordering on *morbid obesity*. What exactly does that mean?"

"It means," said Juliette, jumping in before their wellness coach could respond, "do something about your weight or you could soon be history." Jeanette gasped audibly.

"According to the CDC, the Centers for Disease Control," said their coach, "the terms *overweight* and *obesity* are labels indicating that a person's weight is greater than what is considered healthy for his or her height. An individual may weigh more than recommended due to muscle, bone, fat, or body water. The term obesity indicates the person has too much body fat. I'm sure you know that obesity is a leading preventable cause of death worldwide, even though plumpness is still seen as a symbol of wealth and fertility in some parts of the globe."

"We're both overweight," said Jeanette, "but how do we figure out if we're obese, or morbidly obcsc, as my doctor put it?"

"Your Body Mass Index or BMI is one indicator. You can access a BMI indicator at the Club 122 Longevity website." (www.Club122Longevity.com)

"The National Heart, Lung, and Blood Institute (NHLBI) guidelines recommend looking at two other factors, as well: your waist circumference, because abdominal fat is a predictor of risk for obesity-related diseases; and high blood pressure or physical inactivity, which are also associated with obesity."

"What are some of the other risks linked with *morbid obesity*?" asked Juliette. "An awful term, it makes me think of dying."

"The term has been around since about 1656. It comes from the Latin root *morbidus* (diseased). And disease can increase one's risk of dying sooner than later. Parrot-owners say you never see obese birds in nature unless they're diseased. Some estimate that if you're 20 percent over your ideal healthy weight, you may be considered obese. If you're 50 percent over your ideal healthy weight, you may be considered morbidly obese.

"Here's how the Bariatric Surgery Center at Highland Hospital in Rochester, New York, puts morbid-obesity risks," said their coach, summarizing:

> *Those who are morbidly obese are at greater risk for illnesses including diabetes, high blood pressure, sleep apnea, gallstones, GERD or gastroesophageal reflux disease, osteoarthritis, heart disease, and cancer.*

This time it was Juliette who gasped. "I had no idea there was even a difference between being overweight and obese. When I said we needed help with size, I was thinking of *portion* size. Recently I read a news article that said Americans are being killed by sugar, fat, salt, fried and processed foods—and *portion size*."

"*Portion* size can impact *person* size. If you're like most people, a serving is the *portion* size you're used to seeing in front of you. Typically, larger portions have larger numbers of calories, and America is notorious for large portions. Some restaurants have increased serving sizes—likely in order to raise meal prices.

"If you aren't careful, you can eat three or four times as many calories as you need in just one meal—and then be tired after you ate because your energy went into digesting food you didn't even need. The number of daily calories a person actually requires can vary depending on gender, bone structure, height, occupation, level of physical activity, and so on.

"Think *portion management*. It's a mindset. You might begin simply by using a smaller plate and bowl. A one-cup serving on a small plate or a half-cup serving in a small bowl looks

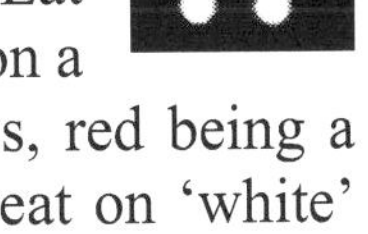

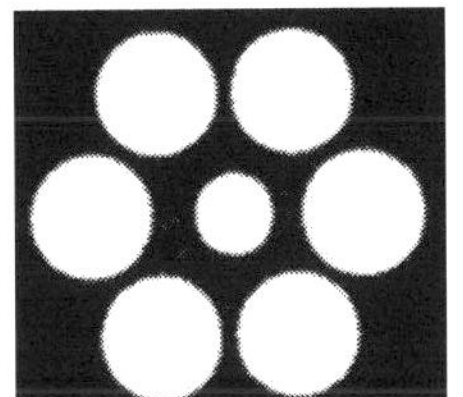

like a lot more food than when served on a large plate or in a big bowl. Eat dinner on a salad plate instead of on a dinner plate. Try using red dishes, red being a signal to *stop*. Many people overeat on 'white' foods. You don't really notice the size of a serving when white foods are served on white plates. White foods show up better on dark colored plates, which help you see the portion size."

"That makes sense," said Juliette, "but how do I know what an appropriate portion is?"

"Recommended portion sizes can range between one-fourth and one cup. The higher the content of fat, sugar, refined products or density of the food, the smaller the serving size. You can compare portion sizes to common objects. It's less precise than measuring, but once you get the hang of it you can estimate quite easily, and that's usually adequate for most people. Make a game of it and have fun. Just keep it simple."

"Common objects?" asked Juliette. "I don't know what you mean."

"Let me show you," their coach suggested, taking several objects from a drawer and placed them on the desk.

"One cup, or eight ounces, is about the size of the average computer mouse, baseball, or your fist.

"One cup is a good size for a serving of broccoli or cauliflower or asparagus or green beans or green peas or a medium white potato or half a large sweet potato. Use that as the basis for lettuce in a green salad, too."

Jeanette looked at her clenched her fist and smiled. "You're right. My fist is about the size of a baseball, or one cup."

The coach continued. "A small muffin is the size of a tennis ball, which is slightly smaller than a baseball).

"Half a cup (four ounces) is about the size of a baseball sliced in two. If that's difficult to imagine, think of a golf ball or a Ping-Pong ball. That's one serving of pasta or legumes or a small banana.

"Picture one serving of grains (pancake, waffle, slice of bread, tortilla, or pita bread) as the diameter of a CD.

"An English muffin, preferably sourdough, is the size of a hockey puck.

"Visualize a pack of playing cards as the portion size for a serving of fish, chicken, or other meat.

"Use a poker chip to represent the serving size for salad dressing, nut butters, cheese or oil. A serving of raw nuts is one ounce or one-eighth of a cup (about 35 peanuts)."

"Depending on the density, fat, and sugar content of a given dessert, use a Ping-Pong ball to represent the serving size. Better yet, forget the *ball* and just eat two or three small bites of dessert—once in a while."

"I could get into this!" Juliette exclaimed. "More tips, please."

Their coach summarized a few more suggestions.

- Remove all food and drink from your home that doesn't match your Longevity Lifestyle. Give them to a food bank or shelter.
- *Out of sight is out of mind.* Lose the candy dish and bags of crackers or chips. If you want food visible, use a fresh-fruit bowl.
- If you are purchasing food in bulk, store the excess at the back of the freezer or out in the garage or in a top cupboard.
- Keep one-cup, half-cup, and quarter-cup measuring containers on your kitchen counter. Use them initially to become familiar with portion sizes and then substitute a mental picture of the portion-size objects. Soon you'll be doing it automatically.
- If you are having home-made granola for breakfast, put a fourth-cup or third-cup serving in a small bowl and put the rest away. Then take 15 minutes to eat that serving.
- When eating broccoli or asparagus, put a one-cup serving on your plate. If you feel satisfied, save the rest for later.
- Serve out what you plan to eat all at once. Remove serving containers from view to make it harder to reach for seconds.

- If you decide to eat a snack while watching TV (air-popped popcorn and an apple), dish out what you plan to eat rather than eating from the package or a larger container.

- Remember the fifteen-minute rule: give your brain time to register satisfaction. Eat slowly, chew each bite well. If you're still hungry eat celery or jicama sticks, an apple, or more salad.

"What about eating out?" asked Jeanette. "Any tips for that?"

"Sure. Try to sit near a window or in a brightly lighted area as people tend to eat more salads in those locations. Dress your salad with lemon juice or a light water-based vinaigrette. Split an order or ask for a take-out container at the start of your meal and put half of your food in it to take home with you."

"Those are helpful ideas," said Juliette. "I think where we stumble is eating fresh stuff. We like variety, hate eating the same thing day after day, so we buy salad fixings and then most of it spoils and gets tossed into the trash bin."

"There are other ways to handle this besides buying food in large quantities and then dumping half out," said their coach. "It can actually be cost effective for smaller households to shop more frequently. Purchase just enough for a meal or two: a cucumber, two zucchinis, a yam, an avocado, three or four apples, one bunch of asparagus, a cluster of grapes, and so on. Some stores now carry small packages of pre-cut jicama or pre-washed green beans or have a bin of unpacked carrots or single stalks of celery. They may cost slightly more per ounce, but you may waste much less food—and money—in the end. Since you won't feel compelled to eat the same thing day after day to use it up, the variety keeps you and your brain interested."

"Just avoid impulse buying," their coach continued, "especially from marketing displays near the cash registers."

"I can shop more often," said Jeanette. "It gets me out of the house. I can *walk* to the store from our apartment and I rarely succumb to impulse buying because it would be too much to carry home." She laughed.

"But we do throw away a lot of food," said Juliette, thoughtfully, "which means we spend a lot of money on stuff we don't eat." She looked at her twin sister, who nodded. "It's just another *mindset*, isn't it? Sure, it may be cheaper by the pound to purchase a bunch of celery but buying 3-4 single stalks at a time means we're much more likely eat them before they go to waste—which will help my waist!"

"If 'confession is good for the soul,' said Jeanette, "I have a confession to make. I binged on chocolate chip cookies the other day. And I mean binged. My neighbor had a cute little puppy. I joked about being its human auntie. When my neighbor called to say the puppy had been run over by a huge garbage truck, I went right out and bought a huge bag of cookies, curled up on the couch, cried and cried, and ate them all. Every last one!"

"I think we figured out what prompted that binge," said Juliette. "When we were little and cut a finger or skinned a knee, mother would make a fuss over us, put on a band aid, and then say, 'Now what will help Jean and Jul feel all better?' We would shout *'Cookies!'* So we'd bake a batch (or two) of Mom's fabulous—albeit high calorie—cookies and eat until we felt 'all better.'"

"That's what I did when I felt sad about my neighbor's puppy dying," said Jeanette. "I ate and ate and ate—trying to feel *all better*."

"Good job connecting the present with the past," said their coach. "It points out the benefits of doing family-of-origin work. Eating cookies filled with sugar and fat releases dopamine in your brain—the feel better chemical—and endorphins, the brain's natural morphine. No wonder you felt better. The brain remembers that and when a similar situation arises, it will prompt you to repeat almost any behavior that made you feel better in the past.

"Rob Liano suggests that before you make a decision, you ask yourself this question: Will you regret the results or rejoice in them?"

"That's a good idea," said Jeanette. "Now that we've the past together with what just happened, I'll be more likely to catch myself before repeating another bingeing behavior."

"Okay, Sis, let's go shopping for smaller portions of fresh stuff," said Juliette, smiling at her twin. And they were out the door.

The equation IQ plus EQ equals what? Chapter 17 contains the answer.

Emotional self-control—
delaying gratification and
stifling impulsiveness—
underlies accomplishment
of every sort.
—Daniel J. Goleman, PhD
Emotional Intelligence: Why It Can
Matter More Than IQ

IQ Plus EQ Equals SQ

Chapter 17

"We're doing quite well with our Longevity Lifestyle," said John, holding a chair for his wife, Joan.

"Except that he flies off the proverbial handle whenever I remind him to follow the program," said Joan. "Especially when he wants ice cream and wants it *now*."

"I did get upset when she suggested I pass on going out last night to buy a gallon of ice cream," said John. "Strangely, I woke up this morning recalling that Dad and his brother both loved ice cream. They resisted all suggestions to lighten up on desserts, period. In fact, Dad got angry whenever Mum tried to fix healthier meals."

"Interesting," said their wellness coach. "According to John Byng-Hall, family scripts are revealed when repeating patterns of family interactions are either observed or described. Earlier we talked about family scripts and this behavior may be part of yours."

"It's a conundrum," said John. "I want to get healthy, and yet I get mad at Joan's reminders."

"Emotions are powerful. They can over-ride your conscious thought in a nanosecond unless you have developed skills to manage them."

"Emotions are physiological changes that occur in both brain and body in response to a stimulus or trigger. The stimulus can be in the external environment or inside, in your own internal environment. Think of them as cellular signals that function much as highway cones alert you to changes in road conditions. Emotions are designed to get your attention, move information from the subconscious into conscious awareness, and provide energy so you can take appropriate action.

"Studies suggest that facial expressions registering joy, anger, fear, and sadness are inborn and may be seen on the face of a fetus during gestation. Of those four core emotions, anger is the emotion designed to get your attention when you perceive that your boundaries have been invaded."

"You mean my *unhelpful* boundary of wanting to be in charge to help me feel safe and resisting being told what to do—even when it's what I want to do?" John shook his head in bewilderment and reached over to take Joan's hand. "I am committed to this Longevity Lifestyle and yet at any given moment when I think about eating something I want right now versus …" His voice trailed off.

"You have a difficult time delaying short–term gratification for a long-term reward," his coach finished the thought.

"Short-term gratification," John mused. "*The New York Times* reported that in follow-up interviews with original participants of the Stanford Marshmallow experiment, those who had gotten a second marshmallow turned out years later not only to be better adjusted socially but also to have scored an average of 210 points higher on their SATs than the most impatient children in the studies."

"Plus," added their coach, "the children who got a second marshmallow were more likely to be closer to their recommended weight-range in adulthood." Joan raised an eyebrow.
"The ability to defer immediate gratification, a learned skill, impacts many areas in life—positively."

"I watched some YouTube clips of researchers repeating the Marshmallow Experiment," said Joan. "It was interesting and sometimes almost painful to watch those four-to-six year olds trying to wait just fifteen minutes to eat a marshmallow."

"If I'd been in that original study, I likely would have been in the two-thirds group who couldn't wait," said John. "My skills related to deferring immediate gratification are not too good." He paused. "Actually, I don't think I have any of those skills."

"An ability to delay gratification is a key component of Emotional Intelligence or EQ. That skill can be indispensable in handling relationships, avoiding conflict, solving problems—and in attaining long-term goals. David Caruso, describing EQ, said that Emotional Intelligence is not the opposite of intelligence, not the triumph of heart over head, but the unique intersection of both.

"In his book *Working with Emotional Intelligence* Dr. Daniel Goleman describes EQ as the capacity for recognizing your own emotions as well as those of others, for managing emotions and feelings effectively in your personal life and in your relationships, and for motivating yourself. He referred to it as the building block of the next fundamental emotional intelligence: being able to shake off a bad mood. In *Handle with Care* Dr. Anabel L. Jensen and colleagues described EQ as a way to recognize, understand, and choose how to think, feel, and act."

John and Joan looked at each other and smiled.

"Up until just a few years ago," their coach continued, "the heart was believed to consist primarily of muscle cells. Now neurons, thinking cells, have been found in the heart. These neurons, 40,000 or more per heart, look and function much like brain neurons.

"Your success quotient or SQ is believed to result from a combination of IQ and EQ, but they don't contribute equally. Estimates are that IQ contributes only about 20 percent to your overall success in life, while EQ contributes 80 percent.

"According to Childre and Martin, authors of *The HeartMath Solution*, and to Dr. Paul Pearsall in *The Heart's Code,* what brain neurons are to IQ, heart neurons may be to EQ."

"My IQ is fairly high," said John, "but I doubt my EQ is."

"Same here," added Joan. "What does a high EQ look like?"

"Every brain is different. Generally, however, in addition to developing positive-mindset and self-talk patterns, self-awareness, and motivational abilities, individuals with high levels of EQ tend to exhibit some specific behavioral characteristics—not necessarily 100 percent of the time, but most of time."

Their coach explained that individuals with high levels of EQ tend to be able to:

- Identify, label accurately, assess intensity, and express emotions appropriately.

- Recognize what the emotion is trying to signal or communicate and take appropriate action.

- Articulate the difference between identifying an emotion and taking action based on it.

- Exhibit effective verbal and nonverbal skills, along with empathy and compassion.
- Handle relationships effectively, avoiding jumping to conclusions, taking things personally, or overreacting.
- Delay gratification with good impulse control.
- Read and interpret social cues and understand the perspective of others.

"I think that when John gets mad I get sad," said Joan. "We get over it pretty quickly but it's still a waste of time and energy."

"That's a typical pattern for many," said their coach, handing them a drawing of the Emotions Staircase. Joan and John looked at the drawing.

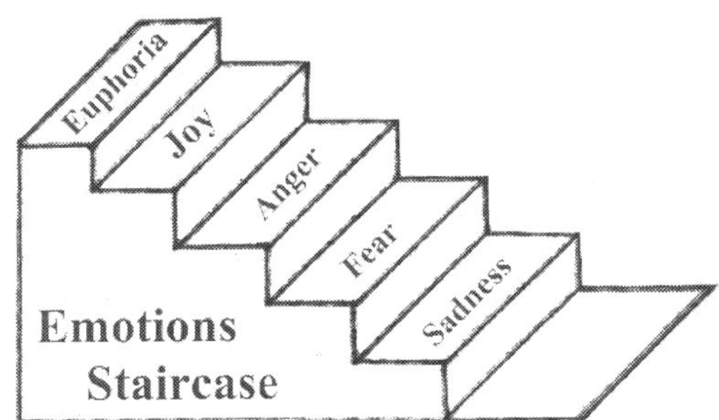

"Males, socialized toward anger, often stop at that step whether or not anger is the appropriate emotion for the situation. Females, socialized toward sadness, often go down to sadness whether or not the situation involves a loss, which means they have a longer climb back up to joy."

"That's exactly what we do," said Joan, shaking her head.

"I'm curious," said Joan "Earlier you said that emotions are just *signals*. That's an interesting way of describing them. Can you expand on that?" Their coach pointed to summaries on the reverse side of the Emotions Staircase.

Euphoria (brief intense joy or elation) is a signal that something especially rewarding or pleasurable is happening. It provides energy to experience special moments that can add spice and excitement to your life. Unmanaged euphoria can prompt a search for activities that provide a continual high through self-medication that alters your neurochemistry.

Joy (happiness, general contentment) is a signal that all is going well. A natural state of anti-depression, joy provides energy to live

life in all its fullness—balanced and productive. Joy is believed the only emotion that has no negative outcomes when maintained over time. Unfortunately, false joy can lead to obsessions, compulsions, addictive behaviors, frustration, and depression.

Anger (rage, bitterness, hate, irritation) is a signal that your boundaries have been breached (e.g., physical, mental, emotional, sexual, spiritual, financial, social). It provides energy to create and implement bona fide boundaries. Without anger you may lack the motivation to take corrective action or tolerate the intolerable. Unmanaged anger can lead to illness, injury, and death.

Fear (anxiety, apprehension, terror) is a signal that you are in danger and it provides energy to take appropriate action. Without fear you may be unable to protect yourself—or those you love—and may become immobile. Unmanaged fear can kill ideas, block creativity, undermine confidence, and escalate into phobias and/or immobilization.

Sadness (anguish, sorrow, misery, despair) is a signal that you have experienced a loss. It provides energy to grieve the loss, heal past woundedness, and recover. Without sadness you may be unable to grieve loss successfully. Unmanaged, it can lead to immune system suppression, depression, and/or immobility. Even apathy. Over time one can develop a slush-fund of unresolved grief that can spill over in spades when another loss occurs.

"My mother died suddenly when I was age fifteen," said John. "That was traumatic and things were rough for a few years. As I think about it now, I doubt any of our family has ever dealt well with my mother's death. We lost a lot when she died. So 'losing ice cream' is another loss. It fits."

"Sometimes childhood trauma can interfere with emotional growth, resulting an emotional age that is far lower than one's chronological age."

"How do I go about learning these EQ skills?" asked John.

"You might begin by evaluating your emotional age. You may need to raise your EQ so it matches or exceeds your chronological age. Learning EQ skills can assist you in maintaining good cognitive brain function and help you avoid behaviors that result in negative outcomes. Pay attention to the behaviors you exhibit and whether or not they result in desirable outcomes. For those that do, identify a healthier behavior and start practicing. EQ skills may also reduce or mitigate the effects of stress, enhance your personal, social, and professional relationships, and provide a sense of personal empowerment."

"I'll try to identify my emotional age," said John. "But what can I do right now?"

"How about building skills in the area of deferring short-term gratification? When you have the urge to go out and purchase ice cream, John, talk it through first. Try this:

> *There's that thought about ice cream again. I know I could choose to have some. What do I want more: a short-term reward or a healthier snack that keeps me moving forward on a Longevity Lifestyle? Hmm. Right now I choose to eat a healthy snack."*

"Sample wording helps," said John. "I can do that. Well, I can starting *learning* that skill." He laughed.

"We're in this Longevity Lifestyle together. I'll commit to having healthier snacks on hand and I'll also commit to refraining from nagging you," said Joan.

"And I'll commit to counting to ten when I feel angry or frustrated with the process of selecting healthier behaviors," said John. After a moment's pause he continued. "I suppose a higher level of EQ would impact my work life positively, too," said John.

"In *Emotional Intelligence at Work,* author Dr. Dahlip Singh, indicates that it does," said their coach. "Singh points out that EQ consists of three psychological dimensions that motivate individuals to maximize productivity, manage change, and resolve conflict. Those three dimensions are: emotional competency, emotional sensitivity, and emotional maturity."

"I guess we're both committed, then," said John. His wife nodded her agreement.

Chapter 18 is next. Meet Rick, who learned how the brain resembles both a three-story building and an automatic transmission.

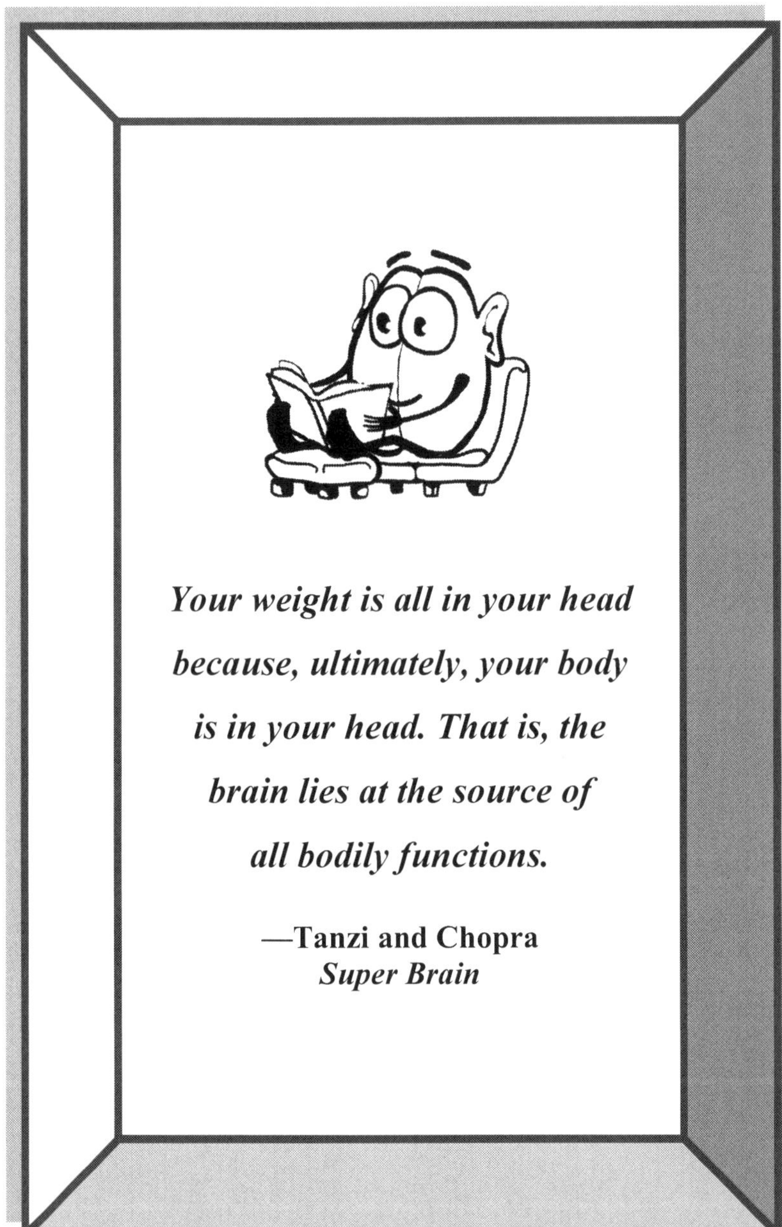

Your weight is all in your head because, ultimately, your body is in your head. That is, the brain lies at the source of all bodily functions.

—Tanzi and Chopra
Super Brain

Room with a View

Chapter 18

"Every time I get anxious about my eating habits or worry about my weight, my brain seems to just shut down," said Rick. "I misplace my goals and fail to maintain my Longevity Lifestyle, which gets my life out of balance in a hurry."

"You're likely describing a natural brain phenomenon sometimes referred to as *downshifting,"* said his wellness coach. "Used appropriately, it can save your life. Used inappropriately, it can negatively impact your thinking."

"My dad used to say that what I didn't know would come back to bite me in the ah-h, posterior," said Rick. "Is that what you're talking about?"

"The word downshifting describes the brain's automatic response to fear, anxiety and worry being forms of fear. When it doesn't feel safe, the brain directs its energy, resources, and attention toward lower brain layers looking for something to promote a sense of safety. For example, the *fight-flight* stress response," his coach explained. As I said, downshifting can be life-saving during situations of actual danger; it is unhelpful when used inappropriately or when your brain gets stuck in a downshifted position. There are a couple metaphors that may help you better understand this phenomenon."

"The first metaphor compares the three brain layers to the gears in an automatic transmission. The vehicle is usually in the third gear when out on the highway but the automatic transmission can gear down based on road and traffic conditions.

"The first brain *gear* is part of the subconscious and primarily focuses on what is happening in the present moment. The second gear, also part of the subconscious, can remind your brain of what happened in the past and may automatically trigger a repeat action. Planning a course of action and following through on your goals, utilizes functions located in the third gear or neocortex (new brain), where there is conscious thought. Ready access to these functions is vital to a Longevity Lifestyle.

"When downshifted, accessing those complex third-level functions becomes difficult and/or inconsistent. You're more likely to be successful when you are consciously mindful, aware, and accessing critical, pre-frontal brain skills. The goal is to avoid unnecessary downshifting by managing your anxious thoughts and upshifting quickly—as soon as you determine there is no imminent danger or it has passed. Look at this drawing."

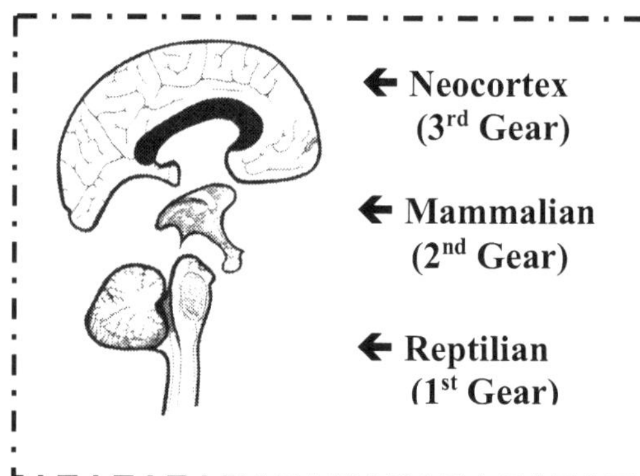

"Got it," said Rick. "An automatic transmission is meant to shift up or down as needed based on driving conditions. And if you are depending on it to upshift automatically and it fails to do so, you can be in a world of hurt—more time, more fuel, a potential hazard on the highway, and maybe even a burned-out engine. Analogous to the brain? Makes sense to me."

"The other metaphor comes from Edward Morgan Forster's book *A Room with a View*."

"My wife and I saw the movie that was made from that book," said Rick. "As I recall, the girl, Lucy I think her name was, wanted a room in the hotel that allowed her to see out over the town rather than a room that had no view."

His coach nodded. "Now imagine the brain as a building with three floors. On the top floor you can hang out over the balcony and see where you have been, identify where you are now, and look ahead to see where you are going. This allows for course-correction, if where you appear to be headed is not where you want go."

"That metaphor is good, too," said Rick. "How do I get upshifted so I can follow my program by design?"

"To upshift you first need to know that you're downshifted. When you take something personally, jump to conclusions, or overreact in a given situation, it's usually a good guess that your brain is downshifted. To upshift, activate a preplanned strategy. I have two.

- "First I try to identify something humorous about the situation and laugh mirthfully. When that occurs I know I'm upshifted since humor and laughter reside in the third brain layer.

- "My other strategy is to think of something for which to be grateful. Studies have shown it's virtually impossible to be fearful (or anxious) and grateful at the same time. I can usually think of something for which to be grateful.

"Identify a couple of strategies for upshifting that will work for your brain and use them as necessary."

"I've had most of these habits for decades," said Rick. "Some are pretty strong."

"Remember, the brain is designed to create habits. When you do something once, the brain begins developing brain software—a *neuron highway*—in case you want to do the same thing again. Once developed, these *neuron highways* cannot be deleted easily per se, since neurons do not multiply and divide as do other cells. That's the bad news if you develop unhelpful habits. You make 'em, you got 'em. For helpful habits, it's the good news. You make 'em, you got 'em."

"What can I do about an unhelpful habit?" asked Rick.

"Create a replacement behavior," his coach replied, "and practice it consistently for at least twelve weeks. By then you're well on your way to the new habit. As you repeat the behavior, the brain coats the neuron highway with layers of insulation known as myelin. Think of myelin as the brain's asphalt or think fiber optics. The neuron highway gets stronger with practice, which results in more layers of myelin. Eventually the replacement behavior can become stronger than the old habit.

"After that replacement habit is well in place, start working on another. When it's in place, work on yet another. That's how you build and implement a Longevity Lifestyle. Rather than collapsing on the couch and snacking, let's say your replacement behavior is to take a 15-minute walk after dinner. Start walking and mark it down on the calendar each day to help chart your progress.

"If you let down your guard, however, you may find yourself once again collapsing on the couch. Should that occur, get right back following your replacement behavior. You will still need to make choices and use willpower to follow through on them."

"Think of yourself as developing *skillpower.* It helps you make those healthier choices. Then access *willpower* to help you follow through on those healthier choices. Willpower is not designed to help you stop doing an undesirable behavior, especially if it gave your brain some type of reward, so be careful how you talk to your brain. Tell your brain often: '*You* are walking for 15 minutes. *You* feel better. *You* look better. *You* are thinking more clearly.'"

Rick looked thoughtful.

"Speak in the present tense, as if it's a done deal. When you speak in future tense—*tomorrow I'm going to*—the brain may think: *That's in the future. I don't need to do anything now. If you still want to do this when tomorrow gets here, then I'll start to help you.* On the other hand, when you speak in the present tense, your brain gets in gear to help you now."

"Doable," said Rick. "I think it's the snacking that really trips me up. I even wake up at night tempted to snack. Go figure."

"In his book, *Breaking the Food Seduction,* author Dr. Neil Barnard writes:

> *Don't seduce yourself. If you're leaving little presents of the very foods you'd like to get away from lying around in your cupboards, that's a sign that you've not made up your mind for a change.*

"Remove all unhealthy snacks from the house, office, and car. Make sure plenty of fresh water, apples, celery, nuts, and other healthier foods easily available."

"That's clear enough," said Rick. "By the way, I like these metaphors. My brain seems to remember them quite easily—a three-gear automatic transmission; a three story building." He paused for a moment.

"You mentioned that some foods contain substances that can be addicting or at least are linked with addictive-like behaviors. I'd like to understand more about that. Do you have a metaphor for how that happens?"

"Let me think," said his coach. "Okay. Here's one that might get the job done. I remember you saying that you have a boat."

"I do have a boat," replied Rick. "A little rowboat that I use on the river near the house." He laughed. "I'm sure that stems from my childhood. I had one as a boy, too. Pretended it was a pirate ship. It even had a little pirate flag. I use my rowboat for fishing. Mostly I row but there is a small 1 horse-power outboard motor in case I need a little extra help because of the wind or current."

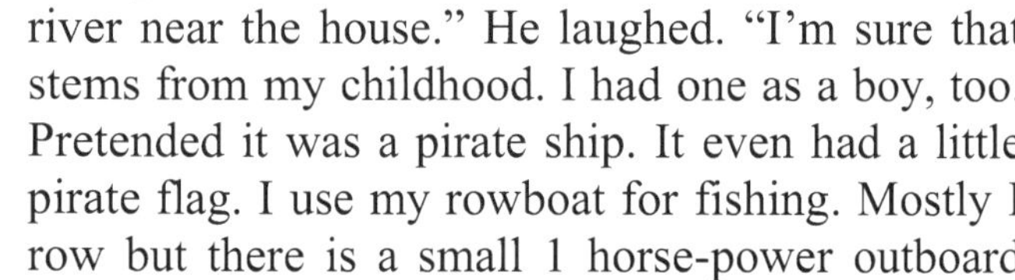

"You've heard the term *receptor molecules*?" asked his coach.

Rick nodded.

"Think of the brain as having a huge marina with many different slips (the receptor molecules) to accommodate the boats. Picture neurotransmitters as boats that need to dock and unload their cargo of neurochemicals. Some boats must always go to a specific matching slip to unload. Others are more versatile in where they can unload.

"For example, alcohol, tobacco, sugar, and other refined and processed simple carbs all appear able to use the same type of slip interchangeably. And the cargo these boats offload, although not identical, tend to produce similar effects in the brain reward system. These effects can become habituating and sometimes addicting, typically due to the dopamine—the feel better substance—that is released when they dock and unload their cargo."

Rick broke in. "That explains the reason I love white potatoes in any form, mounds of pancakes and pasta. And cheese. Lots of cheese. My wife makes fabulous Mexican food slathered in cheese, along with baskets of chips, salsa, and guacamole. When we go out to eat, I top off with flan and a couple of sodas. I'd sure hate to give all that up."

"It may be more about modifying them. Think modification and substitution. Remember, you can retrain your taste buds in just a few weeks."

His coach mentioned several examples.

- Corn tortillas (steamed) are better than flour tortillas.
- Basmati brown rice is better than white.
- Whole beans are better than refried beans made with lard or lots of oil.
- Baked chips are better than deep-fried.
- Turkey or chicken with the skin removed or lean meat is better than ground beef or pork.
- White cheeses are better than colored and non-dairy cheeses likely are even healthier.
- Avocado can substitute for the feel of dairy cheese. Half a pound of cheddar cheese can contain 900 calories with 75 grams of fat, over half of which is saturated. Half an avocado can contain only 135 calories with 15 grams of fat, over 75 percent of which is *unsaturated*, a far preferable fat.

"Use your favorite seasonings—herbs, cumin, chili peppers, cumin, whatever—and still enjoy foods you love," his coach continued. "Some sprinkle flakes of nutritional yeast (not to be confused with Brewer's yeast) on food. Think abundance, not deprivation. Focus on what you are eating and enjoying and not on what you used to eat that helped pack on unwanted pounds and increase your risk for disease."

"I'm sure we can figure out ways to make healthier dishes," said Rick. "My wife is already collecting new recipes. My doctor did tell me to take a walk after I eat. Said it would help with digestion and increase my stamina. He suggested starting out with 10 minutes and gradually working up to 30. My wife takes our dog for a walk every day after dinner. I think I'll start going with them. I tell you our neighbors will faint—and I mean faint—when they see the *three* of us out walking!" Rick laughed heartily.

"You see? You're already getting creative about strategies that will work for you. Yes, exercise can help you increase your stamina but Researchers at Laval University in Quebec found many other benefits. It not only burns calories, it can help reset your appetite levels, enhance your mood, and reset or improve your sleep cycle. After just three weeks of exercise, study participants saw a dramatic improvement in their insulin sensitivity. Peak after-meal insulin levels dropped by more than 20 percent. In fact, exercise can help you feel so much better that it motivates you to stick with healthier habits and maintain them. Just be sure to find a way to have fun."

"I used to golf," said Rick, musingly. "Quite enjoyed it, 'though I always used a golf cart. Unfortunate, that." He chuckled. "When I've built up some stamina from walking, my doctor has challenged me to a golf game—without a cart. I'm on my way!"

"Remember sleep," said his coach. "Plenty of sleep. Feeling rested can help you maintain your Longevity Lifestyle."

"You know creating a Longevity Lifestyle involves hard work," said Rick.

"Almost everything in life that is worthwhile takes some hard work," his coach replied. "That reminds me of a quote attributed to Stephen King: *Talent is cheaper than table salt. What separates the talented individual from the successful one is a lot of hard work.*

"I figure everyone with a functioning brain is talented enough to create and maintain a Longevity Lifestyle—if he or she wants to. It all goes back to mindset, choice, and willpower."

"You know what?" asked Rick, pausing by the door. "It's taken me a while but I think I'm on the third floor of my brain—in *a room with a view*. And by crikey by gum, I like what I see. Remind me again how I alter an old habit."

1. Identify the habit that needs to be altered.

2. Select a healthier replacement behavior.

3. Make sure you have a positive mindset and self-talk patterns.

4. Use willpower to implement the replacement behavior.

5. Reward yourself for your successes.

"You can do this," said his coach.

Rick nodded and smiled. "I know and I am."

When it comes to curves and constipation, some like the first, most dislike the second, and few want to even talk about it. Get acquainted with Todd and Tami in Chapter 19.

Lack of activity destroys the good condition of every human being, while movement and methodical physical exercise save it and preserve it.

—Plato

Curves and Constipation

Chapter 19

"Tami here just joined Curves," said Todd, holding out a chair for his attractive partner. "So I signed up at a gym. I could stand to drop a few pounds."

"That's great," their wellness coach replied. "The unneeded pounds you pack around can impact every facet of your life including your risk for:

- Decreased energy and increased fatigue
- Health challenges such as cancer, stroke, heart attack, and other chronic diseases—and decreased longevity

"And that doesn't include your increased risk for requiring additional closet space to store several sets of clothes in different sizes, or the whack to your self-esteem, or the recycling discouragement, or the loss of hope and enthusiasm, or a variety of health challenges."

"The trainer seems knowledgeable," said Todd. "Funny. First thing he cautioned me to avoid over-exercising, said that over-exercising decreases the benefits and stresses both the brain and the body. Not that there's a huge danger of that." He and Tami laughed.

"The trainer suggested limiting my exercise to no more than 40 minutes at a time for one type of exercise, like the treadmill or weights. He also suggested a 20-minute break after one type of aerobic exercise before beginning another set or another type of exercise. Does that sound reasonable?"

"It certainly does," replied their wellness coach. "You want to *strengthen* your brain and body, not break them down."

"The trainer also told me that high intensity intermittent training is more effective that some of the older recommendations for hours of continuous exercise. That was a new concept." Todd continued. "Both the treadmill and the stationary bike have built-in programs that take you through high intensity intermittent training. The trainer kept talking about physical exercise being necessary for my brain, too. But I thought exercise was about my body."

"It is about your body," said his coach. "But it definitely is about your brain, too." Todd raised an eyebrow.

"Your brain has no muscle tissue per se, and physical exercise enhances blood flow to the brain. This not only brings increased amounts of oxygen, glucose, and nutrition to brain tissues but also washes away accumulated waste products. Many people have no idea how closely physical exercise is tied to brain function. Dr. Candace B. Pert points this out in her book *Your Body is Your Subconscious Mind*."

> *The most important function of exercise is to stimulate and cleanse the body-mind so that it is free to do its best work. You can enhance the benefits of your daily exercise by linking it to something you enjoy, such as listening to your favorite music on headphones while walking.*

Their coached continued. "A study of retirees who exercised regularly showed that after four years they had maintained nearly the same level of blood flow in the brain, while those who chose not to exercise had evidenced a significant decrease in blood flow. An important component of a Longevity Lifestyle, exercise has been found to help combat apathy—sometimes seen in the elderly—through the release of dopamine and endorphins."

"I'm not yet a retiree," said Todd, "but I'd like to be in good shape when that time comes."

"Then you need exercise. It helps strengthen your body's muscles—but you already knew that. What you might not know is that it can decrease your risk for heart disease, vascular disease, and diabetes. It also stimulates the release of dopamine, the *feel-better* brain chemical that fuels pathways for the brain reward system. Dopamine levels tend to decrease with age so physical exercise becomes even more vital.

"And you need exercise for your brain, too. It has been touted as one of the best things you can do for it. Your brain tends to function best when the body gets regular physical exercise—when the heart is pumping hard and circulating the blood through your brain. Not only does that improve overall brain function but also helps protect against cognitive decline. Studies of men and women over age 65 found that those who exercised were less likely to lose their mental abilities or develop symptoms of dementia. But start now. In *The Owner's Manual for the Brain*, Dr. Pierce J. Howard points out that benefits are aligned with long-term exercise."

"Great," said Tami. "No fly-by-night exercise starts and stops for me. I signed up my plump little self for an entire year at Curves, because I tend to use whatever I've paid for."

"What about constipation?" asked Todd. "I've fought it my entire life. Thought exercising would take care of everything. It hasn't—but I didn't want to ask the trainer."

"Problems with constipation are common—unfortunately. Physical exercise is important, but so is an adequate intake of water and of fiber."

"Fiber? Remind me," said Todd.

"You may recall that carbohydrates typically are grouped into a trio of main categories: simple, complex, and fiber. You need some of all of those. Found mainly in fruits, vegetables, whole grains, and legumes, fiber includes parts of plant foods that your body does not absorb. Many think of fiber primarily for its ability to relieve constipation, but fiber provides many other health benefits, including lowering your risk for heart disease and diabetes, and helping you maintain an optimum weight.

"Different from macronutrients that provide calories for your body to digest, fiber passes through your bowel relatively unchanged and leaves the body in your bowel movements. Fiber is commonly classified as insoluble (it doesn't dissolve in water) or soluble (it does dissolve in water). Soluble fiber may also help reduce the absorption of cholesterol into the blood stream."

"I didn't know that!" exclaimed Tami. "How much do we need?"

"The FDA recommends between 20-30 grams a day, although most Americans get less than half of that. In 2012 The Institute of Medicine provided fiber guidelines broken out by gender and age. Take a look at this chart." The coach pointed to a chart on the wall.

	Under Age 50	Over Age 51
Males	38 grams	30 grams
Females	25 grams	21 grams

"And while Todd copes with his constipation; I deal with my Irritable Bowel Syndrome," said Tami. "The doctor told me to increase my intake of fiber but I'm unclear about the type of fiber to eat and what it really does for IBS."

"The ENS or Enteric Nervous System has been found to contain neurons—at least a million. Some scientists now call the ENS a 'second brain.' In fact, IBS is now being referred to as an enteric neuropathy: *enteric* referring to the bowel and *neuropathy* indicating that the nerves are functioning sub-optimally. Patricia Raymond, MD, assistant professor of clinical internal medicine at Eastern Virginia Medical School in Norfolk, points out that fiber can function like an on-off switch for IBS.

- "Soluble fiber can slow down movement in the digestive tract, helping with diarrhea
- Insoluble fiber can speed up movement in the digestive tract, alleviating constipation."

"Hey, now that we have a clue," said Todd, "we'll both eat more fiber. More insoluble fiber for me to help with constipation and more soluble fiber for Tami to help her with IBS."

"Some foods such as oats and legumes contain both types of fiber," said their coach. "I think of them as two-for-one foods."

"I do remember my doctor telling me that fiber-rich foods take longer to digest so eating them can help decrease hunger pangs," said Tami. "That'll be a bonus. He also mentioned FOD something but I missed …" Her voice trailed off.

"FODMAPs," said their coach. "It's an acronym coined by a group of researchers who were studying several types of digestive disorders. The acronym stands for *fermentable oligo-, di-* and *mono-saccharides,* and *polyols*—types of short-chain carbs."

Tami laughed. "You aren't expending me to remember what that acronym stands for, are you?"

Their coach laughed. "No, of course not. Commonly found in modern Western diets, these short-chain carbs are poorly absorbed in the small intestines and easily fermented by bacteria. FODMAPs include:

- Fructan in wheat
- Fructose in some fruits and artificial sweeteners
- Lactose in some dairy products
- Galactans in some legumes

"FODMAPs may exacerbate the symptoms of digestive disorders in conditions such as inflammatory bowel disease, irritable bowel syndrome, non-celiac gluten sensitivity, and functional gastrointestinal disorders. In some individuals, their bowel symptoms may be due to FODMAPs more than to gluten."

"You mentioned cholesterol," said Todd. "Now there's another unsolved puzzle in my mind. Another black hole." He laughed.

"Cholesterol is the name for a waxy-like substance that is vital to your health, although high levels of cholesterol can increase your risk of heart disease and stroke. Your liver makes most of the cholesterol you need—to keep cell membranes intact; make insulation (myelin) for nerve cells; form bile that helps digest fats; and create hormones such as testosterone and estrogen."

"The two main types of cholesterol are:

- HDL or high density lipoprotein, generally referred to as healthier cholesterol

- LDL or low density lipoprotein or LDL, sometimes called lousy cholesterol.

"According to the American Heart Association, LDL is found in foods that contain saturated fats, as in animal-based products; and in foods containing trans fats, found in commercially prepared products that contain hydrogenated or partially hydrogenated oils and shortening."

"Oh," said Todd. "That's the reason a Longevity Lifestyle recommends minimizing foods that contain LDL and including those that contain HDL."

"There are a number of Internet sources that provide lists of foods along with their cholesterol content. Search the Internet and you can stimulate your brain at the same time," said their wellness coach.

"I can find those lists," said Tami. "I like to search the internet."
"I'm still curious about the link between physical exercise and the brain," said Todd. "Tell me more about that."

"As your brain ages, it becomes more vulnerable to damage. Physical exercise has been called a general antioxidant, helping to repair damaged cells—especially damage from free radicals. Almost any type of physical exercise can improve your brain's performance. Individuals who are aerobically fit may have an intellectual edge with concentration, creativity, and problem-solving. Physical exercise can help you maintain an optimum weight, as well."

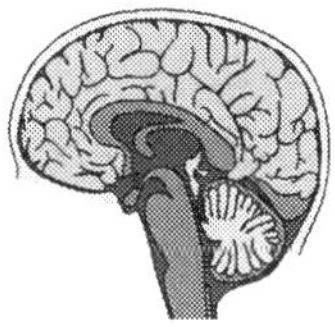

"Being overweight can raise your LDL cholesterol and lower your HDL—unhelpful for brain, body, and heart. The good news is that physical exercise can help reverse that.

"But to be really healthy," their coach continued, "the brain needs more than physical exercise. It needs brain aerobic exercises, as well."

"Brain aerobic exercises? They'd need to be portable, whatever they are, because I'm on the go a lot," said Todd.

"Many are portable. Audio books, for example, as well as hard copy books. Read aloud for at least 10 minutes a day. An anti-aging strategy, it exercises more parts of the brain (compared to reading silently to yourself) as well as the mouth, tongue, teeth, and larynx or voice box. You see, hear, and articulate the information, which makes it more likely you'll recall it."

"Reading aloud? I like it when Tami reads aloud while we're driving," said Todd. "Makes the time fly by."

"Reading aloud helps *my* brain," said Tami. "But I want a partner with a well-functioning brain, too, not just brawn—although the brawn isn't bad, mind you." She looked over at Todd and smiled appreciatively.
"Guess I need a well-functioning brain to keep up the brawn!" said Todd. He and Tami both laughed.

"There are Internet programs, too," said their coach. "Lumosity.com, BrainHQ, and Posit Brain are three examples."

"The bottom line is use it or lose it! Aim to obtain 30 minutes of challenging mental exercise every day. Play word games, Sudoku, crossword puzzles, brain benders, and simple math problems with the goal of beating your own time, and so on."

"Dr. Richard Restak points out that physical exercise prepares your neurons to connect with each other, while mental stimulation allows your brain to capitalize on that readiness. Think big picture for brain exercises. You may be doing some already."

Their coach listed several more examples.

- Interact regularly with others. The more social ties, the less your brain abilities tend to decline.
- Practice relaxation techniques to help interrupt the release of stress-stimulating neurochemicals. Meditate and visualize regularly.
- Yawn. It is a powerful neural-enhancing tool in brain areas involved in generating social awareness and creating feelings of empathy.
- Develop a sense of hope, optimism, and a belief in a positive future.
- Smile and laugh often to strengthen the brain's neural ability to maintain a positive outlook.
- Stay intellectually active to strengthen neural connections throughout your frontal lobes.

"Got it," said Tami. "We can do this."

"We're on it," said Todd. "See you next week."

Do you know the so-called *miracle* ingredient that can make cheap unpalatable food edible at virtually no cost? Turn to Chapter 20, meet Xavier, and find out.

There is a mountain of compelling research showing that plant protein allows for slow but steady synthesis of new proteins, and is the healthiest type of protein.

—T. Colin Campbell, PhD
The China Study

Three Pillars of Hedonia

Chapter 20

"We've been buying low-fat foods for the Forestry station," said Xavier. "You know: cookies, crackers, dairy products, salad dressing, and you name it; basically whatever we can find. We thought low-fat foods would be healthier. With what I've been hearing lately, however, I'm starting to wonder."

"Low-fat or non-fat dairy products are preferable choices," said his wellness coach, "because they do have a lower fat content. Other processed *low-fat* foods may be lower in actual fat, as well, but fat makes food taste better. In order to make low-fat foods palatable, manufacturers typically add other ingredients to compensate; sugar, fat, and salt—sometimes referred to as the Three Pillars of Hedonia or pleasure. Many processed foods also contain highly refined white flour, so eating those *low-fat* foods not only may provide less than optimum nutrition but also may result in weight gain. In most cases you're better off avoiding processed foods, especially those touted as low-fat."

"Added sugar, fat, and salt!" exclaimed Xavier. "I didn't know that. Speaking of salt, we have to keep large shakers on the tables. Some of the guys add salt before they even taste the food. They've told me they'd rather have food taste too salty than the other way around. How much salt do we need, anyway?"

"Good question," said his coach. "You do need some sodium to keep your brain and body working properly. Based on the amount required to meet the sodium needs of most healthy and moderately active individuals, the Institute of Medicine has set Adequate Intake levels for sodium at 1500 mg of per day. However, estimates are that more than 95 percent of American men and 90 percent of Canadian men ages 31 to 50, and 75 percent of American women and 50 percent of Canadian women in the same age range regularly consume salt in excess of the upper limit of 2300 mg per day."

"Salt does help food taste better. I'll give you that," said Xavier. "Without it, food can taste rather blah."

His coach nodded. "That's because you taste salty foods throughout your entire mouth. Unlike sugar or sweetness, human beings are not born with a preference for salt. Studies have shown that the development of a liking for salty tastes is related to early dietary experiences during infancy. Most babies dislike salt until at least six months of age. With continuing exposure, however, they soon start to like it—even crave it."

"Instead of buying low-fat products, should we be trying to cut out salt?" asked Xavier.

"Not necessarily. Our understanding of healthy sodium intake is actually changing. Dr. George E. Guthrie has pointed out that the sodium-potassium ratio is now believed to be much more important than simply limiting one's sodium intake. Studies have shown a relationship between consuming too much sodium (salt)—and too little potassium—and an elevated blood pressure. The typical age-related increase in blood pressure that is seen in most Western countries is now thought partly due to an insufficient intake of potassium."

"My mother has high blood pressure," said Xavier. "She's not only on a low-sodium diet but also takes medication to lower her risk of heart attack and stroke."

"I've heard physicians quote studies that show the importance of an appropriate sodium-potassium ratio, which may reduce the incidence of sodium-related health problems such as increases in blood pressure," said his coach.

"In fact, a low sodium diet—without an appropriate sodium-potassium ratio—may not be as helpful as was once thought. Heart disease is the leading cause of death in America and stroke is the third leading cause. High blood pressure is a risk factor for both. When the sodium-potassium ratio is brought into an appropriate range, blood pressure may begin decreasing within a few days to a few weeks for some people."

"I don't know much about potassium. What is it?" asked Xavier.

"Potassium is an element. You may recall from high school that its symbol is a 'K.' Potassium ions are necessary for the function of all living cells and a key mechanism in nerve transmission. Potassium depletion in animals, including humans, can result in various cardiac dysfunctions."

"So what can I do to get a better sodium-potassium ratio?" asked Xavier.

"Include more potassium-rich foods in your menu. There are many options including Shitake mushrooms, chick peas or garbanzos, bananas, beans (mung beans, white beans, Lima beans, lentils), yams, butternut and acorn squash, dried prunes and apricots, tomatoes, cucumbers, avocados, chard, and spinach."

"I wonder how the salt trend got started," said Xavier. "Do you know?"

"The Chinese are credited with discovering salt some 5,000 years ago. They found it could be used to preserve food, a boon with no refrigeration and often little available ice—if any. With refrigeration, salt was no longer needed for preservation of food. But the food industry learned quickly that salt accentuates flavors in food; it even makes sweet tastes taste sweeter.

"According to Michael Moss the food industry considers salt a magical ingredient because it provides such a burst of flavor and can make cheap unpalatable food edible at virtually no cost. It can even mask specific metallic or chemical after-tastes that may be present in soft drinks and processed foods. Salt can trigger thirst, as well, so keeping processed foods salty can also increase sales of soft drinks. And, like fat, salt can extend the shelf life of processed foods. It adds crunch to chips, crackers, and frozen waffles, and helps food retain moisture."

"I'll bet that's the reason some of the guys put handfuls of coarse salt on their steaks before they barbeque—to make cheaper cuts of meat taste better." Xavier laughed. "And speaking of steaks, can you give me a rundown on proteins, in a nutshell, that is?"

"Well, nuts *out of the shell*," said his coach, smiling. "Preferably raw and dry-roasted nuts, and nut butters made with nuts only, free of other additives such as hydrogenated oils. Proteins break down into amino acids that promote cell growth and repair. They help you feel satisfied longer because they typically take longer to digest than carbohydrates."

"And how much protein do we actually need?" asked Xavier.

"Recommendations vary, but the usual is about 55 grams of protein for most men and 45 grams for most women. Some individuals actually eat more protein than they need, which can be a stressor for the body."

"When I think of protein I think primarily of meat, chicken, dairy, and eggs. I'd forgotten about nuts. What are other good sources?"

"There are many other protein sources, some especially favored by vegetarian and vegan eaters."

His coach listed examples.

- Chick peas or garbanzos. They have 15 grams of protein in one cup. Think hummus.

- Quinoa, which includes all 9 essential amino acids and contains 8 grams of protein per cup.

- Sunflower, sesame, poppy, and chia seeds. Two tablespoons of chia seeds contain nearly 5 grams of protein.

- Legumes. Four ounces of beans contain as much protein as an ounce of broiled steak; a cup of green peas has about as much as a cup of milk. Lentils, another legume, have 18 grams of protein per cup and are low on the Glycemic Index.

- Edamame, Seitan, tofu (especially forms such as Tempeh, Miso, and Natto, reportedly considered the *breakfast of champions* by the Japanese.). Even raw spinach and broccoli contain some protein.

"I forgot about tofu and Tempeh, too," said Xavier.

"I could mix Tempeh or tofu with scrambled egg whites, add a bit of turmeric for color, and use that for a breakfast dish. I could easily vary it by adding onions and other veggies and seasonings." He paused.

"I've been reading labels—okay, I started reading them rather recently—and we've switched to Tamari soy sauce because it's gluten-free. Turns out two of the crew are gluten intolerant."

"Keep reading labels," said his coach. "It's often amazing what you can learn!"

"One of the crew always makes instant oatmeal for breakfast when it's his turn to cook. *Always.* Me? I like variety."

"Variety is good," said his coach. "And speaking of oatmeal, it's a rich source of complex carbs. Instant varieties cook quickly but also digest quickly. This can cause a rapid rise in blood sugar followed by a low that can make you want to eat again. Old-fashioned and steel-cut oatmeal are less processed. This helps blood sugar levels stay steadier and satisfies hunger for a longer period of time.

"Breakfast is an important meal, you know. It boots up your brain for the day ahead, much like you would boot up a computer at the start of a work day. Missing breakfast is not good for any brain, male or female. However, it may even be worse for males. Reportedly, males can lose up to 40 percent of their energy efficiency by noon if they begin their work day with an empty stomach."

"Some of the crew eat breakfast but it's inconsistent," said Xavier. "My goodness! We can't afford to lose 40 percent of our energy efficiency by noon."

"No one can," replied his coach.

"As the old saying admonishes:

- "Eat like a King at breakfast,
- "Eat like a Prince at lunch,
- "And eat like a Pauper at dinner or supper, depending on the label you use."

"Most people are less active in the late afternoon and evening hours. Calories ingested later in the day or evening are more likely to be stored as body fat rather than burned for energy."

"And those calories literally go to *waist.* Ours!" exclaimed Xavier.

"That's right." His coach laughed. "Now, tell me more about the forestry camp."

"It's in a beautiful location. There's a central office building with a kitchen and eating area in the basement. And then there are two bunk houses where the rangers sleep. The boss makes a schedule every month, and we guys take turns doing KP, two at a time on a seven-day rotation. We shop, cook, and clean up, although everyone is expected to bring their dirty dishes back to the kitchen.

"Our menus have been heavy on burgers slathered in cheese, pizza, spaghetti and meat balls, pasta, hash browns and eggs, pancakes, steak, mashed potatoes and gravy. Tastes good, but maybe not such healthy choices considering what I'm now learning." Xavier grimaced.

"You know, I can fix some of this," he continued, "'cause I do most of the shopping. Several of the fellows really hate shopping. I don't mind it. And in all fairness, the guys really do want to be healthier.

"Well, most of us do. That's one reason I'm here meeting with you. And I, for one, want to know more about nutrition for a Longevity Lifestyle."

"If anyone can *fix* some of this, as you put it, you likely can, with your male fix-it brain." His coach smiled. "And it sounds to me that you enjoy both your work and the crew."

Xavier nodded. "It's a good group of guys and meal times can be a hoot. Everyone wolfing down their food, telling jokes, unwinding. But collectively the two dozen of us have put on over 250 pounds this year. When I take this information back, they'll get on board, especially if I've done the leg work. Well, most of them will. A couple of the guys are proclaimed *gluttons*." He laughed. "It's like watching a couple of machines work when they eat."

"Proclaimed gluttons? Then something must not be working well for them," said his coach. "I tend to agree with a comment by Peter De Vries: gluttony is an emotional escape and a sign that something is eating the person. *Wolfing* down food in just a few minutes can be a factor that contributes to weight gain. When your brain and body are in homeostasis, balance, the brain typically signals it has had enough to eat after about fifteen or twenty minutes into your meal.

"When you wolf down your food, in just a few minutes you may eat several hundred more calories than you really need before satiation kicks in. It's easy to ingest a couple thousand calories at a single meal when you eat too fast and when the food is dense and high in simple carbs.

- "Slow down.
- "Chew thoroughly.
- "Take your time!"

"Thanks, coach," said Xavier. "Longevity Lifestyle, here I come. I'm on my way to healthier eating and, right now, to do some healthier shopping."

Filled with enthusiasm, Xavier left the office and trotted off down the hall.

Do you know what lower-income people tend to do that higher-income people don't?

Marvin found out.

So can you, in Chapter 21.

Water deprivation kills faster than lack of any other nutrient.

—Linda Boeckner and Kay McKinzie
Water: The Nutrient

Case of the Gold Stars

Chapter 21

"I've had several soft drinks every day—for years," said Marvin. "I heard on the news that, depending on the amount of soda guzzled, a person might add as much as a pound per week to their waist line. A pound!"

"According to Heath Herrera, owner of Fitness Revolution in San Marco, and the home of HH Fitness Boot Camps, drinks loaded with sugar contribute directly to weight gain. Period," said his wellness coach. "One 20-ounce glass of cola can contain the equivalent of 16 teaspoons of sugar, which is nearly three times the maximum daily sugar intake recommended by the American Heart Association.

"Soft drinks containing caffeine and sugar mimic the effect of amphetamines, providing a temporary energy boost. The 'high' shoots up blood sugar levels but is followed by a rebound 'low,' as blood sugar levels fall. Such dramatic fluctuations in blood-sugar levels can damage both the brain and immune system organs, contribute to health problems in the long term, and even accelerate the process of aging."

"My buddy recently switched to diet drinks figuring they'd help him lose weight," Marvin said. "They haven't. Not so far, anyway. In fact, he's gained. Go figure!"

"Diet sodas may be free of calories, but they're not free of health-related consequences. Confusing the brain with artificial sweeteners may also result in weight gain. A 2010 experiment in rats found that those who were fed saccharin-sweetened yogurt ate more rat chow, gained more weight, and had more body fat than those who ate the same amount of yogurt containing glucose, a natural sugar.

"A study that followed more than 400 diet-soda drinkers for 10 years showed that their waist sizes increased 70 percent more than non-consumers. Those who drank 2 or more diet sodas per day increased their waist sizes 5 times more than those who avoided diet drinks entirely. That's one reason a Longevity Lifestyle recommends avoiding sodas of any type: regular or diet."

"My waist can testify to that," laughed Marvin. "What a *waste*!"

"Using brain imaging techniques, San Diego researchers found diminishing activation in a brain area (known as the caudate head) as consumption of diet sodas increased. The caudate head is associated with food motivation and the brain reward system. Decreased activation of this brain region has been linked with an elevated risk of obesity.

"Unfortunately, alternative beverages such as fruit drinks, sodas, energy drinks, sports drinks, and sugary drinks appear largely to have replaced water in the lives of many Americans. Estimates are that half the population above the age of two years consumes sugary drinks on any given day. Consumption of soft drinks now exceeds 600 twelve-ounce servings per person per year. And as waist sizes grow, so do health risks for diabetes, heart disease, and cancer."

“Since the late 1970’s,” his coach continued, “soft-drink consumption has doubled for females and tripled for males. Males between 12-19 years of age have the highest soft-drink consumption, averaging half a gallon a day, or 160 gallons a year. And low-income persons tend to consume more sugary drinks in relation to their overall diet than those with higher incomes.”

“That reminds me. “I brought you a little something.” Reaching into a paper bag beside his chair, Marvin removed a mega-jug of Mountain Dew and set it on his coach’s desk. “You’ll make short work of this.”

There was a moment of complete and utter silence as the coach stared at the 64-ounce bottle. Marvin tried to keep a straight face. He really did. But it was more than the man could manage. After just a moment or two he burst into peals of laughter, laughing until tears ran down his cheeks.

“Oh! If only you could’ve seen your face,” Marvin howled, slapping his knee. “Last week I quit drinking sodas of any type, regular or diet. I still had this bottle at home and thought it would make a good joke. Just wait ‘til I tell my buddies. They’ll love it!”

“It was very funny, Marvin,” said his coach, joining in the laughter. “You sure had me going there for a minute. I was thinking to myself, *Short work? That’s 64 ounces! Twice what my stomach can hold comfortably. That one bottle contains about 70 teaspoons of sugar—nearly one and a half cups—and more than 900 calories. What was the he thinking? How can I explain graciously that I simply cannot drink this stuff?*”

“It was priceless, that’s what it was,” said Marvin, finally gaining his composure. “Especially when I already know that water is your beverage of choice. I’ll be laughing about that for years. You’re a good sport!”

"One of America's *drinking problems* involves a failure to drink enough water, which often leads to dehydration. By the time you experience thirst you're likely already dehydrated. Symptoms can include dry mouth, dry skin, sense of thirst, sleepiness, headache, decreased urine output, and constipation. Dehydration increases the production of free radicals, too. These damaged molecules can wreak havoc in many ways.

"You may be interested to know that aging and water consumption appear to be directly related," said his coach. "The body's water content tends to decrease with age. According to Dr. Mu Shik Jhon, outward signs of aging, such as wrinkling and withering, are indicators of what is happening inside the body. At the cellular level, aging causes a shift in the ratio of water inside versus outside the cells. As the volume of water inside the cells is reduced, the cells *wither*.

"In his book *Your Body's Many Cries for Water* Dr. Batmanghelikj explains that water is the body's main source of energy. Water flows through cell membranes providing electrical energy much like turbines in a hydroelectric plant. Sufficient water is important in order for ongoing energy, especially during the aging process. A lack of water is one of the most common causes of daytime fatigue."

"That reminds me of an old Greek proverb," said Marvin. "It goes something like this: I fear the man who drinks water and so remembers this morning what the rest of us said last night."

His coach chuckled.

"Dehydration is reversible, right?" asked Marvin.

"Most of the time dehydration can be reversed by drinking enough fluids to replace that which was lost. But not always."

"Dehydration can actually be a life-threatening condition—especially for the very young and the very old—and typically requires prompt medical attention, sometimes including hospitalization. A 1 percent level of dehydration can result in a 5 percent decrease in cognitive function. And just a 2 percent drop in your brain-body water supply can trigger a variety of symptoms such as fuzzy short-term memory, difficulty with basic math problems, and trouble focusing on smaller print such as seen on a computer, iPad, or mobile-phone screen."

His coach continued. "A team of scientists in Britain scanned the brains of teenagers after they had done an hour and a half of cycling. Those who had exercised in sweat-inducing clothing, had lost about two pounds of fluid in sweat—and their brain tissue had shrunk away from their skulls."

"Whoa!" exclaimed Marvin. "Serious stuff, that brain shrinkage."

"Those who had lost the most weight from perspiration showed the most brain shrinkage. In subsequent activities to test their ability to plan and solve problems, this group of participants did as well as those who had dressed more lightly to minimize sweating, but scans of the participants who wore the sweat-inducting clothing showed their dehydrated brains were forced to work harder. Immune system function can be impaired by dehydration, as well, because every organ in the body requires water to do its job."

"But we get some fluid from food," said Marvin. "I mean soups and stews and coffee and such."

His coach nodded. "According to the Mayo Clinic, food provides about 20 percent of one's total fluid intake on average. That percentage may go up slightly in cold weather if you are eating hot soup on a regular basis."

"Juices and other liquid beverages contribute as well. However, water is still a best bet because it's calorie-free, inexpensive, usually readily available, and requires no digestion."

"Growing up, we had plenty of milk and fruit juice but we didn't drink much water, so I didn't really learn to like it. Still don't."

"Learn to like it now," said his coach. "Unfortunately, sensations for hunger and thirst are similar and easily confused. Parents often feed children when they are thirsty, instead of giving them water to drink. This teaches them to eat for both sensations. In adulthood, many are thirsty but think they are hungry so they snack instead.

"Or they drink some food, like milk, fruit juices, sodas, or other sugary drinks. Your brain is composed largely of fluid, between 80-90 percent; and your body is 60-70 percent fluid. Both need a daily supply of water. Consume your calories through food and make water your beverage of choice."

"Are there general guidelines about how much water I should drink each day?" asked Marvin. "Like the old 8-glasses-a-day rule?"

"There are a couple of guidelines," said his coach. "Unless you must limit water intake due to a medical condition, some recommend aiming to drink half your body weight in ounces of water each day."

"Half my body weight!" exclaimed Marvin. "Did you say *half*?"

"In *ounces*," his coach reiterated. "For example, if you weigh 150 pounds, drink 75 ounces of water every day. That's a little over nine 8-ounce glasses. Depending on the weather and your activity level, you may need slightly less or a fair amount more."

"Oh," said Marvin, laughing. "The bit about *ounces* went right over my head. Learning to drink water will be a steep learning curve."

"Add a slice of lemon to your water and tell your brain how much you like the taste," his coach suggested, smiling. "You may be surprised at how good pure water can taste."

"What's the other guideline for avoiding dehydration?" asked Marvin.

"Rather than compulsively trying to count glasses of water, a more helpful guideline for some is to aim for two pale urines per day. That does mean that you have to pay some attention to the color of your urine."

"I can do that," said Marvin. "No sweat. And I'm committed to creating and maintaining a Longevity Lifestyle, now that I'm learning what to do and what to tell myself. I just never really understood before."

"You might try another tip," said his coach. "In *Hexagonal Water: The Ultimate Solution*, Pangman suggests that drinking a glass of water 20 to 30 minutes before each meal helps the body distinguish between sensations of thirst versus hunger. This is important for those who are trying to maintain optimum weight, since many people tend to eat less at a meal when they drink water first. The water helps suppress hunger. It also can help the body to burn fat.

"At a brain symposium several years ago, I heard a speaker emphasize the important relationship of water to brain function. He said, 'Think of it this way. Your brain must have water to do its job. If you don't give it a good supply, your brain will direct the body to steal some fluid from elsewhere in your body. At any given time your bladder has the largest potential reservoir of fluid—urine. That puts a different spin on the term *pee brain.*' The crowd loved it! Recalling his words helps remind me to drink water on a regular basis, not just to thirst."

"Well!" said Marvin, emphatically. "I'm completely uninterested in being a *pee brain*! Water is going to be my beverage of choice. My wife is charting my weekly waist circumference. And my weight. She says I'll get a gold star every time they decrease. I'll ask her to add drinking water to that list and then her I want a gold star for that, too." He and his coach had another good laugh.

"If your wife wants to give you gold stars, take them and have fun with them. They could be more helpful than you might think. The brain loves rewards and tends to repeat behaviors for which it gets a reward."

"I'll pick up a package of gold stars on my way home," said Marvin. "My wife will get a kick out of that." He paused. "I'm fortunate, you know. My wife is my biggest supporter. She's learning how to fix food in a healthier way and doing a good job—for both of us. I'm actually learning to like it. The food. Who knew? Now for the water …"

And Marvin was out the door, going for gold.

Chapter 22 is coming up next. Meet Angela who has been hauling around something potentially deadly.

Sleep is the interest we have to pay on the capital which is called in at death; and the higher the rate of interest and the more regularly it is paid, the further the date of redemption is postponed.

—Arthur Schopenhauer
19th Century
German Philosopher

Out of the Sand

Chapter 22

"Maybe my head is buried in the sand, in a manner of speaking," said Angela, but sometimes I wonder if trying to keep my weight within optimum limits is really all that important, other than helping me look trimmer, of course." Angela was nothing if not honest.

"Hauling around excess fat can be dangerous and potentially deadly," said her wellness coach. "It can lead to brain atrophy—shrinkage—something I'm sure you'd like to avoid. Loss of brain tissue has been linked to cognitive decline, which can be a problem for everyone. However, women who are obese throughout life may be at even higher risk for losing brain tissue, perhaps due to increased secretion of cortisol over the years. Multiple studies have shown a relationship between obesity and ischemia (inadequate blood flow), hypertension (high blood pressure), and heart disease. These conditions contribute to an unhealthy cardio-vascular system and a higher risk for dementia."

"That happened to my mother," said Angela. "She died last year at age 60 from complications related to diabetes. I sure miss her."

"It can be traumatic when a woman loses her mother," said her coach, "especially when it's an untimely death."

"Not that it isn't difficult for a male, mind you. But when a woman's mother dies that maternal line is broken, and the daughter now becomes the older generation. It can put mortality in a slightly different perspective."

Angela nodded. "It was traumatic. Very traumatic. Mom and I had become good friends in adulthood. Learning about the risks of obesity is going to help me pull my head out of the sand. I wish we had understood a Longevity Lifestyle earlier. Not just for my mother and me but for my daughter, as well. She's even heavier than her twin brother—and he's quite overweight!"

"Research has shown that children—at almost any age—are far more likely to copy what their parents *do* than what they *say*," said her coach. "You are developing and role-modeling a Longevity Lifestyle. Your life is changing for the better and as it improves, your twins will notice the improvements. They may ask you what you are doing differently, which can give you the opportunity to make a few appropriate comments. Remember, they are adults, so avoid nagging or repeating your advice. Lead by example."

"I can do that," said Angela, yawning.

"Do we need to talk about sleep?" Angela shrugged.

"Dement and Vaughan in their book *The Promise of Sleep* identified sleep deprivation as the most common brain impairment in our 'sleep-sick society.' Dr. Dement, a Stanford professor, regularly challenges his students to figure out how much sleep their brain needs and then adopt a sleep-smart lifestyle. Each brain has an optimum number of hours of sleep that it needs on a daily basis. Infants generally require about 16 hours, teenagers 9. There are exceptions, of course, but most adults need 7 to 8."

"How do you figure out how much sleep you need?" asked Angela.

"Guess how much sleep your brain might need and identify the time you want to wake up in the morning. Say you think your brain might

do best with 8 hours sleep and you need to up by 6:00 am. Add on an extra hour to allow your brain to become accustomed to actually getting sufficient sleep and go to bed at 9:00 pm every night for at least a week (or 10:00 pm if you don't have to get up until 7:00 am). Eventually, when it has had sufficient sleep, your brain will start waking up spontaneously—without needing an alarm clock—and will not protest about your crawling out of bed. After a few nights of your brain waking up spontaneously, make note of the number of hours. That typically represents your brain's optimum sleep needs. Then make sure you give your brain that amount."

"I thought I'd trained myself to need less sleep," said Angela. "In fact, I was quite sure of it!"

"Cheating successfully on the amount of sleep your brain needs is a myth. You may 'get by' on less sleep for a while, but eventually your brain and your immune system will have to pay the piper. Without adequate sleep you risk accumulating a sleep debt that can be difficult to pay back, especially if it becomes too large. Mental skills suffer severely from sleep deprivation, even more so than physical skills. Loss of sleep, even for a few hours during one night, can interfere with needed repairs to your neurons, lower the production of neurotrophins (neuron food), and prompt one's immune system to function less effectively.

"Less than 7 hours of sleep at night has been associated with a decrease in overall blood flow to the brain. Studies have shown a growing link between sleep duration and a variety of serious health problems including high blood pressure, negative moods and behaviors, safety issues, obesity, diabetes, hypertension, and depression. What you think you achieve by reducing your sleep is likely an illusion, both in the amount and quality of work performed."

"When sleep deprived, studies have shown that one's concentration is only 70 percent of what it is on days when the brain is well-rested. Studies at the MRC Cognition and Brain Sciences Unit in Cambridge showed that drowsiness alters awareness in much the same way as a common form of brain damage known as hemispatial neglect.

"According to James B. Maas, MD, author of *Power Sleep,* healthy sleep is the single most important determinant in predicting longevity—but our modern culture has become a case study in sleep deprivation. At least 70 million Americans are estimated to suffer from chronic, long-term sleep disorders. They often turn to sleeping pills, which may help in some ways but which can be habituating and typically interfere with one's quality of sleep."

"I know I'm probably sleep deprived, but there's so much to do," wailed Angela. "I simply couldn't get it all done if I slept for 6 or 7 or 8 hours every night." She paused. "My cat, on the other hand, always seems to be sleeping. I wish it could sleep for me!"

"You may want to revisit what you think you need to 'get done.' Lack of sleep is independently associated with weight gain, particularly in younger age groups. Studies at Columbia University found that people who get insufficient sleep tend to eat an extra 300 calories a day—ice cream being the favorite. Both men and women eat more protein-rich foods on short sleep, but only women ingested more fat—averaging 31 more grams of fat after sleeping for just 4 hours."

"I didn't realize there was a link between sleep deprivation and a desire to eat. Thirty-one more grams of fat after sleeping only 4 hours? Ouch! Although I hate to admit it, I often get only 4 hours of sleep a night. Hmmm."

"Sleep deprivation alters your hormonal balance. Your body releases more cortisol (a stress hormone) and ghrelin (the hormone that increases appetite) and less leptin (the hormone that tells you to stop eating). Over time, this imbalance can contribute to immune-system changes, insulin resistance, and weight gain."

"My husband and I are in the habit of munching potato and tortilla chips with sour-cream dip before his bedtime. And we usually top it all off with a bowl of ice cream. Is that really so horrible?"

"Is what really so horrible?" asked her coach, laughing.

"The sour-cream dip, the potato and tortilla chips, the ice cream, or eating just before going to bed? I suppose it all boils down to how well you want to sleep at night—and how much you want to manage your weight. Digesting food requires your body to work, which generates heat, which warms up the body. The body doesn't sleep well when it's hot. Let me say it again: you lose sleep and your hormones become unbalanced, which can increase your risk for immune-system changes, insulin resistance, and weight gain."

"Okay, I get the part about sour-cream dip and ice cream—sugar and fat and eating late at night, which makes my digestion keep on working," said Angela. "But potato and tortilla chips?"

"Figure that 6 large deep-fried tortilla chips or 20 potato chips contain 2 teaspoons of oil and have 150 calories. If you choose to eat chips, read labels carefully—even if you must carry a magnifying glass around with you—and make healthier choices. *Baked* multigrain vegetable chips (e.g., sweet potato) likely have more nutrients and considerably less fat."

"I can do that but what can I do to get more sleep?"

Her coach mentioned several strategies.

- Go to bed at the same time each night and get up at the same time each morning, and keep weekday and weekend sleeping routines as similar as possible.

- Develop relaxation techniques to quiet a *racing mind.* Practice them at bedtime or if awakening during the night.

- Train yourself to associate specific restful activities with sleep (e.g., warm bath or shower, reading) and make them part of your bedtime ritual.

- If you lost an hour of sleep the night before, get in a 15-minute power nap the following afternoon.

"Those are helpful," said Angela. "Do you have any more tips you can share?"

- Eat protein for lunch rather than dinner. Eating high-protein foods in the evening can disrupt the production of serotonin, the mood-regulating chemical that also helps you sleep.

- Open your mouth to simulate (or stimulate) a yawn. (Cats and dogs yawn regularly.) Do this four times before you go to bed. Find something to laugh about, too. An old Irish proverbs says that a good laugh and a long sleep are the best cures in the doctor's book.

- Get physical activity during the day. Leonard da Vinci said that a well-spent day brings happy sleep. When your muscles are tired, they push you to sleep.

- About half an hour before bedtime, stretch out your arms the way you did as a child. Stretch several times and tell yourself that it's bedtime.

- Minimize alcohol intake. A few hours after drinking a glass of wine or beer, the alcohol converts to aldehydes, stimulants that can accentuate worry and anxiety. Alcohol can also lead to one waking up after just a few hours of sleep and/or to restless sleep.

- If you're a coffee drinker and struggling with sleep, try drinking your coffee at breakfast and avoiding it for the rest of day. The half-life of caffeine (the time required for the body to eliminate one-half of the total amount of caffeine) is about 6 hours. A cup of regular coffee after lunch will leave half its caffeine still running around in your body at 6 p.m. and a quarter still circulating about 12 midnight.

"The National Sleep Foundation website offers tips for obtaining restful sleep," said her coach. "You also might refer to *Breaking the Food Seduction* by Dr. Neal Barnard. And Dr. Mary O'Brien has packed her book *The Healing Power of Sleep* with a great deal of valuable information. She points out that Americans slept nearly 10 hours a night prior to Edison's invention of the first commercially practical incandescent light bulb. A mere 30 years later (1910) sleep time had fallen to about 9 hours a night. And less than a 100 years later, 2002, average nightly sleep was in the 7-hour range, with millions trying to make it on only 5 or 6 hours.

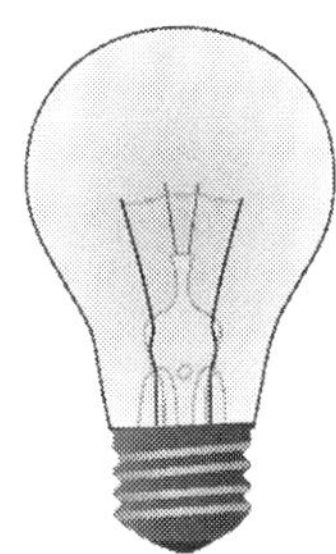

"Human physiology hasn't changed simply because electric light is readily available. Most adults still need 7 to 8 hours of sleep each night. Listen to your body. Pay attention to how you feel. If you ignore the whispers of fatigue you may eventually be assaulted by the shouts of exhaustion as your brain and body struggle to get your attention. Better to give them the rest they need now."

"This is not good news," said Angela, wide-eyed.

"That depends. It is particularly good advice, given the apparent association between insufficient sleep and weight gain. And it is wonderful news if it motivates you to get more centered about a balanced lifestyle. Every period of exhaustion is followed by a corresponding period of depression, which can challenge you at your points of vulnerability. Then, your brain is simply too tired to help you stay motivated."

"Sleep is essential to mood, memory, creativity, immune function, cognitive performance, and weight management."

"I thought we needed less sleep as we get older," said Angela. "Is that a myth or just wishful thinking?"

"It is a common misconception that sleep needs decline with age. In fact, research demonstrates that our sleep needs remain constant throughout adulthood. According to the National Sleep Foundation, although sleep may become more fragile in older people, the need for sleep does not decrease with age."

"My husband has been encouraging me to have someone come in for a few hours a couple times a month to do the heavy housework," said Angela. "I've been resisting his suggestion thinking 'I can do that myself.' In light of this information, however, he may have had a good idea. A strategy that could help me keep my life in balance."

"No one can 'do it all,' as you put it—and that includes you."

"I know one thing," said Angela, smiling. "Starting tonight, I believe I'll be in bed by eleven rather than staying up half the night trying to 'get it all done.' Eleven o'clock is my husband's bedtime. He'll be surprised. Actually, more like shocked!" She chuckled. "I'll give you an update next week."

"Good for you," said her coach. "It's like the old proverb says:

> *"You can't become what you can't believe but you can become what you can believe."*

"If you believe you'll be in bed by 11 o'clock, you can make it happen."

Do you know about the 20:80 Rule? Nell and Mark learned about it. You can, too, in Chapter 23.

If you ask what is the single most important key to longevity, I would have to say it is avoiding worry, stress, and tension. And if you didn't ask me, I'd still have to say it.

—George F. Burns

Crash and Burn or Not

Chapter 23

"I'm the poster boy for hair on fire and running at top speed on the proverbial treadmill!" exclaimed Mark as he and Nell took seats across from their wellness coach. "Juggling employee schedules is a real challenge, to say nothing of a headache. Some seem to regularly call in sick on weekends and holidays. Makes me wonder if they are really too *sick* to work." He sighed.

"The stress is further complicated by the sedentary nature of my job. I'm often too busy to take breaks and usually eat at my desk while working on the computer. My weight and blood pressure have climbed steadily over the past five years. I can't even remember what it felt like to be less stressed."

"I'm stressed—and depressed—from worrying about Mark," said Nell, wiping her eyes. "I'd hate being a widow."

"The brain is the first body system to recognize a stressor and it reacts with split-second timing," said their coach, "triggering the stress response. In fact, the brain can stimulate the stress response for up to seventy-two hours after a traumatic event—real or imagined. I'm sure you already know that unmanaged chronic stress can lead to illness, as well as contributing to attitudes such as hostility, fear, and depression."

"Effective stress-management strategies are critically important for both of you. However," said their coach, looking directly at Nell, "studies by Rita Valentino, PhD, have shown that women are twice as vulnerable as men to many stress-related disorders, including depression and PTSD. The female brain appears to respond to stress differently. Researcher Dr. Debra Bangasser says that even in the absence of any stress, the female stress signaling system is more sensitive from the start.

"Doc Childre, author of *Freeze Frame*, describes how stressors can stimulate the release of stress hormones: adrenalin, noradrenalin, and cortisol. Adrenalin released during stress can trigger the release of fat into the bloodstream, which provides extra energy for a bona fide emergency. But when there is no real emergency the liver converts the fat into cholesterol—increasing cholesterol levels is not a desirable goal.

"Childre also points out that the stress response creates specific hormonal imbalances that can damage brain cells and may even lead to Alzheimer's disease. Stress stimulates the release of the hormones adrenaline, noradrenaline, and cortisol. Unchecked, chronic stress—along with attitudes like hostility, anger, and depression—can lead to sickness and death. Adrenaline released during stress can stimulate the release of fat cells into the bloodstream. This provides extra energy if it was a real emergency. If not, the liver converts the fat into cholesterol.

"In his book *Why Zebras Don't Get Ulcers,* Dr. Robert M. Sapolsky explains how physical exercise helps burn off stress hormones and boost endorphins. When doing sedentary activities, ergonomic specialists recommend getting up from your chair every thirty minutes and doing thirty seconds of physical exercise."

"We're not getting any younger," said Nell, "and we want a long, healthy life together But Mark needs to make it to retirement!"

"An ancient proverb says *'it's not how old you are that matters—but how you are old'*. Living a long time is one goal. Thriving while you are alive is another. Both are important."

Mark nodded. "Unfortunately, I feel older than my chronological age. Some days, a *lot* older."

"Dr. Michael F. Roizen indicates that there is a relationship between stress and aging," said their coach. "Studies have shown that the faster you rev up your body with stress, the more quickly you age. Physically, chronic stress alters immune responses. And according to Dr. Benjamin V. Treadwell you may accelerate your biological age by as many as 17 years by being exposed to what you perceive to be a high psychological stress for prolonged periods of time.

"There is hope," their coach continued. "Dr. Mark P. Mattson, author of *Diet-Brain Connections: Impact on Memory, Mood, Aging and Disease*, puts it this way:

> *'The good news—if we take it seriously—is that many of the same factors that reduce one's risk for cardiovascular disease and diabetes also reduce the risk for age-related neurodegenerative disorders.'*

"To make matters worse," said Mark, "our church activities seem to cluster around sitting and eating. *Sitting* and *eating!* Potlucks, pancake breakfasts, picnic barbecues, ice-cream feeds, strawberry shortcake parties, fish fries, corn roasts, banquets…"

"Mark's right," said Nell. "A couple weeks ago I mildly protested the amount of fried foods weighing down the serving tables at potluck. One of our friends blew off my concerns, saying, 'Relax, Nell. It's all fried in vegetable oil. Besides, people who eat together stay together.'"

"I believe the saying refers to people who *laugh* together," said their coach. "The same thing may apply to people who eat together, too, but it's important to factor in the type and amount of food being ingested. Eating large quantities of unhealthy food may eventually keep people together all right—in the hospital, if not in the cemetery."

"That's a humorous way of putting it," said Nell.

Their coach continued. "Studies at Northwestern University have shown that those who regularly attend religious services are significantly more likely to become obese by the time they reach middle age. Jeff Levin, Director of Baylor University's Program on Religion and Population Health, has hypothesized that attendees may be 'sitting around passively instead of being outside engaging in physical activity.'"

"Have you heard about the *Daniel Plan*?" Mark asked suddenly.

"Yes. I read an article that was published in the 'Orange County Register.' Reportedly, the Daniel Plan was developed by Rick Warren, pastor of the Saddleback church, in collaboration with Doctors Mehmet Oz, Daniel Amen, and Mark Hyman."

"I heard about it on the news," said Mark. "The Amen Clinics found that brain health is highly linked to physical health, so these docs teamed up in an effort to help improve the health of church attendees."

"Brain health is linked with physical health," agreed their coach. "When a person's weight goes up, function in the prefrontal cortex—the most human and thoughtful part of the brain—goes down. The Daniel Plan utilizes such health strategies as keeping a food journal, drinking water throughout the day, getting sufficient amounts of sleep, ingesting high quality calories, and obtaining regular physical exercise."

"Some 15,000 people became involved in the plan," said Mark, "and collectively they lost a quarter of a million pounds in 52 weeks. I got the idea that the plan was named after Daniel, an Old Testament writer who balked at eating the King's food."

"Remind me of the details," said Nell. "I'm a bit hazy. By any chance was that the same Daniel of the *lion's den* fame?"

Their coach nodded. "The story actually begins with Nebuchadnezzar. Born around 630 BC, he became king of the Chaldean or Neo-Babylonian Empire. One of the most powerful monarchs of his dynasty, Nebuchadnezzar is credited with creating the Hanging Gardens of Babylon, which must have been a sight to behold. He also engaged in many military campaigns designed to increase the wealth, size, and importance of his Empire.

"It was on one of those military conquests that Nebuchadnezzar destroyed the famous King Solomon's Temple in Jerusalem. As was customary at that time, Nebuchadnezzar took prisoners along with spoils of war. Daniel and three of his friends were among the group of captives that went back to Babylon with the King. Nebuchadnezzar accorded some of the captives the so-called honor of eating the same menu that was served at the King's table. Daniel and his three friends took one look at what was being served and told themselves *don't think so.* But what to do?

Negotiating with the King's steward, they asked for a trial period during which they would eat herbs, (likely vegetables, fruits, and legumes) and drink water as their beverage. At the end of ten days, the steward would evaluate whether these four performed as well or better than the other captives."

"And what they ate and drank made a positive difference," said Mark. "I doubt the King's fare would be recommended today for good health. Certainly not for a Longevity Lifestyle!"

"Correct on all accounts," said their coach. "At the end of ten days, the four young men were more healthful looking and had better complexions as compared with those who had been scarfing down what was served at the King's table. Therefore, the steward agreed that Daniel and his three friends could continue on their menu of choice.

"Three years later, all the captives were tested. When the King personally interviewed Daniel and his four friends, he found them to be ten times wiser than the other students and wiser even than their teachers. Because of this, the King made them special advisors to his court. The story of Daniel and his three friends may be one of the earliest recorded about the relationship between mental and physical health and the types of food and beverages ingested."

"You know," said Nell, "I could challenge the members of my potluck committee to draft and guidelines for the types of healthier foods we'd prefer to provide. Right now we're heavy on 'white' stuff: mashed potatoes, white bread and rolls, mac 'n cheese, potato salad, pasta, white-flour cakes and pies, plus fried chips with ranch dip and fried chicken. If it's white or fried, we've got it," she concluded, laughing ruefully.

"And we could stand for at least part of our choir rehearsals instead of sitting," offered Mark.

"You're being creative," said their coach. "Every little bit helps!"

"Back to stress," said Nell. "Obviously, we both need help managing it. Do you know of more research?"

"Neuroscientist Dr. Andrew Newberg—based on new evidence from brain-scan studies and a wide-reaching survey of people's religious and spiritual experiences—has concluded that prayer and spiritual practice can reduce stress.

"Just twelve minutes per day of meditation or prayer—a form of meditation—may slow down the aging process. Intense prayer and

meditation can permanently change numerous structures and functions in the brain, altering your values and the way you perceive reality.

"Newberg also points out that the contemplation of a Higher Power as loving rather than as punitive, has been found to reduce anxiety and depression and increase feelings of security, compassion, and love. In and of itself religious fundamentalism may be personally beneficial, but the prejudice often generated by extreme beliefs can be stressful and can permanently damage the person's brain."

"All I know is there are lots of kinds of stress," said Mark. "Every time I turn around I bump into one type or another."

"Stress is often described in three general categories: Eustress, Distress, and Misstress."

Their coach described the categories.

- Eustress is desirable stress such as obtaining additional education, marrying, getting a promotion at work, welcoming a new baby into the family (or twins or triplets), planning a surprise birthday party, hosting a holiday celebration, or taking a vacation. Eustress is considered a positive type of stress because it can help you grow and develop. Typically you have some choice around eustress events or situations.

- Distress is undesirable stress like a fire, earthquake, or other natural disaster; being fired, bankruptcy, or having a family member or friend die unexpectedly. Daniel Goleman in *Primal Leadership* says that distress erodes mental abilities and makes people less emotionally intelligent. People who are upset have trouble reading emotions accurately in other people, decreasing the most basic skill needed for empathy and thus impairing their social skills.

- Misstress, hidden stress, is the third category. It includes such things as long commutes, prolonged sitting in front of a computer, overeating, or living an unhealthy lifestyle. The stress tends to accumulate and can produce outcomes as undesirable and damaging as outright distress.

"Dr. Al Siebert has pointed out something very interesting about stress, said their coach: *There is no stress in any situation until the individual human feels strain—and this differs for every brain. The distress perceived is less the result of what actually exists objectively, and more about what an individual brain perceives is happening.*

"According to Dr. Herbert Benson, stress does not cause pain, but it can exacerbate pain and make it worse. Much of chronic pain is 'remembered' pain. It's the constant firing of brain cells leading to a memory of pain that lasts, even though the bodily symptoms causing the pain are no longer there. The pain continues because of the neurological connections in the brain itself."

"Those are new thoughts," said Mark. "Different strokes for different folks can apply to an individual's personal perception of stress. Say, do you have a favorite stress-management strategy? An *effective* stress-management strategy," he amended.

Their coach laughed. "I can certainly share one of my favorite strategies and it is effective for me."

"I think of the *20:80 Rule* as a universal antidote to stress. It comes from work by Epictetus, a 2nd Century Greek Philosopher, who believed it's not so much what happens that matters as what you think about what happens. A profound concept, that. My guess is that it's as relevant today as it was back then, if not more so.

"Stressors are believed to interact with the brain in a predictable equation. An estimated 20 percent of any negative effect to one's brain and body is due to the event or situation itself, while 80 percent is due to your perception of the event, the importance you place on it and the weight you give to it. Bottom line, even when you can't do anything about the 20 percent, you can do something about the 80 percent—because you create your own perceptions."

"I'm embracing that *20:80 Rule!*" said Mark. "It's a dandy metaphor. I can already see how that could work for me. And I'm definitely interested in creating and maintaining a Longevity Lifestyle—starting right now."

"Me, too," Nell affirmed. "On both accounts. I know we can influence some improved behaviors at our church."

"Such as distributing healthier guidelines for church potlucks and standing for part of your choir rehearsals," said their coach.

Mark and Nell left the office, holding hands and smiling.

Chapter 24 is next. George reappears to get tips about *forewarned is forearmed.*

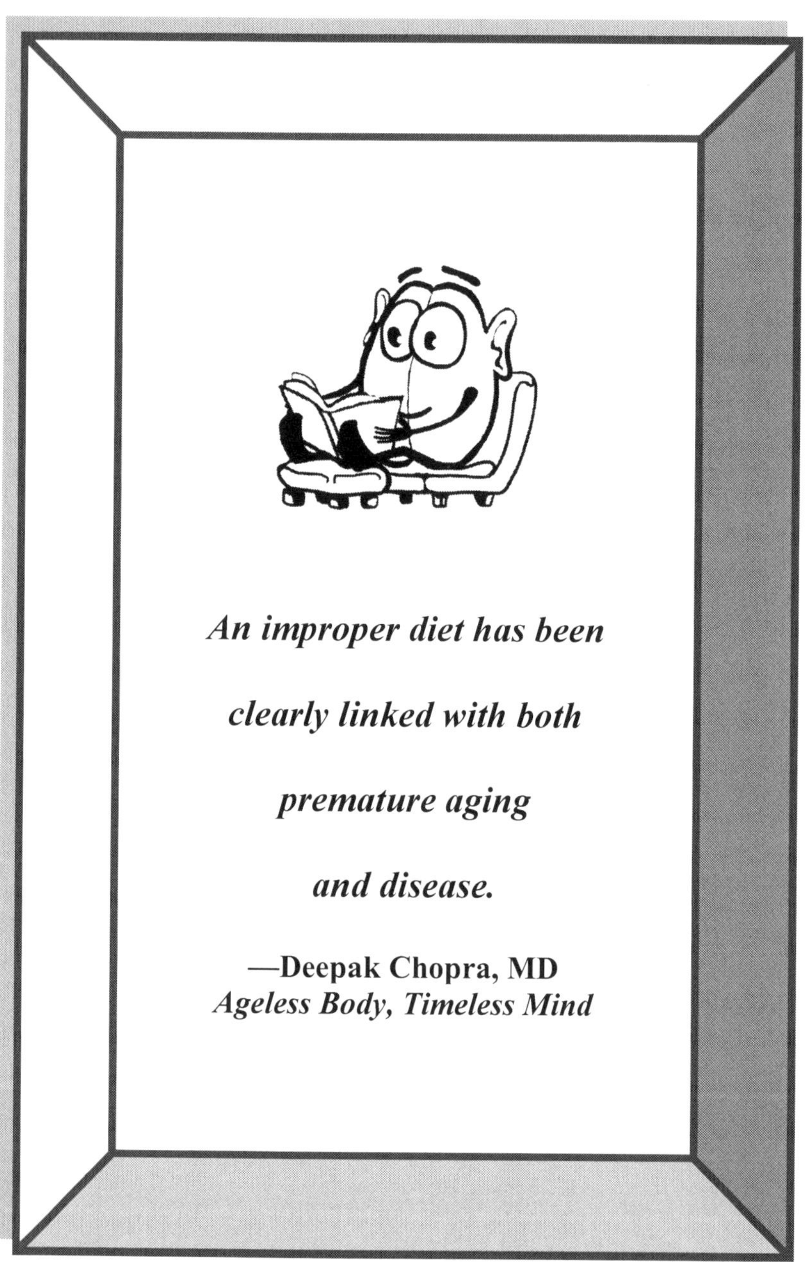
An improper diet has been
clearly linked with both
premature aging
and disease.
—Deepak Chopra, MD
Ageless Body, Timeless Mind

Forewarned is Forearmed

Chapter 24

"I dropped by to tell you that I'll be working in South America for the next few months," said George. "An opportunity to further hone my Spanish." He smiled. "And to say that that my colleagues have noticed, ah-h-h …" his voice trailed off.

"Have noticed how good you look and how much more energy you have," said his wellness coach. "And how clearly you are thinking. It's hard to miss, George. You've dropped nearly 47 pounds in 14 months and buffed up your muscle tone. Give yourself due credit. You look great!"

George smiled, acknowledging the affirmation. "One of my assignments is to give a monthly talk to employees about a Longevity Lifestyle. Thinking about that, I recalled an earlier discussion we had about challenges people might face in creating and implementing a long-term lifestyle change. You used the phrase *forewarned is forearmed;* said that individuals tend to meet challenges more successfully when they are aware of problems that might arise. Those potential challenges would make good topics for my talks. I'd appreciate your going over them again, so I can jot down a few notes."

"I'll be happy to do that. It's a bit like recognizing that your fuel gauge registers below a quarter of a tank. Knowing this gives you the opportunity to stop and fill up in a timely manner. Likewise, identifying some of the challenges that others have encountered and surmounted successfully can help you do the same.

"Recently I compiled a list of a dozen myths, mindsets, or traps. I'll give you a copy."

George's wellness coach reviewed the points with him.

1. If a little is good, a lot is better

False. Serving sizes have increased dramatically over the past decade. Sodas are sold in 64-ounce containers even though the average stomach capacity is only 32 ounces. Mega-burgers could feed several, to say nothing of mega-cookies or huge slices of pie or mammoth wedges of cake. Some people overexercise and actually injure their bodies in an attempt to compensate for increases in caloric intake or in an attempt to drop pounds quickly.

According to the American College of Sports Medicine, physical activity alone is largely ineffective for losing weight because of the high volume of activity that would be required. The addition of regular exercise to a reduction in caloric intake does spare muscle mass, but it only marginally increases short-term weight loss.

On the flip side, studies have shown that a long-term exercise program can help you maintain an optimum weight. That's worth its *weight* in gold.

2. A mindset of extremes is the way to go

Nada. *All-or-nothing* thinkers tend to live in a black-or-white world. They often overgeneralize, taking one isolated event and assuming that all future events will be the same. They use words such as *always* and *never,* rather than *sometimes* or *occasionally*, a mindset that can sabotage an exercise program. For example:

- If you can't do everything today, then there's no point in doing anything.
- If one exercise falls short of your goal, then your entire program is going to fail.
- You ate half-a-dozen donuts, so there's no point in exercising at all; might as well give up altogether.

Stop it! In reality, life is filled with gray areas. Doing something is better than doing nothing.

3. You must always eat meals with the family

Not necessarily. It can be important to interact with the family at meal time, but there is no rule that says you have to eat a whole meal every time you sit down at the table. You can opt for a salad or an apple, munch on jicama and celery sticks or drink a cup of green tea, and still engage with the family or read aloud while they eat—something humorous or fun. You may be amazed at how much they look forward to this once or twice a week. One mother read *Anne of Green Gables* aloud over dinners. The kids loved it. Another read Patrick Taylor's *An Irish Country Doctor* only to have the whole family beg, *Read it again. Puleese!* The sky is the limit. Be creative. Eat sometimes; read sometimes.

4. Females can eat as much as their male counterparts and still maintain an optimum weight

Not likely. Although the strength of a woman's abdominal muscles equals those of a comparably-sized male, females have only one third the upper body strength and half the lower body strength. About 40 percent of the male body consists of muscle fibers, which burn five more calories per pound than fat—even at rest. Females have a greater fat-to-muscle ratio and simply cannot ingest the same number of calories and still expect to remain within their desired weight range. It can be a source of discontent when a couple embark on a similar journey toward health and he loses weight faster than she does. On the other hand, the muscles in the female body are better equipped to deal with changes in hormonal levels and water retention. Think menstruation and pregnancy. Male muscles lack this advantage. Consequently, males tend to experience greater levels of muscle aches and pains when they become ill with a cold or the flu.

5. A mindset of 'shoulds' keeps you on track

False. Thinkers who rely on *should* statements tend to have rigid rules and often apply information in a rigid and self-limiting style. They place themselves under considerable stress in an attempt to live up to their own self-imposed unrealistic expectations or those of others. They often limit themselves unnecessarily (e.g., "I *should* cancel a visit to my aunt's because she has no exercise equipment and I *should* work out every day"). There are many ways to exercise without using exercise equipment! Get rid of the *shoulds* and be creative in discovering flexibility options in differing environments.

6. Females cannot maintain an optimum weight with their body type

False. You will remember, however, that the optimum daily calorie range for the average female is several hundred calories lower than that for a comparable male.

- Eat healthy balanced meals, with foods in as natural a state as possible.

- Drink a glass of water twenty or thirty minutes before each meal to keep you hydrated and lower the likelihood of eating because you are thirsty.

- Regulate portion sizes. A fourth to a half cup is a serving for denser foods; one cup is a serving size for less dense foods, such as steamed or raw vegetables.

- Eat when you are physiologically hungry. Eat slowly. Chew your food well. Put your utensil down between bites. Minimize desserts and take only two or three bites when you choose one.

- Make water your beverage of choice. Avoid all sodas, colas, diet drinks, and sugary fruit drinks. There are 100 calories in a glass of orange juice and only 60 in an orange. Eat the orange!

7. Willpower over-rides negative self-talk

False. Just try using willpower to stop old behaviors—to *not* do something—and you're in for the battle of your life. You'll likely lose because what you resist persists, especially when what you are resisting gave your brain some type of reward. Work by Dr. Daniel Wegner and his *don't think about the white bear* phenomenon has made that clear. Tell yourself what you want to have happen as if it's a done deal and stop focusing on what you do not want to have happen. Use willpower to follow through on the new or healthier replacement behaviors you have selected.

Creating and maintaining a Longevity Lifestyle requires frequent reminders to your brain about where you are going and how you are getting there. It's easy to get off schedule for a day or two and *forget* to get back on track. When you wake up in the morning, remind yourself of your goals and the strategies you are applying to be successful. Applaud yourself for your gains; reward your brain with affirmations. Nothing feeds success like success—not even food.

8. You can never do too much for others

Wrong. Even good things taken to an extreme can result in negative outcomes. Some overextend doing things for others that those individuals can and more properly need to be doing for themselves. Some try to give and give in an effort to feel better about themselves. Some try to do too many good things or attempt to do everything flawlessly. They lose sleep by over-volunteering, trying to keep everyone happy, or failing to practice good self-care. Dump that myth. Strive for balance, *every* day in *every* way. An empty cup has nothing of value to give away. Keep your cup full first and then share from an overflowing abundance.

9. Lose a few pounds and you can revert to your old favorite habits

Not if you want to maintain your gains. You always give up something to get something. Reverting to your old habits will return you to the outcomes they produced. Dr. David Katz points out in *Disease-Proof: The Remarkable Truth about What Makes Us Well* that lifestyle is the best medicine. As brain and body return to a more desirable state of balance, neurochemicals and hormones may also move toward homeostasis. If hunger is not the problem, then eating is not the solution. Leave your old habits in the dust of your Longevity Lifestyle even as you embrace the new and healthier behaviors.

10. Focusing on the negative helps you learn

False. This type of mindset leads individuals to magnify all negative experiences and gloss over all positive experiences as if each were a fluke. They seem oblivious to the three positive things that just happened, concentrating on and emphasizing the one that went wrong. Gradually they filter out all positives, developing a worldview of disasters and disappointments. Eventually, they seem to recognize only negatives. Even when trying to solve a problem, they respond to most suggestions with: *Yeah, but that won't work.* Because of this they rarely try other option and often simply keep doing what they did before, all the while hoping for a different outcome.

11. A mindset that catastrophizes is helpful

False. People with this mindset imagine the worst possible scenario, then expect it to happen. They tend to jump to the conclusion that everything will be worse than imagined—and what they imagined was pretty horrific. Rather than learning to think ahead and weigh *possibility versus probability*, initiating preventive strategies whenever possible, they seem to look for disaster, almost willing it to happen. And if it does occur, they say, "I knew it! I told you so!" Some throw up their hands and refuse to even problem solve, believing that everything in life is beyond their capability. They stop trying to learn or fail to apply new information, believing it won't work anyway. Think positive can-do thoughts.

12. Hanging out with those who are not following a Longevity Lifestyle has little impact on you

False. Social support systems are important for long-term success. The key word here is *support.* Individuals who are not on a similar journey, don't value what you are doing, or who are not sufficiently actualized to support your health choices (especially when they make less healthy decisions for themselves) can derail you. Within a period of three years you are at high risk for picking up the habit patterns of those with whom you associate. To be successful, you may need to limit time spent with such individuals and carefully orchestrate the environment so it works for you. It is often preferable to invite people to your home where you have more control over the environment. If you go to their place, make careful food and beverage selections, remembering the importance of portion sizes. Offer to bring veggie munchies and baked crackers to add to the spread. As you role model looking good, feeling better, and thinking more clearly, some might even get on board with you.

"That is exactly what I needed," said George, placing the copy in his briefcase. "I'll check in with you when I return. Thanks again. And I do mean *thank you*! The information you've shared with me has been life-changing in so many different ways."

"Email if you have questions," said his coach. "I believe you'll do very well."

Move on to Chapter 25. Meet Pax and Pen and find out what they learned about the link between gratitude and health.

At times our own light goes out and is rekindled by a spark from another person. Each of us has cause to think with deep gratitude of those who have lighted the flame within us.

—Albert Schweitzer

Elixir of Gratitude

Chapter 25

"Life is really irritating and I mean *really* irritating," said Pen, dropping into a cushioned chair. Pax nodded in agreement.

"You know, I thought a Longevity Lifestyle would smooth out the things that bother me," Pen continued, "but it hasn't. At least not completely. The doctor told me this morning—rather bluntly, mind you—that I need to work on forgiveness and gratitude. I ask you, what do forgiveness and gratitude have to do with a Longevity Lifestyle?"

"Perhaps more than you may have realized," said their wellness coach. "Life will always contain irritants—from the pebble in your shoe to the neighbor's barking dog or crowing rooster. When you focus on irritants, they can turn into proverbial mountains rather quickly. When you concentrate on irritants, that's what goes into your working memory (what you are consciously focusing on at the moment). Since the brain wants congruence and because it perceives that what you put in your working memory is important to you, it immediately begins searching its memory banks for similar incidents from the past. Any event or situation that you found irritating. And before you know it …"

"Before you know it, all you seem to notice are life's irritants," said Pax, interrupting.

"Metaphorically, think of your brain as a camera that continually records the things on which you choose to focus. What pictures are you putting into your brain's working memory? What is being transferred into your long-term memory?"

"The doctor said I'd be far better off to stop whining and start being thankful—which irritated me no end! I thought that was rude, but maybe he was right. Maybe I've developed a bad habit of looking for what's wrong instead of what's right." Pen sighed.

"The doctor was direct," said Pax. "But as I think about it, he's got a point. He mentioned studies showing a link between forgiveness, spirituality, gratitude, and health. Do you know of some?"

"Dr. Herbert Benson has identified what he calls the physiology of forgiveness®. An inability to forgive people's faults (or your own) is harmful to one's health, relationships, and maybe even to longevity. The question is: can you afford unforgiveness? The cost is high.

"Ruminating about faults, mistakes, and perceived injuries keeps your mind occupied with the event, situation, or los s. It can keep you stuck and derail you from moving forward successfully, negatively impacting your health and wellbeing. As Desmond Tutu point out: *'Without forgiveness there is no future.'* Want a healthier future? Choose to practice forgiveness. Mahatma Gandhi said that the weak can never forgive—forgiveness is the attribute of the strong. Pretty powerful words, those."

"I'll admit that I've hung onto a lot of perceived injuries and injustices," said Pen, "whining and complaining about them—which solved nothing, of course but which made them all seem even worse. It also helped me feel like a victim."

"A victim mindset burns up norepinephrine (a chemical that impacts mood and stress), stops emotional growth, and blocks recovery. Typically, it involves a sense of helplessness and hopelessness. Sometimes it also includes a perception of being *special* because of being injured. Everyone experiences injuries in life. Period. So being injured doesn't make one special.

"Choosing to move from a position of victim to one of survivor, on the other hand—now that's a badge of honor. Choosing a survivor mindset helps you recover, heal wounds from the injury, grow up emotionally, role model more effectively, and assist others more appropriately. Actually, refusing to forgive can be compared with taking poison and expecting it to kill the other person."

"Oh, that's good!" exclaimed Pax. "I need to remember that. I've been quite unforgiving at times. And more than once I've jumped on the band wagon right along with Pen, reinforcing negative perceptions instead of helping to reframe them."

"All human beings make mistakes," their coach pointed out. "Most people do the best they can at the time with what they know. What's important is to learn from your mistakes and move on gracefully. Be clear that forgiving doesn't mean forgetting. You let go of the hurt feelings while still remembering the lessons you learned. Choosing to forgive yourself and others can be life-saving. And the person who does the forgiving appears to benefit the most."

Pen nodded. "And the link—as the doctor put it—between unforgiveness and health?"

"A variety of undesirable consequences have been associated with unforgiveness."

Their coach listed several.

- Increased heart rate and higher blood pressure

- Higher stress levels along with a higher risk for depression, heart disease, stroke, and cancer
- Increased muscle tension and muscle fatigue
- Suppressed immune system function
- Elevated adrenaline and cortisol (stress hormones)
- Impaired neurological function and memory

"Not pretty," said Pen. "I can relate to some of those undesirable consequences. I'm guessing the reverse is also true?

"Good guess. As Bernard Meltzer put it, when you forgive, you in no way change the past, but you sure do change the future. The benefits of forgiveness include at least these:

- Healthier relationships
- Lower blood pressure
- Less anxiety
- Less hostility and stress,
- Fewer symptoms of depression
- Lower risk of alcohol and substance abuse
- Increased compassion, kindness, and peace of mind
- Enhanced mental, physical, emotional, and spiritual health."

"The question remains: in terms of health and longevity, can you really afford to be unforgiving?"

"When you put it that way, Coach, the cost is very high," said Pen ruefully. "Too high, actually. I'm rather tired of hanging on to some of these resentments. And when I look at them from the perspective of a bigger picture, they're downright ludicrous."

"I heard a PBS special not long ago suggesting the every brain is innately spiritual," said Pax. "I supposed they were referring to religion."

"Maybe not," their coach replied. "Newberg and Waldman in their book *Why We Believe What We Believe* point out that the human mind may be naturally calibrated to embrace spiritual perceptions. Although often considered to be synonymous, spirituality and religiosity are differing concepts. I'll give you a couple definitions, although I encourage you to craft your own and personalize them to fit your brain.

- "Religion involves a choice to affiliate with specific theologies (rules, rituals, rites, or dogma) that have been endorsed by an organization.

- "Spirituality encompasses the spirit in which you live life; your ethical and moral choices; helping you understand and find purpose and meaning in life, a sense of awe for something greater than yourself; and a vision to achieve the highest possible levels of healthiness and longevity.

"According to Dr. Benson, 22 of 27 studies he reviewed correlated improved health in those who attended religious services. In *Mind over Medicine* Dr. Lissa Rankin points out that individuals who attend religious services regularly live 7.5 years longer (almost 14 years longer for African-Americans) than those who never or rarely do so."

"Those who are part of a spiritual community have also been shown to have lower blood pressure and a reduced risk of cardiovascular disease, lower rates of depression and suicide, lower rates of substance abuse, and stronger immune systems."

"That's a substantial list of benefits," said Pax, impressed.

"A strong spirituality is being linked with a variety of healthy benefits including lower depression rates and enhanced relationships," their coach continued. "Your level of spirituality may also impact the way you care for your brain and body. If you believe that a brain and body have been leased to you for use on this planet, you may be more likely to care for them as carefully, consistently, and thoughtfully as you would a leased high-end vehicle. Hone your spirituality in whatever way works for you. Some like to meditate or pray (a form of meditation). Include activities that trigger a sense of awe.

"No wonder the doctor told me to stop whining and start being thankful," said Pen. "I need to develop some healthier habits."

"Practice gratitude," their coach suggested. "It's *good medicine*. The word gratitude describes a state of mind that acknowledges when bad things happen but looks for the lesson or gift. Studies have shown that fear and gratitude cannot coexist simultaneously in the brain. In his book *Thanks!* Robert Emmons points out that people who practice grateful thinking reap emotional, physical, and interpersonal benefits. They tend to take better care of themselves and engage in more protective health behaviors like physical and mental exercise, healthy eating, and regular physical examinations.

"You might begin by keeping a gratitude journal, hard copy or electronic. People who keep such a journal report fewer illness symptoms, feel better about their lives as a whole, and are more hopeful about the future."

"A gratitude journal," said Pen thoughtfully. "I think I'd like to try that."

"Grateful people tend to be more optimistic, a characteristic that researchers say boosts immune system function. You can move up your set point to some degree for both happiness and gratitude—in all likelihood enough to have a measurable effect on both your overall outlook and health. Studies at the University of Connecticut showed that patients who identified benefits from their heart attack—such as becoming more appreciative of life—lowered their risk of having another heart attack.

"Edward Diener, PhD, professor at the University of Illinois at Champaign-Urbana and also known as Dr. Happiness, has studied life satisfaction of people from various cultures. He found, for example, that people in India living in poverty report low levels of life satisfaction. But so do a high percentage of people in affluent Japan. This suggests that an emphasis on materialism may be at least partially to blame.

"Research by Martin Seligman points out that individuals who write 'gratitude letters' to a person who made a difference in their lives score higher on happiness, and lower on depression—and the effect lasts for weeks.

"Studies by David DeSteno at Northeastern University in Boston have shown that gratitude reduces impatience, even when real money is at stake. The effects of gratitude are differentiable from those of the more general positive state of happiness. Although different, gratitude and happiness may actually reinforce each other, positively impacting mindset, self-talk, and communication.

Thanks

"Oprah Winfrey put it this way:

> *Be thankful for what you have; you'll end up having more. If you concentrate on what you don't have, you will never, ever have enough."*

"Okay. That does sit. I'm on board," said Pax. "My goal is to focus on the positives in life rather than on the negatives. And I plan to do some Internet research on aspects of spirituality. That topic intrigues me." He paused. "Growing up I had some unfortunate experiences with rigid religiosity. Equally unfortunate, perhaps, I threw out the proverbial baby (in this case, spirituality) with the religious bathwater. I'm starting to think that spirituality and gratitude may be kissing cousins."

"You may have something there," said their coach, smiling.

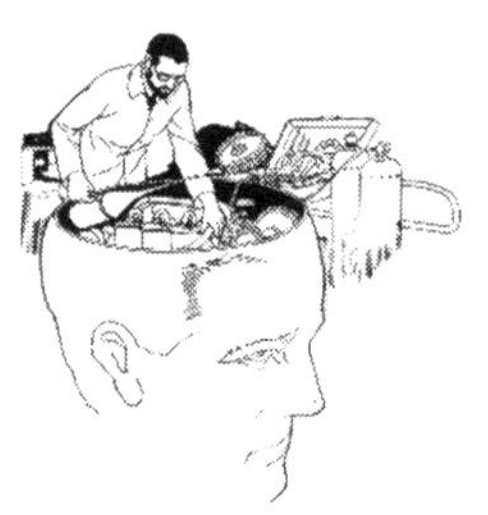

"According to Melanie Greenberg, PhD, a clinical psychologist, life coach, and expert on life change, developing a gratitude practice can open your heart and rewire your brain."

"Wow!" exclaimed Pen. "I'm doing an about-face and heading in a healthier direction." She looked at Pax.

"Good-bye unforgiveness—hello forgiveness. So long whining—come on in gratitude. From now on, I choose to be thankful for something every single day."

"No doubt you've heard of the Native American Shawnee Warrior, Tecumtha, often referred to as Tecumseh," said their wellness coach.

"A proponent of gratitude, he has been quoted as saying:

> *When you rise in the morning, give thanks for the light, for your life, for your strength. Give thanks for your food and for the joy of living. If you see no reason to give thanks, give thanks anyway."*

"I've certainly benefited from being mindfully grateful on a daily basis," said their coach, smiling. "I'm also discovering a great deal of personal fulfillment in doing random acts of kindness. Often it's just some small thing that makes a difference in someone else's life. When you stay alert for opportunities, somehow they pop up right in front of you. I've been the recipient of random acts of kindness myself and know how good they can make you feel."

"Random acts of kindness," mused Pax. "Another good idea. I am starting my gratitude journey right now. Thank *you* for pointing us toward a new and healthier direction—a Longevity Lifestyle."

THANK YOU

Pax and Pen left the office looking a great deal less irritated than when they'd arrived. It was a good start.

Turn the page to Chapter 26. The last chapter. Meet Debi, Dana, and Darla. Discover what the triplets asked their wellness coach to do for them.

Who you spend time with
is who you become.
Change your life by
consciously choosing to
surround yourself with
people with higher
standards.
—Tony Robbins

One, Two Three—Go!

Chapter 26

"Guess what, Coach? We wore name tags this time," said Debi, laughing. The triplets, Debi, Dana, and Darla, shrugged off their coats and, sure enough, each wore a gold-colored name tag.

"What a relief," said their wellness coach, chuckling. "I'd about given up trying to tell you three apart, especially when you dress alike and wear your hair in the same style. How did your parents know who was who and which was which?"

"We wore beaded name bracelets," said Dana. "Dad initially suggested wrist tattoos, joking that with three girls there weren't even any differing body parts to help tell one from the others. Our parents replaced the hospital name tags with beaded name bracelets—on both ankle and wrist in case one broke. Good thing we had short names!"

"We wanted to see you today for two reasons," said Darla. "First, to tell you we're taking a trip to Peru. At last! It's been on our bucket list for ages. We've always wanted to trek through Machu Picchu, and after two years of a Longevity Lifestyle we're finally healthy enough to go. It's so exciting!"

"That is exciting news! I have a big bucket list, myself. And a trip to Machu Picchu is on that list."

"And second," chimed in Debi, "would you be willing to give us a list of key points related to a Longevity Lifestyle?"

"We'd like to take them with us on the trip," said Dana, "and talk about them, keep them fresh in our minds, so to speak."

"You are wise women," said their coach. "I applaud you for recognizing the importance of reinforcing your strategies through regular review and repetition. That can be very helpful in maintaining a Longevity Lifestyle. I started compiling just such a list when I really got on board myself with a Longevity Lifestyle. The more I learned, the more key points I added to my list. Now there are over two dozen Nifty Nuggets, as I call them."

The coach handed each woman a sheet of paper on which were printed 25 Nifty Nuggets.

Debi, Dana, and Darla looked at the list.

"This is great," said Debi. "A treasure chest of Nifty Nuggets!"

"I think we should each take turns reading the Nifty Nugget aloud," said Darla. "Remember, Coach, you're the one who told us that reading aloud for 10 minutes a day was an anti-aging strategy. We've been taking turns reading aloud when we're on vacation—sometimes even when we're home. It's a gas. Stories sound different when you hear them read aloud."

"I've got a better idea," said Debi. "Well, at least it's another idea," she amended quickly, seeing one of Dana's eyebrows rise toward her hairline. "Let's all four of us read the Nifty Nuggets aloud together. Like a speech choir, sort of. You could use some more reading-aloud brain stimulation, couldn't you, Coach?"

Clearing their throats, the four began reading aloud in unison.

Nifty Nuggets

1. Everything starts and ends in the brain. Yours. Because every brain is unique, the Longevity Lifestyle you create will also be unique. It needs to fit you. This makes it easier to maintain for your lifetime. Join *Club 122 Longevity* and become a lifetime member. Talk the talk and walk and walk.

2. Pack a *PAC Mindset* (Positive, Active, and Creative) and take it with you everywhere. As Mark Twain put it, the secret of getting ahead is getting started. The secret of getting started is breaking your complex overwhelming tasks into small manageable tasks, and starting on the first one Then keep on keeping on.

3. Mindset is key. Both a negative mindset and a positive mindset are self-fulfilling. If you think you can or you think you can't, you are right! Embrace an affirming mindset that says: *You are doing this.* Weight management is less about food and more about mindset—what happens in your brain.

4. Self-talk follows mindset. Stop talking about what you want to avoid or give up and talk instead about what you are doing as if it's a done deal. Use a positive communication style that helps program your brain for success. What you tell yourself makes all the difference in the world.

5. Recognize when your brain and body *need* food and eat when your body is physiologically hungry. Drink water to stay well hydrated. Avoid using food and beverages to self-medicate due to unmanaged emotions and feelings. Develop sound strategies for managing your emotions and feelings effectively without bingeing on comfort foods. Eat a good breakfast, a moderate lunch, and a small dinner. Experiment with two meals a day on the weekends.

6. All human beings self-medicate to feel better. Identify your patterns of self-medication, (e.g., food, beverages, and addictive behaviors). If they are not resulting in desirable outcomes, create new replacement behaviors and use willpower to implement them, one at a time. Be vigilant and keep your life in balance.

7. Get moving and keep moving. Avoid *death by sitting.* Exercise is vital to both brain and body health and plays a role in retarding the onset symptoms of aging. Stay active at every age. Doing something is far better than doing nothing and you can do something. Set challenging and realistic low-high range goals; and follow through on them. Aim for 30 minutes of physical exercise at least 5 days per week.

8. Physical exercise helps to *boot up* your brain. Include variety: aerobic, strengthening, stretching, and balance exercises. Avoid over-exercising in an attempt to get a high from the natural endorphins that are released during exercise. Develop a balanced program. Physical exercise is the single most powerful tool you have to optimize your brain function.

9. Healthy carbs provide energy for body, brain, and nervous system. Minimize ingesting empty calories, (e.g., sugar, refined or highly processed foods, sodas, and alcohol). Eat a variety of foods in as natural a state as possible. Balance the calories you take in against those you expend—but focus on a Longevity Lifestyle rather than on compulsively counting calories.

10. Select nutritious foods—in as natural a state as possible. Eat at regular times when you are physiologically hungry, and make your meals a pleasant experience. Take your time, chew your food well, and savor it. If you are in a rush or in the midst of a stressful situation, drink a glass of water and wait to eat until things are calmer. Or simply eat very lightly.

11. Avoid overeating, especially of poor quality foods such as high fat, high sugar, and refined processed foods—which can trigger hormonal imbalances and increase your risk of insulin resistance, visceral fat accumulation, and type 2 diabetes. Increase your intake of fiber (soluble and insoluble) preferably from whole, intact foods.

12. Avoid all trans fats and minimize the use of saturated animal fats. Select monounsaturated and polyunsaturated fats primarily from plant sources—but in moderation, as they are still calorie dense at 9 calories per gram. Use vegetable oils extracted without the use of heat and solvents. Develop positive self-talk patterns to help manage cravings for the unhealthy foods and beverages that are no longer part of your life.

13. Appropriate physical activity and exercise are key to lowering your risk for stroke, heart disease, and type 2 diabetes—and improving your brain function. Focus on lifestyle rather than weight loss. Select foods that are low on the Glycemic Index and that have a low Glycemic Load.

14. Stop thinking *deprivation.* Instead, picture the nutritious food that you now ingest to energize both your brain and body. All calories are not created equal. Select quality calories in fresh fruits, vegetables, grains, seeds, and raw or roasted unsalted nuts. Avoid eating empty calories in the form of refined and processed foods. Slow and steady wins.

15. Manage portion size—which impacts person size—and avoid being killed by sugary, fatty, fried, refined, and processed foods. Ditch the candy dish, fried chips/crackers, and sodas. Remove anything from your home, office, or car that might sabotage your success. Keep only what you have chosen to eat and drink. Think: *out of sight is out of mind.* Rather than living to eat, learn to eat to live. It's a personal choice. Yours.

16. Emotions are powerful. Learn to identify them quickly and accurately and obtain the information they provide. Choose carefully the feelings you want to maintain. Raise your Emotional Intelligence as it can contribute 80 percent or more to your success in life—IQ only 20 percent. A higher EQ also may help you to be more patient and able to delay gratification as needed.

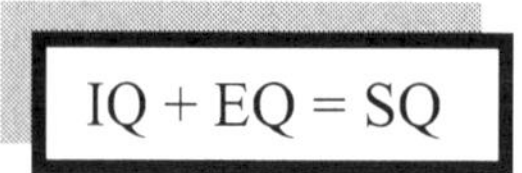

17. Have at least two strategies at the ready to help *upshift* your brain as needed. Avoid unnecessary downshifting by managing your thoughts. If you do downshift, upshift as soon as you determine there is no imminent danger or that it has passed. Develop *skillpower* to help you make healthier choices and then activate *willpower* to help you follow through.

18. Your body energy is closely connected with your thoughts and internal mental pictures. Affirming thoughts and feelings add energy to your system, while negative thoughts and feelings deplete your energy. Develop a growth mindset along with a positive style of thinking and speaking.

19. Use regular physical exercise to help maintain an optimum weight. Prevent or resolve morbid obesity—it's lethal for brain function! Eat foods that contain soluble and insoluble fiber (a type of carb) to combat intestinal problems. Be aware that bowel symptoms may be due to FODMAPs more than to gluten. Include regular brain exercises, too, because everything starts and ends in the brain.

20. An appropriate sodium-potassium ratio may reduce the incidence of sodium-related health problems such as increases in blood pressure. Be prudent about your use of salt and make sure to include foods that are a good source of potassium. Read labels regularly, even if you need to carry a magnifying glass. You may be amazed at what you can learn—and avoid!

21. Avoid sodas of any type: regular as well as diet. Both have been linked with obesity. Make pure water your beverage of choice and drink sufficient amounts every day to minimize dehydration, which can be lethal to cognitive brain function. Stop being a *pee brain.* Give yourself *gold stars*—metaphorically if not literally—to encourage your brain. Reward yourself in healthy ways for improved behaviors.

22. Metaphorically, pull your head out of the sand and recognize that hauling around excess fat can be dangerous and potentially deadly. Lack of sleep is linked with weight gain. Sleep is essential to mood, memory, creativity, immune function, cognitive performance, and weight management—and is an important determinant in longevity.

23. There is a relationship between stress and aging—the faster you rev up your body with stress, the faster you age. Develop effective stress-management strategies. Important for every brain, they're especially critical for the female brain because of how it responds to stressors. Live the 20:80 Rule every day.

24. Identify unhelpful myths related to wellness and aging. Think ahead. *Forewarned is forearmed.* You tend to meet challenges more successfully when you have identified potential problem. Change your life for the better by consciously hanging out with people who are also on a Longevity Lifestyle journey.

25. Choose to forgive—yourself as well as others. *Learn from your mistakes and move on gracefully.* Practice grateful thinking on a daily basis and reap emotional, physical, mental, and interpersonal benefits. Keep a gratitude journal. Consider doing random acts of kindness. Hone your personal spirituality—it impacts how you care for your brain and body and how you relate to others and to the planet.

"What a great set of Nifty Nuggets," said Debi, as they finished reading the list. "You know, when I started a Longevity Lifestyle, I thought it would involve depriving myself of things I liked to eat. Now I know that weight management is less about food and more about what happens in my brain. I'm developing a growth mindset and practicing affirming, positive, can-do self-talk."

Dana nodded. "I've been using the 20:80 Rule. It's a great stress-management strategy for me. I've found it to be amazing, actually, like *reframing* a painting and seeing how different it looks."

"I've been doing family-of-origin work and identifying the *script* I was handed at birth. It's been helpful and more fun than I expected," added Darla. "Talking with family members definitely has been worthwhile. I actually feel closer now to some of them."

Their coach nodded. "Adlai Stevenson believed that we can chart our future clearly and wisely only when we know the path that has led to the present. Sir Winston Churchill once quipped that *the further backward you look, the further forward you can see.* Everyone absorbs family patterns of behavior. In a sense, your ancestors are within you in the form of cellular memories stored in the cell nucleus—from perhaps three or four generations back in your biological line. These memories can influence your choices, preferences, and behaviors. Nevertheless, while cellular memories can push you toward specific types of behaviors, you choose whether or not to act upon those urges."

"Learning to identify when I am physiologically hungry versus thirsty or emotionally upset has been huge for me," said Debi. "Keeping a food journal help me to identify my negative eating patterns has assisted me in reducing my penchant for emotional eating."

"I've been working with my brain about my sugar cravings," said Darla. "The Longevity Lifestyle strategies have helped me pretty much eliminate many of them. I won't go so far as to say it was easy, but I will say you were right: first and foremost it's about mindset."

"Think of cravings as your brain demanding a reward," said their coach, "something that made you feel better in the past. Acknowledge the craving and avoid thinking deprivation, which typically leads to bingeing. Instead, use positive self-talk, skillpower, and willpower to follow through on your healthier replacement behaviors. Let the principles of a Longevity Lifestyle settle into your brain. Turn the information you learn into knowledge, then practically apply it wisely to identify, select, and maintain healthier options."

"One thing that turned my life around," said Dana, "was deciding to get enough sleep—and then actually doing it." She laughed. "It wasn't as hard as I thought it would be once I made the decision."

"Sleep can make more difference than many people realize," their coach agreed. "Each period of exhaustion is followed by a corresponding period of depression, which can challenge you at your weakest point and sabotage your Longevity Lifestyle. Exhaustion is associated with decreased levels of serotonin.

"No surprise, the way you perceive your brain and body will impact the way you care for them. Some perceive that their brains and bodies are leased to them for use on this planet, and they care for them much as they would a leased high-end vehicle. Others picture their brain and body as a temple of inestimable value, viewing themselves as both caretaker and guardian. Those individuals will likely care for their living edifice, their leased humanity, much differently from those who live for the moment with little thought for the future."

"You mentioned the need to be flexible," said Debi, "especially when we travel—and we plan to travel as much as we can for as long as we can."

"In a storm, the bendable trees often are the ones that survive. When you can't follow the program exactly as you have crafted it, figure out how to do part of it even if in a slightly different style or manner. Hone your ability to be flexible. Doing something is far better than doing nothing!

"Trying to do too many things at once can derail even the most dedicated brain. Build your skills at a slow and steady pace. If one strategy isn't effective, select another. There are endless ways to spin the bottle. Be creative in figuring out what works for your brain, what is realistic, and what you will sustain. In the final analysis it is you and your brain working together that results in success. Others have done this. So can you."

"I know, said Dana. "It all starts in the brain. Mine!" The triplets laughed.

"Generally, those who have a good support system are healthier and live longer than those who don't. Be careful about who you spend time with. Your choices can enhance or sabotage your success. Avoid abusing your own brain and body and refuse to accept abusive behaviors from anyone else. If you find yourself in an abusive situation, seek help to protect yourself. Be willing to leave the abusive environment, if necessary."

"Thanks, Coach," said Debi. "We're our own best support system, although we also have a group of wonderful friends. And, by the way, we have reduced the amount of time we are spending with several acquaintances. That alone has made a positive contribution to our being successful."

"We'll check in with you when we're back from our trip," said Darla. "Too bad you aren't coming along. We'd have a blast!"

Bucket List

"I'm sure we would. You three are a blast yourselves, to say nothing of the destination. As I said, Machu Picchu is on my bucket list. One of these times it'll happen. Meanwhile," said their coach, "I'll be looking forward to hearing about your experiences."

Debi, Dana, and Darla left the office with their coach's final words in their minds:

"Expect challenges. Everyone has some. They may resemble some of the myths, unhelpful mindsets, and traps you have already identified or may be a variation on one or more. They might even represent something quite different. Nevertheless, the basic principles of a Longevity Lifestyle apply. Make them work for you. The secret of getting ahead is getting started. Once you have started, keep on keeping on, one step at a time. In the words of Christopher Robin to Pooh, in Alan Alexander Milne's *Winnie-the-Pooh:* 'you're braver than you believe, and stronger than you seem, and smarter than you think.'"

Happy travels on *your* Longevity Lifestyle journey.

Or, as they say in Peru, *que tengas buen viaje!*

You can escape from a trap
only when you recognize
and acknowledge that
you're in one—and choose
to take the steps that are
necessary to free yourself.
—Old Proverb

Appendix

Longevity Lifestyle Components

Develop a positive mindset. It provides the direction for your Longevity Lifestyle. Maximize a can-do attitude. If you have an *enemy outpost* of negativity inside your brain, get rid of it. Avoid worry and anxiety. They can trigger the stress response.

Take responsibility for your self-talk. Tell your brain what you are doing as if it's a done deal and stop talking about what you don't want to have happen. Avoid using words such as *don't* and *can't* and *shouldn't.* Remember that you tend to communicate with others in the way you talk to yourself.

Get optimum amounts of sleep for your brain. Take a 15-minute nap during the day if you missed sleep the night before. Sleep deprivation can negatively impact you and your life by draining your energy, accelerating aging, suppressing both brain and immune system functions, and triggering weight gain.

Stay well hydrated. Dehydration is deadly. It can increase the production of free radicals, which can wrinkle your internal organs much like they wrinkle your skin. Many eat when they are actually thirsty. Learn to tell the difference between genuine physiological hunger and thirst. Generally drink enough pure water to have one or two pale urines per day. Drink a glass of water 15-30 minutes before you eat.

Protect your brain. Avoid trauma in every way possible (e.g., avoid pugilistic sports, arrange your environment to prevent falls, wear a helmet when bike-riding and for other sports activities such as skiing and skate-boarding). If you smoke, stop; if you don't smoke, never start and do what you can to avoid inhaling *side-smoke*. Avoid excessive radiation, toxins and poisons, vehicle exhaust, air pollution, and infections insofar as it is possible to do so. Protect your brain mentally, too. Be careful what you put into it. You only have one brain and neurons do not multiple and divide and replace themselves as do most other body cells. Take care of them!

Get moving. Minimize *sitting* and maximize physical activity. Aim to exercise for thirty minutes each a day, in sections of 10 or 15 minutes, if you prefer. Physical activity and exercise help tone your body and promote balance (homeostasis). Include a combination of stretching, aerobic, balance, and flexibility exercises. Variety is key to keep your brain interested and motivated. Select activities you enjoy and have fun doing them by yourself or with others.

A healthy body without a healthy brain is less than half the picture. Engage in a minimum of 30 minutes a day of active, challenging, mental activities. Include a variety of brain aerobic exercises to keep your mind interested and alert. Read aloud for 10 minutes every day—to yourself, your pet, or others. Minimize *passive* mental activities such as zoning out in front of the TV and maximize active mental picturing. Listen to books on tape. Play games, travel (locally or abroad) to expose your brain to new sights, sounds, smells, and environments. Include music in your life and favorite hobbies. Hone your creativity in any way that works for you.

Obtain moderate exposure to natural light. Flood your home with sunlight but minimize direct exposure to bright sun. Avoid sunburn, tanning parlors, and ultraviolet light as they can increase your risk for skin cancer and are believed to suppress immune system function. When in natural sunlight, consider wearing dark glasses consistently to lower the risk of macular degeneration, especially during the bright portions of the day.

Emphasize a Mediterranean cuisine. Read labels carefully. Lean toward plant-based unrefined and unprocessed foods. Eat when you are physiologically hungry. Minimize *empty* calories and maximize *nutritious* calories. Minimize *chew-less* foods and maximize *chewy* environment. When you choose dessert, take two or three bites only. After a couple bites you're eating from memory anyway; taste-bud intensity falls quickly when eating bites of the same food so rotate bites of what you eat.

The brain loves variety. As the old saying goes: *a change can be as good as a rest.* Schedule regular opportunities for play, relaxation, and fun. Hone your sense of humor. Figure out what tickles your funny bone and make time for it. Laugh mirthfully a minimum of thirty times per day. Very happy people reportedly laugh between 100 and 400 times a day—and they tend to be healthier and often very long lived. Be serious about life but avoid taking every little thing too seriously. Life is relatively short (a potential 122 years against eons). Make your life count and have fun in the process.

Choose your friends carefully. Your network of social connections is more predictive of obesity than the presence of genes associated with being overweight. Studies estimate that within a space of three years you are at higher risk for exhibiting the habit patterns of those with whom you hang out, especially for obesity, smoking, and happiness, to name just three. On the flip side, hanging out with people who embrace a Longevity Lifestyle can increase your likelihood of success.

Manage stressors effectively. Unmanaged stress pours out stress hormones, including cortisol and adrenalin, which can kill brain cells (contributing to dementia), accelerate aging, suppress immune system and brain functions, and trigger eating outside of nutritional balance. Engage in family-of-origin work to identify common patterns and habits that may be impacting your behaviors now. Live the 20:80 Rule: Only 20 percent of the negative impact to your brain and body is due to the event or situation itself; 80 percent is due to your perception of the event and the weight you give to it.

Learn to identify core emotions quickly and accurately, recognizing the information they bring from your subconscious to your conscious mind. Learn to manage them effectively. Choose the feelings you want to maintain over time. Since feelings follow thoughts, change your thoughts to change your feelings. Minimize *emotional* eating as a crutch to feel better. Avoid denial about addictive-like behaviors. Remember that the biggest 'cure' for one addictive behavior is another addictive behavior. Get help to create new, healthier habit patterns, as needed. Raise your level of Emotional Intelligence or EQ. Estimates are that IQ contributes only 20 percent to your overall success in life while EQ contributes at least 80 percent. Do the math!

Hone your own personal spirituality and life vision. Do something every day that evokes a sense of awe in your brain and your spirit. Be grateful. Gratitude has been shown to help delay gratification. Assist others, volunteer, give back to the community, and do random acts of kindness on a regular basis. Interact with selected individuals who have positive mindset and self-talk patterns, have a good sense of humor, are smart, supportive, and are following a Longevity Lifestyle.

Mediterranean Way

Multiple studies tout the benefits of the *Mediterranean Way*—at least the traditional cuisine and way of life. Key components of the Mediterranean Way fit quite well with a Longevity Lifestyle.

Following are some key components.

1. Make physical activity (movement) part of your normal day. Physical activity is defined as any bodily movement produced by the skeletal muscles that results in caloric expenditures. Exercise is considered a subcategory of physical activity that results in improvement of one or more facets of physical fitness.

2. Slow down and take pleasure in what you are doing. An attitude that focuses on the healthy pleasures of life rather than being overly or rigidly concerned about what is "good for me" provides more health benefits. It's all in the attitude.

3. Engage regularly in social interaction. Carve out some personal time for relaxation and reflection, but social interaction is beneficial, as well. Be sure to schedule opportunities to talk and laugh with others, share discussions about life and living, and engage in interesting and enjoyable activities together.

4. The basics of Mediterranean cuisine include:

    - Vegetables: colorful variety, fresh or frozen

- Legumes: lentils, peas, and beans
- Fruits: colorful variety, fresh or frozen
- Nuts: a dozen or so including walnuts every day (preferably raw or dry roasted without oil or salt)
- Cereals: if they are whole grain and as unprocessed as possible
- Breads: try sourdough instead of commercial-yeast breads
- Olive oil: use light for cooking and extra virgin for salad dressings
- Avocado: use in moderation in place of mayonnaise and cheese in sandwiches, casseroles, or tacos
- Water: make it your basic beverage
- Wine: if you choose to use alcohol, make it red and practice informed moderation
- Dairy: use sparingly and make it non-fat or low-fat. According to Richard W. Hubbard, PhD, a Loma Linda University protein researcher, "Milk is just liquid meat."
- Meat, fowl, and fish: less is more so use as condiments rather than as a main dish. Move toward plant-based proteins to reduce your risk of mercury poisoning, exposure to arsenic-laced products, and disease-causing organisms.

Studies have shown that a greater adherence to traditional Mediterranean cuisine is associated with a significant reduction in total mortality. (See Selected Bibliography)

Shopping and Eating Reminders

Use this as a guide when shopping for items that align with your Longevity Lifestyle.

Additives

AVOID food additives whenever possible; foods containing artificial colors, flavors, and/or preservatives; foods that have been sprayed with insecticides.

Beverages

AVOID artificially flavored, colored, sweetened or diet drinks, and non-dairy creamers

Use pure water. Minimize use of canned fruit and vegetable juices (eat the whole fruit and vegetable). Minimize use of caffeinated beverages and alcohol (go easy and choose red).

Chips

AVOID deep-fried anything such as fried corn or potato chips.

Select baked chips containing vegetables, nuts, and whole grains, free from hydrogenated oils and trans fats.

Dairy

AVOID butter; ice cream and toppings; colored cheeses.

If using dairy products, select non-fat or low-fat products.

Eggs

AVOID egg yolks and fried egg products.

If using, poach, boil, or bake egg whites. Use egg substitutes when available and appropriate.

Fats

AVOID shortening, lard; all hydrogenated and partially hydrogenated oils and fats, margarines, and trans fats.

Use healthier fats sparingly (e.g., cold-pressed virgin olive, coconut oil); spray-on forms for stir-frying; and reduce amounts in cooking and baking).

Fish

AVOID deep-fried fish or sea food.

Use sparingly (e.g., fresh white-fleshed fish; broiled or baked) to reduce exposure to mercury.

Fowl

AVOID all deep-fried fowl.

Use sparingly as fowl may be more dangerous than red meat in some areas. Bake, boil, or broil and remove skin prior to eating.

Fruit

AVOID canned and sweetened fruit.

Use fresh or frozen, (preferably unsweetened), stewed, dried (preferably unsulfured).

Grains

AVOID refined white-flour products, white rice, and other highly processed foods; crackers and snack foods with hydrogenated fats; most ready-to-eat cereals due to high sugar content (make healthy granola).

Use whole grains. Select unsweetened minimally processed cereals (e.g., old fashioned and steel cut oats); whole seeds (e.g., sesame, chia, hemp, flax, teff, and sunflower); baked vegetable-grain crackers or chips free of trans fat and hydrogenated oils. Minimize use of wheat and corn products.

Legumes

AVOID refried beans containing lard or high concentrations of other fats.

Use all types of legumes cooked in water with minimum amounts of salt. If using canned beans, make sure to rinse well and drain to remove excess sodium.

Meats

AVOID fatty cuts, especially of red meat products.

Less is more. If red meat is used, select lean cuts and use as a condiment rather than as a large main dish. Move toward plant-based proteins to reduce your potential exposure to arsenic-laced products and disease-causing organisms.

Nuts

AVOID nuts roasted with oil and salt.

Use a variety of raw or dry roasted (unsalted) nuts.

Seasonings

AVOID excessive use of very hot spices.

Use all types of herbs (e.g., garlic, onion, rosemary, parsley, cinnamon, marjoram, cayenne, dill, curry). Experiment.

Snacks

AVOID snacks with a high Glycemic Index or Glycemic Load.

Choose healthy snacks with a low Glycemic Index or Glycemic Load (e.g., celery, jicama, carrot sticks, fresh fruit) when you choose to have a snack.

Soups

AVOID canned or dairy-cream soups; commercial bouillon; fat stock.

Use soups and stews made fresh. Season with herbs.

Sugar

AVOID refined sugars; high fructose corn syrup; regular prepared syrups; milk chocolate; candy; artificial sweeteners.

Use sparingly pure unfiltered honey, unsulfured molasses; pure maple syrup; and dark chocolate in moderation.

Vegetables

AVOID deep-fried vegetables.

Use raw, fresh, and frozen (avoid overcooking); baked or boiled sweet potatoes, yams, squash; steamed veggies.

♥ 12 Steps of a Longevity Lifestyle

1. I acknowledge that I developed some unhelpful habits that have resulted in a variety of undesirable outcomes. As such, my life has become unmanageable and my health is suffering. I experience difficulty in selecting nutritious foods and in maintaining an optimum weight. I tend to overeat and be too sedentary, all of which have increased my risk for illness, disease, and dementia, and have even placed my potential longevity at risk.

2. I believe that a Higher Power (as I understand a Higher Power) can place resources in my path to help me create, implement, and maintain a Longevity Lifestyle successfully. I know that it is my responsibility to embrace these resources and use them to increase my knowledge, insight, creativity, and determination. I understand that while others can support and encourage me, I am responsible for thoughts I maintain, feelings I hang onto, actions I take, and behaviors I choose to exhibit.

3. I ask for clarity of vision as I embark on this journey to select and implement healthier behaviors, for wisdom to make positive choices, and to use willpower appropriately as I follow through on the healthier replacement behaviors I have selected. I realize there are no quick fixes or instant solutions and that slow and steady wins this type of race. I am becoming more patient. When I make a mistake because I am human, I acknowledge it, learn from it, and get right back on track.

4. I am entirely ready to develop and implement a Longevity Lifestyle that includes healthier replacement behaviors (even though some of my old unhealthy behaviors helped me feel better for short periods of time because they triggered my brain's reward system and altered neurotransmitter and hormone ratios). I have a growth mindset, a can-do attitude, and practice positive self-talk. I speak affirmingly to myself using the second person *you*, and upshift quickly when I recognize my brain has downshifted.

5. I am open to increased understanding and to opportunities as they present themselves. Rather than wasting time pounding my head on closed doors or giving up and returning to unhealthy habits, I look for the doors that are open and grasp those opportunities. I understand the difference between *simple* and *easy*, knowing that a Longevity Lifestyle is relatively simple although not always easy to implement and maintain. I have removed foods, beverages, snacks, and anything else from my environment that would make it *easier* for me to slip back into old habits.

6. I take personal responsibility for my behaviors and for my contribution to situations of conflict and misunderstanding—especially those that involve jumping to conclusions, taking things personally, or overreacting. I refrain from wasting time and energy in blaming myself or others, knowing most people do the best they can at the time with what they know, myself included. Honing my spirituality and an ability to experience a sense of awe has helped me respond with kindness to myself and others, while my boundaries help protect me as needed.

7. I engage in family-of-origin work to identify both genetic and epigenetic factors that have contributed to my unhealthy lifestyle. I also recognize and gratefully acknowledge the helpful patterns that came to me through my generational inheritance. I am reworking the script that was handed to me at birth so it better matches me and my Longevity Lifestyle. I am proactive in recognizing myths, negative mindsets, and traps—in a timely manner—that in the past could and would have derailed me from my chosen path.

8. Although I am cognizant both of the past and my specific plans for the future, I strive to live in the present moment, gradually increasing mindful awareness of my thought patterns, choices, and emotions and feelings, and am committed to utilizing them appropriately. I take time for myself to reflect on my journey, identifying what is working well and what I need to restructure in order to help me be more successful. I practice *healthy selfishness* and take good care of myself.

9. I am making a list of individuals I have harmed (including myself) because of unhealthy habits. When possible, I am making amends, except when to do so would be injurious and unhelpful. I regularly interact with a group of supportive individuals, believing that social interactions can help in maintaining a Longevity Lifestyle. I am increasing my level of Emotional Intelligence. I practice gratitude on a daily basis, knowing that fear and gratitude cannot simultaneously co-exist in my brain. I understand that an attitude of gratitude helps me to delay gratification and makes it easier for my brain and body to function in balance. I select carefully the people with whom I spend the time, knowing that close association increases the risk of picking up their habits.

10. I practice vigilance on a daily basis, taking personal inventory of my choices and behaviors, evaluating their outcomes as either undesirable or positive and desirable. I promptly admit when I have made a mistake and immediately take steps to course correct. I smile and laugh often, being serious about life but purposing to avoid taking its vagaries too seriously. This helps me manage stressors more effectively, especially as I concentrate on the 80 percent of the 20:80 Rule.

11. I seek through contemplative meditation or prayer (a form of meditation) to improve my conscious awareness, to gain wisdom and energy, and to make healthier choices. I choose to adopt the recommendations of a Longevity Lifestyle, selecting options and alternatives that work for my brain and body. I am grateful for the opportunity to embrace graceful aging (many others have not had that opportunity). My attitude is more positive and I no longer fear the aging process, knowing that 70 percent of how long and how well I live is in my hands.

12. I share my experience with others as appropriate, encouraging them in their quest for health and longevity, even as I consistently practice and exhibit these principles in my life on a daily basis. I realize that as my brain and body improve, role-modeling is the most effective way to pass along what I am learning. I enjoy and am grateful for this new way of thinking. I rejoice as I experience improvements in my mental, emotional, physical, and spiritual health. I am feeling better, looking better, and thinking more clearly. Life is good.

Based loosely on *The 12 Steps of Alcoholics Anonymous*

Obesity Pandemic

The word *epidemic* typically describes a condition in which contagious diseases spread rapidly among many people. Data from the 2011-2012 National Health and Nutrition Examination Survey [NHANES] revealed that a whopping 68.5 percent of Americans were overweight and 34.9 percent were obese. Obesity is now being called a *disease.* That meets part of the definition of an epidemic, but is obesity contagious?

Apparently so. Tanzi and Chopra in *Super Brain* point out that in the social network of family, coworkers, and friends, simply relating to someone with a weight problem makes it more likely that you'll have one. Data collected by social scientists have shown that if one person becomes obese, the likelihood of a friend following suit increases by 57 percent. If a sibling becomes obese, the chance that another sibling will become obese increases by 40 percent. An obese spouse increases the likelihood that the other spouse will become obese by 37 percent. And so on.

Enters the word *pandemic,* from the Greek *pandemos,* meaning that it pertains to all people. National epidemics of obesity have joined forces and have become *pandemic*, sweeping the globe.

Data released by the Central Intelligence Agency's World Fact Book (July, 2013) listed the top fifty countries with high rates of obesity. Those with the most serious obesity rates were identified as being located in the South Pacific. American Samoa, for example, where 74.6 percent of the residents are obese. Among the world's largest countries, the most obese country in the Western Hemisphere is Mexico (Estados Unidos Mexicanos), with an obesity rate of 32.8 percent. It recently surpassed the United States of America, which has an obesity rate of 31.8 to 34.9 percent, depending on the source of the statistics.

Obesity is linked with more than 50 diseases—50!—including type 2 diabetes, heart disease, some forms of cancer, and dementia. According to the American Diabetes Association, a person is diagnosed with diabetes every 20 seconds in the USA, most with type 2 diabetes. If people continue to gain weight and remain inactive, estimates are that within 30-40 years 1 in 3 Americans will have some form of diabetes, a terrifying statistic for patients as well as healthcare professionals and health systems.

Obesity often begins with a slow, almost imperceptible weight-creep. A few ounces here, a pound there. Insidious, to say the least. On average, people tend to gain about a pound between mid-November and mid-January from ingesting more calories than they used. *But it's only a pound!* Right. But many hang onto that pound for dear life. Tenaciously. In 10 years these individuals can be 10 pounds heavier just from packing on a pound per year. And if they repeat that gain for anniversary and birthday celebrations, weight-creep can move up to a steady weight-crawl.

This obesity pandemic may be less an accident and more the result of careful marketing. Data published by the Euromonitor from the Global Market Information Database (2002) estimate that Americans consume close to 50 billion liters of soda per year. Sodas have beaten out commercial white bread as the number one source of calories contributing to weight gain. Watch almost any sports event on television and count the ads for beverages.

There are other contributors, as well. Nancy Appleton, PhD, in *Lick the Sugar Habit,* points out that the average American consumes 20 pounds of artificial sweeteners per year, which can actually increase one's appetite by stimulating the salivary glands, thus defeating their original purpose. According to Julia Ross, MA, in *The Diet Cure,* artificial sweeteners can contribute to compulsive eating, an increased craving for sweets and fatty foods, and an increase in weight. Ingredients in Aspartame reportedly compete with Tryptophan and can block its conversion into serotonin, while saccharin can cause an increase in overall consumption of sweets.

There is trend toward getting less physical activity. Dr. Edward Archer and colleagues examined 45-year trends in time use and physical activity energy expenditures in a nationally representative sample of mothers in the USA. The results, published in the Mayo Clinic Proceedings, 2013, showed that household chores in 1965 consumed nearly 28 hours per week. In 2010, this had fallen to 13 hours, resulting in a reduction of approximately 360 calories expended per day. At the same time, hours spent watching television and using other electronic devices doubled in that time period, going from 8 hours per week in 1965 to 17 hours per week in 2010. This has resulted in a further reduction of daily calories expended.

Similar changes have been observed in the workplace. A 2011 study by Timothy S. Church and colleagues entitled "Trends over Five Decades in U.S. Occupation-Related Physical Activity and Their Associations with Obesity" estimated that since 1960 the mean daily energy expenditure due to work-related physical activity has dropped by more than 100 calories per day in both men and women. A more sedentary lifestyle appears to have impacted weight gains around the world.

How is the obesity pandemic viewed by big business? As an opportunity. The word on the street is that with 7 billion pounds of *overweight* in the U.S., entrepreneurs see a new market and are going creative. Longer needles are needed to go through more adipose tissue. New toilet seats will have to support weights of up to 1,200 pounds and shower sizes increased. Bed frames may have to be reinforced, dining and lounge chairs strengthened; car and airplane seats expanded. And so on. In addition to an intake of high-fat foods and high caloric beverages, experts credit sedentary lifestyles for an increase in obesity. Only 20 percent of adults in America participate in regular aerobic and muscle-building exercise. The typical obese female gets an average of 1 hour of vigorous exercise per year; while obese males, an average of 4 hours. Not nearly enough to realize the benefits of exercise.

Participants in a recent seminar on how to create and implement a Longevity Lifestyle, expressed many reasons for making conscious decisions to take back their lives and health. For example:

- I want to look and feel good, think clearly, and avoid chronic illness and dementia. I am unwilling to settle for fatigue, muddy thinking, weight problems, and chronic illness.

- I'd like to live a long life, but my family is riddled with diabetes, heart disease, and cancer. I understand that genetic factors do not equal inevitability, however, and that lifestyle plays about a 70-percent role. That's where I'm putting my time, money, and energy!

- I'm frightened of dementia. Most of my aunts are relatively uneducated about healthy living, markedly overweight, and already showing signs of mental decline. I want a healthier life, and I choose to do whatever it takes to make that happen.

Do these comments represent a cross-section of the general population? Yes. The difference is that these individuals are choosing to do something proactive about their hopes, fears, and health challenges, and do it for the rest of their lives. They are interested in creating and implementing a Longevity Lifestyle—and the physical, mental, emotional, spiritual, and social empowerment that comes from being happy, healthy, and successful. Plus, they want to role-model that.

Given a reasonable level of physical and mental health and sufficient financial resources, most people would like to live a long time—to see their grandchildren, nieces and nephews, and maybe even great-grandchildren grow up. They'd like peace of mind, knowing they've done their best, and that their efforts have resulted in a better life than otherwise expected. And, in the process, they have set the stage for their biological offspring to have similar opportunities.

What are the options for those who want to avoid becoming aligned with the obesity pandemic? Hands down, prevention is always better than cure. And those who already are pandemic statistics?

Clearly, the horse has left the barn, to quote an old saying. While prevention cannot undo the past, it can minimize replicating damage in the future and may even mitigate existing injury. The brain and body are quite resilient. It often takes months of mis-living before symptoms of imbalance show up in the form of illness and disease.

Likewise, steps taken today may result in improvements down the line—and sooner than you might think. Author Jean Carper in her book *Your Miracle Brain* indicates that ingesting proper nutrients can have an almost immediate impact on brain cells and brain functioning. So it *is* doable. Success involves identifying unhealthy (often automatic) habits and replacing them with healthier habits, which can then become automatic. It requires the practical application of strategies that have been shown to be effective, while avoiding those that have not. It demands daily vigilance along with a lifetime commitment.

In order to stop this obesity pandemic, each person–each brain and body—must become a committee of one and 'be the change' each would like to see in the world.

Your choices each day determine what outcomes happen in your life. It is choice, not chance, that will determine your life. An unstoppable life begins by taking responsibility for your choices.

—Thomas Narofsky

Authors and Resources

Everything begins in your brain. That includes your health. Use your brain to create and maintain a Longevity Lifestyle—because it matters.

—Sharlet M. Briggs

Sharlet M. Briggs, PhD, has been interested in brain function and its impact on communication and behaviors for over a quarter of a century. Emerging research from brain-imaging studies has opened a new window into organizational performance. She uses her expertise in community presentations, facilitating business groups, providing seminars and workshops, and counseling leaders.

Having been affiliated with healthcare for most of her career, she understands the challenges, roadblocks, and opportunities faced by business leaders in the challenging arena of healthcare.

Briggs has an earned Master's in Counseling and an earned doctorate in Christian Clinical Psychology.

Dr. Briggs holds the senior executive position of Chief Operating Officer for a large hospital affiliated with Adventist Health.

Passionate about the positive contributions that brain-function information can make when practically applied, Briggs speaks internationally.

A published author, books she has coauthored include:

- *Adventures of Aimi*
- *Adventures of Stella*
- *Age-Proofing Your Brain*
- *Age-Proofing Your Memory* (four versions)
- *Brain Secrets—of Successful Parenting*
- *Busting Your Brain's Bad Behaviors*
- *Longevity Lifestyle Matters* series

  Longevity Lifestyle Matters—Keeping Your Brain, Body, and Weight in the Game

  Longevity Lifestyle Matters—Companion Notebook

  Longevity Lifestyle—Facilitator Guide and Companion Notebook

Briggs and her husband, David O. Eastman, who has a background as a CIO for a healthcare network, make their home in California.

Authors and Resources

With appropriate motivation, education, practical application, and the right use of their brains, individuals may feel better, look better, think more clearly, and live healthier lives—longer.

—Steve Horton

Steve Horton, MPH, PhD Candidate, is enthusiastic about health and wellness, believing that a Longevity Lifestyle is not only possible but also can be effective and enjoyable. Even fun.

His goal is to provide educational resources in a stimulating, easy-to understand, and practical-to-apply format. When implemented as part of a life-time commitment, the information and strategies can help people in the community become more aware of simple lifestyle changes they can make to benefit their overall health, avoid preventable diseases, and reduce symptoms associated with chronic illnesses to the extent possible.

Horton has two earned Master's: a Masters of Divinity from Andrews University and a Master's in Public Health Education from Loma Linda University. Currently he is completing a doctoral program.

Horton is CEO of Pacific Health Education Center, headquartered in Bakersfield, California. PHEC alumni are located in fifty-four countries around the world. PHEC exists to promote health and prevent disease through education.

Their goal is to establish Centers of Health around the world that address the needs of people in the community. Currently, sister schools are located in Cuba and India.

As Vice Chair of the board for San Joaquin Community Hospital in Bakersfield, California, Horton is actively involved in community health, motivating and empowering people to self-correct.

He holds certification as a Disaster Relief Chaplain and has served as director for health and wellness programs in multiple venues. Horton regularly produces retreats and seminars related to health, wellness, personal growth, and family life worldwide.

His life is inspired by a personal desire to help heal lives, restore people to health, and prepare individuals to live at least 122 years.

Horton is a coauthor of the *Longevity Lifestyle Matters* series:

> *Longevity Lifestyle Matters—Keeping Your Brain, Body, and Weight in the Game*
>
> *Longevity Lifestyle Matters—Companion Notebook*
>
> *Longevity Lifestyle—Facilitator Guide and Companion Notebook*

Horton and his wife, Dr. Kimberly Horton, Chief Operating Officer for a large healthcare system, make their home in Northern California.

Authors and Resources

You only get one brain and one body to last your entire lifetime. Your health rarely improves by chance—it can improve by incremental positive change and your recommended preventive maintenance program is a Longevity Lifestyle.

—Arlene R. Taylor

Arlene R. Taylor, PhD, a leading speaker on brain function, is sometimes referred to as the *brain guru.* She specializes in simplifying this complex topic so individuals can more easily grasp and implement practical strategies that can help them thrive. A sought-after speaker, she presents seminars internationally.

Taylor is founder and president of Realizations Inc, a non-profit corporation that engages in brain function research and provides related educational resources. She has a Master's in Epidemiology and Health Education, and two earned doctorates.

Taylor has worked with health and wellness programs for decades, including the McDougall Program at the St. Helena Center for Health, the Smoke Free Life program, and multiple addiction recovery programs. She also has spoken at Cardiac Health Improvement Programs (CHIP), and for diverse programs related to weight-management, abuse, addiction, and recovery. Taylor believes your health is the best investment you can make. It can pay unbelievable dividends but there are no quick fixes. It is a life-long process—and it is doable.

A member of the National Speakers Association, Taylor is listed with the Professional Speakers Bureau International. She is a recipient of the *American Medal of Honor for Brain-Function Education*, #22 of 100, American Biographical Institute Inc, 2001.

Taylor's free quarterly online Brain Bulletin, provides current brain-function information, brain aerobic exercises, questions and answers, and other helpful resources. To receive SynapSez® sign up at the website. www.arlenetaylor.org

Books that Taylor has authored or coauthored include:

- *Adventures of Aimi*
- *Adventures of Stella*
- *Adventures of the Alabaster Owl*
- *Adventures of the Jungle Bully*
- *Adventures of the Littlest Dolphin*
- *Age-Proofing Your Brain*
- *Age-Proofing Your Memory* (four versions)
- *Back to Basics*
- *Beyond the House of Silence*
- *Brain Benders*
- *Brain Secrets—of Successful Parenting*
- *Your Brain Has a Bent (Not a Dent)*
- *Longevity Lifestyle Matters* series

Brain Blog

Follow Taylor's blog. Access it through her website www.arlenetaylor.org or via have it sent to you automatically or read it on Facebook at:

Arlene R. Taylor PhD Brain Function Specialist

Club 122 Longevity

Club 122 Longevity was named in honor of Jeanne Louise Calment, a French woman who was born 21 February 1875 in Arles, France, and died 4 August 1997—a lifespan of 122 years, 164 days. Her life demonstrates the old adage, *you'll get farther if you aim higher.*

Members of *Club 122 Longevity* are committed to aiming higher. Continually learning, they turn information into knowledge and then daily apply it to creating and maintaining a Longevity Lifestyle.

Everything starts and ends in the brain. All things being equal, the health and functionality of the brain impact the health and functionality of the body. Together, brain and body influence a person's weight, which in turn impact the brain and body organs. These three basic components—brain, body, and weight—continually influence each other. Portrayed as a simple shape of three lines and three points, the *Club 122 Longevity* logo illustrates this ongoing, three-way collaborative.

To add a bit of longevity trivia, it is recorded that the 'unflappable' Mrs. Calment, at age 85, took up fencing—offering one more creative way to *aim high!*

Join! Take advantage of information and resources available through Club 122 Longevity. Invite your family members and friends to join, too.

Club 122
LONGEVITY™

www.Club122Longevity.com

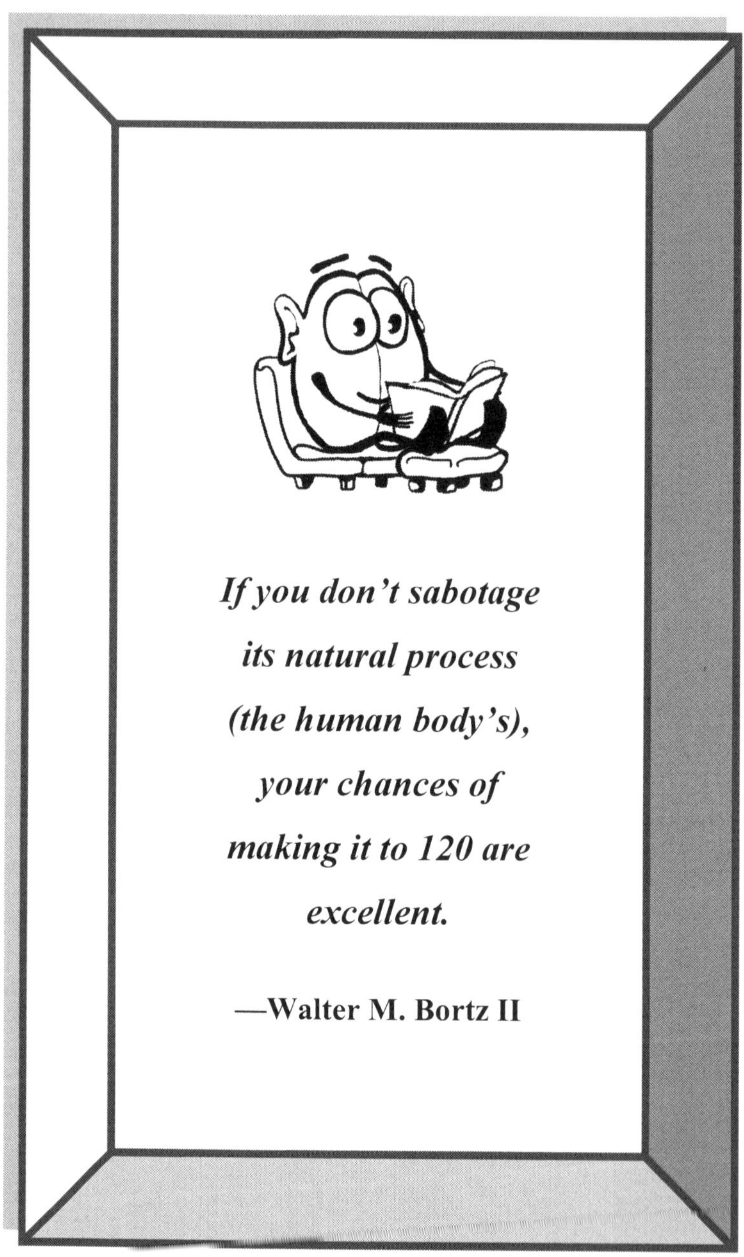

If you don't sabotage its natural process (the human body's), your chances of making it to 120 are excellent.

—Walter M. Bortz II

Selected Bibliography

Almonds and heart disease http://www.aston.ac.uk/about/news/releases/2014/june/research-show-almonds-reduce-risk-of-heart-disease/ (Accessed Oct '14)

Amen, Daniel G., MD. *Change Your Brain Change Your Life.* NY:Times Books, 1998.

Anderson, Sylvia. Editor, Insider Health. *New Study: High Fructose Corn Syrup Prompts Considerably More Weight Gain.* 2010.

Appleton, Nancy, PhD. *Lick the Sugar Habit*. NY:Avery Penguin Putnam, 1996.

Archer, Edward, PhD, et al. "Maternal Inactivity: 45-Year Trends in Mothers' Use of Time." http://www.mayoclinicproceedings.org/article/S0025-6196(13)00828-8/fulltext (Accessed Oct '14)

Avena, Nicole M., et al. "Sugar and Fat Bingeing Have Notable Differences in Addictive-like Behavior." *Journal of Nutrition*, March 2009, 139:623-628.

Bangasser, Debra, PhD, and Rita Valentino, PhD. "Stress Hormone Receptors Are Less Adaptive in the Female Brain." (Accessed 11 '14) http://www.nimh.nih.gov/science-news/2010/stress-hormone-receptors-less-adaptive-in-female-brain.shtml?WT.mc_id=twitter&sms_ss=email

Barnard, Neal D., MD. *Breaking the Food Seduction.* NY:St. Martin's Griffin, 2004.

Barnard, Neal D., MD. "Big Food About to Lose Its Biggest Defense: Food Really Is Addictive." http://pcrm.org/search/?cid=2111 (Accessed Oct '14)

Barnard, Neal D., MD. "Breaking the Food Seduction." http://www.pcrm.org/good-medicine/2003/summer/breaking-the-food-seduction (Accessed Oct '14)

Batmanghelikj, Fereydoon, MD. *Your Body's Many Cries for Water*, 3rd Edition. VA:Global Health Solutions, Inc.; 2008.

Batmanghelikj, Fereydoon, MD. *Water: For Health, for Healing, for Life: You're Not Sick, You're Thirsty!* NY:Grand Central Publishing, 2003.

Belly Fat and Health (Accessed Mar '15)

http://www.clinicaladvisor.com/are-testosterone-and-belly-fat-linked/article/314590/

Belly Fat may Cause Memory Loss | Medindia http://www.medindia.net/news/belly-fat-may-cause-memory-loss-126185-1.htm#ixzz36uxWRoER

http://www.rush.edu/rumc/page-1298331111509.html

Geopp, Julius, MD. "Low Testosterone Promotes Abdominal Obesity in Aging Men." http://www.lef.org/magazine/2010/10/Low-Testosterone-Promotes-Abdominal-Obesity-Aging-Men/Page-01

Benson, Herbert, MD., with Marg Stark. *Timeless Healing: the Power and Biology of Belief.* NY:Scribner, 1996.

Benson, Herbert, MD, and Miriam Z. Klipper. *The Relaxation Response.* NY:HarperTorch, 2000.

Blue Zone - Longevity Research (Accessed 12 '14)

http://en.wikipedia.org/wiki/Blue_Zone

http://www.bluezones.com/

Body Mass Index calculator www.club122longevity.com/tools/bmi

Boeckner, Linda, S. *Water: The Nutrient.* (Accessed Oct '14) http://www.ianrpubs.unl.edu/epublic/live/g918/build/

Bortz, Walter M. II. *We Live Too Short and Die Too Long.* NY:Select Books, 2007.

Bortz, Walter M., II. *Next Medicine.* UK:Oxford University Press, 2011.

Boston Sports Club. (Accessed Oct '14) "Use Shorter Workouts to Build Consistency." http://www.sparkpeople.com/resource/fitness_articles.asp?id=645

Brand-Miller, Jennie, PhD, et al. *The Low GI Shopper's Guide to GI Values 2014.* MA:Da Capo Lifelong Books, 2013.

Brand-Miller, Jennie, PhD, et al. *The New Glucose Revolution Low GI Guide to Losing Weight.* MA:Da Capo Lifelong Books, 2005.

Brynie, Faith Hickman. *101 Questions Your Brain Has Asked About Itself But Couldn't Answer, Until Now.* CT:Millbrook Press, 1998.

Campbell, T. Colon, PhD, with Thomas M. Campbell II. *The China Study—The Most Comprehensive Study of Nutrition Ever Conducted.* TX:BenBella Books, 2006.

Carbohydrates

Harvard School of Public Health Nutrition Source. Harvard School of Public Health. 29 Nov 2006.

USDA recommendations
http://www.cnpp.usda.gov/Publications/DietaryGuidelines/2010/DGAC/Report/D-5-Carbohydrates.pdf

Carder, Dave, M.A., et al. *Unlocking Your Family Patterns: Finding Freedom from a Hurtful Past.* IL:Moody Publishers, 2011.

Carper, Jean. *100 Simple Things You Can Do to Prevent Alzheimer's.* NY:Little, Brown and Company, 2010.

Cellular Memory (Epigenetics)
www.arlenetaylor.org - Brain References - Cellular Memory

Childre, Doc. *Freeze Frame*. CA:Planetary Publications, 1994, 1998.

Childre, Doc, and Howard Martin. *The HeartMath Solution.* CA: Harper SF, 1999.

Cholesterol (Accessed Oct '14)

Centers for Disease Control and Prevention
http://www.cdc.gov/cholesterol/

http://www.livestrong.com/article/29357-foods-containing-ldl-cholesterol/

http://www.dietaryfiberfood.com/cholesterol/cholesterol-high-avoid.php

Church, Timothy, S., et al. "Trends over 5 Decades in U.S. Occupation-Related Physical Activity and Their Associations with Obesity." (Accessed Oct '14) http://connection.ebscohost.com/c/articles/73816545/trends-over-5-decades-u-s-occupation-related-physical-activity-their-associations-obesity

Club 122 Longevity (Accessed Mar '15)

www.club122longevity.com

www.longevitylifestylematters.com

Daniel Plan. (Accessed Oct '14) http://www.ocregister.com/articles/brain-335531-plan-daniel.html

Deckersbach, Thilo, PhD, et al. Division of Neurotherapeutics, Harvard Medical School, Boston, MA. Sept 2014. "Pilot randomized trial demonstrating reversal of obesity-related abnormalities in reward system responsivity to food cues with a behavioral intervention." (Accessed Feb '15) http://www.nature.com/nutd/journal/v4/n9/full/nutd201426a.html

Dement, William C., MD, PhD, and Christopher Vaughan. *The Promise of Sleep: A Pioneer in Sleep Medicine Explores the Vital Connection Between Health, Happiness, and a Good Night's Sleep*. NY:Dell, 2000.

Department of Health and Human Services and United States Department of Agriculture. *Dietary Guidelines for Americans 2010,* 7th Edition. MD:U.S. Government, 2010. (Accessed Oct '14) http://health.gov/dietaryguidelines/dga2010/DietaryGuidelines2010.pdf

Diabetes Prevention. (Accessed Mar '15)

Harvard School of Public Health. "Simple Steps to Preventing Diabetes." *The Nutrition Source.* http://www.hsph.harvard.edu/nutritionsource/diabetes-full-story/

Diener, Edward,PhD, and Robert Biswas-Diener, PhD. *Happiness.* NJ:Wiley-Blackwell, 2008.

Dweck, Carol S., PhD. *Mindset: How we can learn to fulfill our potential.* NY:Ballentine Books, 2006.

Eagleman, David. *Incognito: The Secret Lives of the Brain.* NY:Pantheon Books, 2011.

Emmons, Robert A., PhD. *Gratitude Works! A 21-Day Program for Creating Emotional Prosperity*. NJ:Jossey-Bass, 2013

Emmons, Robert A., PhD. *Thanks! How the New Science of Gratitude Can Make You Happier.* NY:Mariner Books, 2008.

Emmons, Robert, and Michael McCullough. "Counting Blessings Versus Burdens: An Experimental Investigation of Gratitude and Subjective Well-Being in Daily Life." *Journal of Personality and Social Psychology* 84.2 (2003): 377–389.

Exercise, Physical Activity (Accessed Oct '14)

http://www.cdc.gov/physicalactivity/growingstronger/index.html?s_cid=tw_ob276

http://www.cdc.gov/physicalactivity/everyone/health/

Stay Fit. Aerobic Exercise. http://my.clevelandclinic.org/healthy_living/exercise/hic_aerobic_exercise.aspx

The Benefits of Physical Activity. http://www.hsph.harvard.edu/nutritionsource/staying-active-full-story/

Healthy Lifestyle Fitness

http://www.mayoclinic.org/healthy-living/fitness/in-depth/exercise/art-20048389?pg=2

Family-of-origin Work

www.arlenetaylor.org/mini-monographs.html

http://loveandlifetoolbox.com/what-is-family-of-origin-work/

http://www.foryourmarriage.org/dating-engaged/marriage-readiness/family-of-origin/

Fats – Centers for Disease Control and Prevention (Accessed Oct '14)

http://www.cdc.gov/nutrition/everyone/basics/fat/unsaturatedfat.html

http://www.fda.gov/Food/ResourcesForYou/Consumers/ucm079609.htm

http://www.cdc.gov/nutrition/everyone/basics/fat/transfat.html

Fisher, Helen, PhD. *Why We Love.* NY:Henry Holt and Company, 2004.

FODMAPs

Magge, S. et al. "Low-FODMAP Diet for Treatment of Irritable Bowel Syndrome." *Gastroenterol Hepatol* (N Y). Nov 2012; 8(11): 739–745.

Muir, J. et al. "The Low FODMAP Diet for Treatment of Irritable Bowel Syndrome and Other Gastrointestinal Disorders." *Gastroenterol Hepatol* (N Y). Jul 2013; 9(7): 450–452.

Shepherd, Sue, PhD, et al. *The Complete Low-FODMAP Diet: A Revolutionary Plan for Managing IBS and Other Digestive Disorders.* NY:The Experiment, 2013.

Food – Can trigger addictive-like behaviors (Accessed Mar '15)

University of Michigan, List of Addictive Food. http://www.ba-bamail.com/content.aspx?emailid=14460&memberid=960267

Yale University. Yale Addiction Scale. Foods are ranked from most to least problematic in terms of addictive-like behavior on a scale of 1 (least) to 7 (most). http://www.yaleruddcenter.org/resources/upload/docs/what/addiction/FoodAddictionScale09.pdf

Barnard, Neal D., MD. "Big Food About to Lose Its Biggest Defense: Food Really Is Addictive." http://pcrm.org/search/?cid=2111

Barnard, Neal D., MD. "Breaking the Food Seduction." http://www.pcrm.org/good-medicine/2003/summer/breaking-the-food-seduction

Food – FDA Food Defects Action Levels (Accessed Dec '14)

http://www.fda.gov/food/guidanceregulation/guidancedocumentsregulatoryinformation/sanitationtransportation/ucm056174.htm#CHPTO

Fontana, David, PhD. *Teach Yourself to Dream*. CA: Chronicle Books, 1997.

Gazzaniga, Michael S., PhD. *Who's In Charge? Free Will and the Science of the Brain.* NY:HarperCollins, 2011.

Giuffre, Kenneth A., MD., et al. *The Care and Feeding of Your Brain: How Diet and Environment Affect What You Think and Feel*. NJ:Career Press Inc, 1999.

Glycemic Index-Glycemic Load (Accessed Oct '14)

http://www.health.harvard.edu/newsweek/Glycemic_index_and_glycemic_load_for_100_foods.htm

http://www.mendosa.com/gilists.htm

"International tables of glycemic index and glycemic load values: 2008" by Fiona S. Atkinson, Kaye Foster-Powell, and Jennie C. Brand-Miller. *Diabetes Care,* Vol. 31, number 12, pages 2281-2283. December, 2008.

Krishnan, Supriya, et al. "Glycemic Index, Glycemic Load, and Cereal Fiber Intake and Risk of Type 2 Diabetes in US Black Women" *Archives of Internal Medicine* 167 (21): 2304–2309.doi:10.1001/archinte.167.21.2304. PMID 8039988. 2007.

Ludwig, Daniel S. "The glycemic index: physiological mechanisms relating to obesity, diabetes, and cardiovascular disease." *Journal of the American Medical Association* 287 (18): 2414–2423. doi:10.1001/jama.287.18.2414. PMID 11988062 (May 2002).

Mofidi, Anita, et al. "The Acute Impact of Ingestion of Sourdough and Whole-Grain Breads on Blood Glucose, Insulin, and Incretins in Overweight and Obese Men." (Accessed Mar '15) http://www.ncbi.nlm.nih.gov/pmc/articles/PMC3317179/

Villegas, Raquel, et al. "Prospective Study of Dietary Carbohydrates, Glycemic Index, Glycemic Load, and Incidence of Type 2 Diabetes Mellitus in Middle-aged Chinese Women." *Archives of Internal Medicine* 6167 (21): 2310–2316.doi:10.1001/archinte.167.21.2310. PMID 18039989. 2007.

Goleman, Daniel Jay, PhD. *The Brain and Emotional Intelligence: New Insights.* MA:More Than Sound, 2011.

Goleman, Daniel Jay, PhD. *Emotional Intelligence: 10th Anniversary Edition.* NY:Bantam, 2009.

Goleman, Daniel Jay, PhD. *Social Intelligence.* NY:Bantam Dell, 2006.

Gordon, Jon. *The Energy Bus: 10 Rules to Fuel Your Life, Work, and Team with Positive Energy.* NY:Wiley, 2007.

Gordon, Jon. *Energy Addict: 101 Physical, Mental, and Spiritual Ways to Energize Your Life*. NY:Perigee Trade, 2004.

Gratitude (Accessed Oct '14)

http://www.cfidsselfhelp.org/library/counting-your-blessings-how-gratitude-improves-your-health

DeSteno, David. "Gratitude - A Tool for Reducing Economic Impatience." http://pss.sagepub.com/content/early/2014/04/22/0956797614529979

Greenberg, Melanie, PhD. http://melaniegreenbergphd.com/marin-psychologist/

Guangwei Li, MD, and David Katz, MD, MPH. April 3, 2014, *The Lancet Diabetes & Endocrinology*, online. (Accessed Oct '14)

Guthrie, George E., MD, MPH, CDE, CNS. "Insalting Your Intelligence? Another Look at Salt and Hypertension." PowerPoint presentations, 2014.

Hafen, Brent Q., et al. *Mind/Body Health*. MA:Allyn & Bacon, 1996.

Health Definition: Preamble to the Constitution of the World Health Organization as adopted by the International Health Conference, NY, June, 1946. (Official Records of the WHO, no. 2, p. 100) and entered into force on 7 April 1948.

Health Determinants (Accessed Oct '14)

http://www.cdc.gov/socialdeterminants/Definitions.html

High Fructose Corn Syrup (Accessed Oct '14)

Princeton University, "High-fructose corn syrup prompts considerably more weight gain, researchers find." http://www.sciencedaily.com/releases/2010/03/100322121115.htm

Bocarsly, Miriam E., et al. "High-fructose corn syrup causes characteristic of obesity in rats: Increased body weight, body fat and triglyceride levels." *Pharmacology Biochemistry and Behavior*, 2010; DOI: 10.1016/j.pbb.2010.02.012

Howard, Pierce J., PhD. *The Owner's Manual for the Brain, 4th Edition: The Ultimate Guide to Peak Mental Performance at All Ages.* NY:William Morrow Paperbacks, 2014.

Jensen, Anabel L., PhD, et al. *Handle with Care: Emotional Intelligence Activity Book.* CA:Six Seconds, 1998.

Jhon, Mu Shik, PhD, and M. J. Pangman. *The Water Puzzle and the Hexagonal Key.* UT:Uplifting Press, 2013.

Kahleova, Hana, et al. "Two large meals a day versus six small meals a day and Diabetes 2." Diabetes Centre, Institute for Clinical and Experimental Medicine, Videnska 1958/9, 140 21 Prague, Czech Republic e-mail: hana.kahleova@gmail.com www.diabetologia-journal.org/files/Kahleova.pdf DOI 10.1007/s00125-014-3253-5

Halpern, Sue, PhD. *Can't Remember What I Forgot.* NY:Harmony Books, 2008.

Kaiser, Jon D., MD. *Immune Power.* NY: St. Martin's Press, 1993.

Katz, David, L., MD, and Stacey Colino. *Disease-Proof: The Remarkable Truth about What Makes Us Well.* NY:Hudson Street Press, 2013.

Kidd, Parris M., PhD. *GPC (ClyceroPosphoCholine) Mind-Body Power for Active Living and Healthy Aging***.** UT:Total Health, 2007.

Khalsa, Dharma Singh, MD, with Cameron Stauth. *Brain Longevity.* NY:Warner Books, 1997.

Klatz, Ronald, MD, and Robert Goldman, MD. *The Anti-Aging Revolution.* 4th Edition. CA:Basic Health Publications, 2007.

Kulinski, Jacqueline, MD., and colleagues. (Accessed Mar '15)

"Too Much Sitting May Up Risk of Coronary Artery Calcification." http://www.medscape.com/viewarticle/841248

Ludwig, David, MD. Ending the Food Fight: Guide Your Child to a Healthy Weight in a Fast Food/ Fake Food World. NY:Mariner Books, 2008.

McGinnis, Alan Loy. *The Power of Optimism.* NY:Harper & Row, Publishers, Inc., 1990.

McGonigal, Kelly, PhD. *The Willpower Instinct: How Self-Control Works.* NY:Penguin Books, Inc., 2012.

McGraw, Phillip Calvin, PhD. *Self Matters: Creating Your Life from the Inside Out.* FL:Free Press Publishing, 2003.

Maas, James B., PhD. *Power Sleep: The Revolutionary Program That Prepares Your Mind for Peak Performance.* NY:Collins Living, 1998.

Macronutrients – Carbohydrates (Accessed Oct '14)

McKiney Health Center, University of Illinois
http://www.mckinley.illinois.edu/handouts/macronutrients.htm

Mahoney, David, and Richard Restak, MD. *The Longevity Strategy.* NY:John Wiley & Sons, Inc., 1998.

Marshmallow Experiment. "We Didn't Eat the Marshmallow. The Marshmallow Ate Us." (Accessed Oct '14)
http://www.nytimes.com/2014/01/12/magazine/we-didnt-eat-the-marshmallow-the-marshmallow-ate-us.html?_r=0

Mattson, Mark P., PhD. *Diet-Brain Connections: Impact on Memory, Mood, Aging and Disease.* NY:Springer Publishing, 2002.

Mediterranean Way, Benefits

Masala, G. "A Dietary Pattern Rich in Olive Oil and Raw Vegetables Is Associated With Lower Mortality in Italian Elderly Subjects." *British Journal of Nutrition.* August, 2007.

Perez-Lopez, F. R.. "Effects of Mediterranean Diet on Longevity and Age-Related Morbid Conditions." *Maturitas*, Oct 20, 2009.

Trichopoulou, Antonia, M.D.., et al "Adherence to a Mediterranean Diet and Survival in a Greek Population." New England Journal of Medicine 2003; 348:2599-2608June 26, 2003DOI: 10.1056/NEJMoa025039

More Evidence Mediterranean Diet May Reduce Stroke Risk
http://www.medscape.com/viewarticle/841359

Moss, Michael. *Salt, Sugar, Fat: How the Food Giants Hooked Us.* NY:Random House, 2013.

Naude, Celeste E., et al. "Low Carbohydrate versus Isoenergetic Balanced Diets for Reducing Weight and Cardiovascular Risk: A Systematic Review and Meta-Analysis. (Accessed Oct '14) http://www.ncbi.nlm.nih.gov/pmc/articles/PMC4090010/

Newberg, Andrew, MD, and Mark Robert Waldman. *How God Changes Your Brain: Breakthrough Findings from a Leading Neuroscientist.* NY:Ballantine, Books, 2010.

Newberg, Andrew, MD., and Mark Robert Waldman. *Why We Believe What We Believe.* NY:Free Press, 2006.

Null, Gary, PhD. *Reboot Your Brain.* NY:Skyhorse Publishing, Inc., 2013.

Obesity, Morbid Obesity, and Overweight (Accessed Feb '15)

http://www.who.int/mediacentre/factsheets/fs311/en/

http://www.weather.com/health/which-country-fattest-20130709

http://www.cdc.gov/obesity/adult/defining.html

National Heart Lung and Blood Institute, Classification of Overweight and Obesity by BMI: http://www.nhlbi.nih.gov/health/public/heart/obesity/lose_wt/bmi_dis.htm (Using Kg)

http://www.life123.com/health/weight-loss/obesity/definition-of-morbid-obesity.shtml

"Pilot randomized trial demonstrating reversal of obesity-related abnormalities in reward system responsivity to food cues with a behavioral intervention." (Accessed Feb '15) http://www.ncbi.nlm.nih.gov/pmc/articles/PMC4183968/

O'Brien, Mary. MD. *Weight Perfect,* 2nd Edition. CA:Biomed General, 2013.

O'Brien, Mary. MD. *The Healing Power of Sleep,* 2nd. Edition. CA:Biomed General, 2011.

Pangman, M. J., MS. *Hexagonal Water: The Ultimate Solution.* UT:Uplifting Press, 2005.

Pawlak, Laura, PhD. *The Hungry Brain.* CA:Biomet General, 2012.

Pearsall, Paul, PhD. *The Heart's Code.* NY:Broadway Books, 1998.

Pert, Candace, B., PhD. *Molecules of Emotion: The Science Behind Mind-Body Medicine*. NY:Simon and Schuster, 1999.

Portion Size. (Accessed Oct '14)

www.ChooseMyPlate.gov

http://www.cdc.gov/healthyweight/healthy_eating/portion_size.html

http://forum.lowcarber.org/showthread.php?t=437612

http://www.rd.com/slideshows/medical-news-april-2014/

Rankin, Lissa, MD. *Mind over Medicine.* CA:Hay House, Inc., 2013.

Ratey, John J., MD, and Eric Hagerman. *Spark: The Revolutionary New Science of Exercise and the Brain.* NY:Little, Brown and Company, 2008, 2010.

Raymond, Patricia L., MD FACP FACG, with assistance from Albert Einstein, PhD. "Smart Diagnosis and Smart Treatment of Irritable Bowel Syndrome." (Accessed Mar '15) http://rxforsanity.com/free-articles/fun-gastro-articles/smart-diagnosis-and-smart-treatment-of-irritable-bowel-syndrome/

Restak, Richard, MD. *Older & Wiser. How to Maintain Peak Mental Ability for As Long As You Live.* NY: Simon & Schuster; 2014.

Restak, Richard, MD. *Mozart's Brain and the Fighter Pilot: Unleashing Your Brain's Potential.* NY:Harmony Books, 2007.

Robinson, Ken, Sir, PhD. *The Element: How Finding Your Passion Changes Everything.* NY:Penguin Books, 2011.

Roizen, Michael F., MD, and Mehmet C. Oz, MD. *YOU: The Owner's Manual (Enhanced Edition)* NY:William Morrow, 2014.

Roizen, Michael F., MD, et al. *Real Age, are You as Young as You Can Be?* NY:Harper Collins, 1999.

Ross, Julia, MA. *The Diet Cure*. NY:Penguin Books, 1999.

Salt – Sodium (Accessed Oct '14)

Guthrie, George E., MD, MPH, CDE, CNS. "Insalting Your Intelligence? Another Look at Salt and Hypertension." PowerPoint®, 2014.

http://www.cdc.gov/features/dssodium/

Institute of Medicine. *Dietary reference intakes for water, potassium, socium, chloride, and sulfate.* 1st edition. Washington, DC:The National Academices Press, 2004.

http://www.iom.edu/reports/2004/Dietary-Reference-Intakes-Water-Potassium-Sodium-Chloride-and-Sulfate.aspx.

Santrock, John, PhD. *A Topical Approach to Life-Span Development.* NY:McGraw-Hill Humanities/Social Sciences/Languages; 6 edition, 2011.

Santrock, John, PhD. Life-Span Development, 13th Edition. NY:McGraw-Hill Humanities/Social Sciences/Languages; 6 edition, 2011.

Sapolsky, Robert M., PhD. *Why Zebras Don't Get Ulcers.* NY:W. H. Freeman and Company, 1994.

Seale, Stuart A., et al. *The Full Plate Diet: Slim Down, Look Great, Be Healthy!* TX:Bard Press; Spi edition, 2010.

Seligman, Martin E. P., PhD. *Learned Optimism: How to Change Your Mind and Your Life.* NY:Vintage, the Random House Group, 2011.

Seligman, Martin E. P., PhD. *Flourish: A Visionary New Understanding of Happiness and Well-being.* NY:Atria Books, Simon and Schuster, 2011.

Seligman, Martin E. P., PhD. *Authentic Happiness: Using the New Positive Psychology to Realize Your Potential for Lasting Fulfillment.* MA:Free Press, 2002

Siebert, Al, PhD, with foreword by Bernie Siegel, MD. *The Survivor Personality.* NY:Perigee Books, 1996.
Singh, Dalip, PhD. *Emotional Intelligence at Work.* NY:Sage, 2000.

Sleep (Accessed Mar '15)

www.sleepfoundation.org

http://www.theguardian.com/science/neurophilosophy/2014/jun/01/sleep-hemispatial-neglect
http://www.rapidrecoveryhyperbarics.com/sleep1.html

Maas, James B., PhD. *Power Sleep: The Revolutionary Program That Prepares Your Mind for Peak Performance.* NY:Collins Living, 1998.

Small, Gary, MD. *The Longevity Bible—8 Essential Strategies for Keeping Your Mind Sharp and Your Body Young.* NY:Hyperion Books, 2006.

Snowdon, David, PhD. *Aging with Grace—What the Nun Study Teaches Us About Leading Longer, Healthier, and More Meaningful Lives.* NY:Bantam Books, 2001.

Sugar Consumption (Accessed Oct '14)
http://www.nature.com/nature/journal/v482/n7383/fig_tab/482027a_T1.html

Tanzi, Rudolph E., PhD, and Deepak Chopra, MD. *Super Brain.* NY:Random House Inc., 2013.

Taylor, Arlene R., PhD, and W. Eugene Brewer, EdD. *Your Brain Has a Bent (Not a Dent),* 3rd Edition. CA:Success Resources International, 2015.

Taylor, Arlene R., PhD, and Sharlet M. Briggs, PhD. *Age-Proofing Your Brain.* CA:Success Resources International, 2009.
Taylor, Arlene R., PhD, and Sharlet M. Briggs, PhD. *Age-Proofing Your Memory.* CA:Success Resources International, 2008.

Taylor, Shelley E., PhD. *Health Psychology*, 8th Edition. NY:McGraw-Hill, 2011.

Tofu, Fermented (Accessed Oct '14)

http://www.whfoods.com/genpage.php?tname=newtip&dbid=36

Townsend, John, PhD. *Who's Pushing Your Buttons.* TN:Integrity Publishers, 2004.

Tracking what you eat and drink (Accessed Oct '14).

www.Dailyplate.com

Treadwell, Benjamin V., PhD. *Maintaining a More Youthful Brain.* "Psychological Stress and Accelerated Aging." Juvenon Health Journal Exerpts, Vol one, 2005.

Visceral Fat. See Belly Fat and Health

Wegner, Daniel M., PhD. *White Bears and Other Unwanted Thoughts: Suppression, Obsession, and the Psychology of Mental Control.* NY:Guilford Press, 1994.

Weil, Andrew, MD. *Healthy Aging: A Lifelong Guide to Your Well-Being.* ME:Anchor Publishing, 2007.

Zied, Elisa, RD. "Want to try LeBron James' Paleo diet? 3 things we get wrong about carbs." http://www.today.com/health/you-try-lebron-james-paleo-diet-3-myths-about-carbs-

1D80087878?__source=xfinity|hero&par=xfinity (Accessed Oct '14)

Zimmer, Carl. "The Dark Matter of the Human Brain." http://discovermagazine.com/2009/sep/19-dark-matter-of-the-human-brain

Zull, James, E., PhD. *The Art of Changing the Brain.* VA:Stylus Publishing, LLC, 2002.

The
End

Made in the USA
San Bernardino, CA
08 May 2015